Taking the Lead

Taking the Lead

Rochester Women in Public Policy, 1970-1990

Sponsored by the Rochester League of
Women Voters

With an Introduction by Lori Sturdevant,
author and Minneapolis *StarTribune* columnist

P★

POLARIS PUBLISHING
An imprint of NORTH STAR PRESS OF ST. CLOUD, INC.
St. Cloud, MN

First Edition: December 1, 2012

Printed in the United States of America

Published by
Polaris Publications, an imprint of
North Star Press of St. Cloud, Inc.
P.O. Box 451
St. Cloud, Minnesota 56302

www.northstarpress.com

Contents

Foreword

This book, a project of the Rochester League of Women Voters (LWV), features twenty-five women who took the lead on issues of great concern to them and their community. The League became interested in and supportive of this project so that they might honor Rochester women who so clearly embodied the LWV mission: to encourage the informed and active participation of citizens in government and to influence public policy through education and advocacy.

The women we have featured dared to be the first to attempt new careers in public life for women. They dared to be the first women elected to various government posts. After election, they dared to speak out on the issues rather than being quiet, ornamental figures. Their stories provide a sampling of what it was like to be breakthrough leaders in Rochester, Minnesota–a middle-sized town in the Midwest–during the 1970s and 1980s, a period of rapid emergence of women into many areas formerly dominated by men. We tell of their successes, setbacks, roadblocks, coping methods, and leadership styles. We recognize those who helped them along the way. We show how these women made Rochester public policy richer because of a fuller inclusion of both sexes in leadership positions.

Taking the Lead has been written by volunteers, most of whom personally know–or knew–their subjects. It contains stories told to them "as the subjects remembered" and enhanced by the voiced memories of others. The material also includes references to official minutes, election results, personal papers, and newspaper articles from various local sources.

There are other Rochester women who made similar public policy contributions, but because they are deceased or they moved from Rochester and we lost track of them, we knew too little to write full chapters. There are still others whose public contributions fell before or after the time frame selected. The book's appendix lists names of some of the women who fall into these categories. Because we know that we have inadvertently omitted others, we've left the final chapter of the book blank so that you might add your own stories about them.

I had the pleasure of knowing nearly all of the *Taking the Lead* women while they were making their contributions. They are my heroes.

Amy Caucutt

Introduction

The speed of social change is usually glacial. But glaciers sometimes fall abruptly into the sea, and the landscape is forever changed. Something akin to an ice field's collapse occurred for the women of Rochester, Minnesota, and places like it throughout the United States in the 1970s and 1980s.

In most years in the 1960s, only two women served alongside 199 men in the Minnesota Legislature. Women with advanced degrees were shunted into secretarial positions. Law firms refused to hire female law school graduates. Female flight attendants were fired upon marriage, as teachers had been in rural Minnesota until the 1950s. Lower wages for women than for men doing comparable work were standard, justified by the excuse that "men are breadwinners." Women who wanted to become doctors were counseled into nursing; those who sought good-paying factory or building-trades jobs were ridiculed–and worse. But most American women weren't reaching for careers in the 1950s and 1960s. They heard and heeded postwar America's message: Stay home. Be doting wives. Have babies. If you want to do more, there's always volunteer work–provided dinner is on the table when your husband gets home.

That was the status circa 1960 of many of the women you will meet on the pages that follow. They were able-bodied, well-educated adults, brimming with vitality and desire to make a positive contribution to their world. For years, they held back. Or they were held back.

Then, beginning in about 1970, everything changed. That's the title of an impressive 2009 book by New York Times columnist Gail Collins: *When Everything Changed: The Amazing Journey of American Women from 1960 to the Present.* The change was sudden and sweeping, quickly moving from the nation's populous coasts to the rural midsection. "It seemed that overnight, everything that America had taken for granted about a woman's role was being called into question," Collins wrote. This book describes how those new questions were answered in a small city in the nation's heartland, eighty miles south of Minneapolis/St. Paul.

What some called "women's liberation" or "the feminist movement" moved so far and so fast because even in places like Rochester, conditions were ripe for women to assert themselves. The U.S. economy was expanding and needed more workers, many of them to fill jobs that women were well suited to perform. The Baby Boom generation was moving through high school and into college; their mothers weren't as tied down by childrearing by 1970, while their family budgets were stretched. Many families required a second income to keep their toehold on the middle class. Improved contraception with the advent of the birth control pill in 1960 helped bring the Baby Boom to an end. The civil rights movement that began in 1955 had by 1970 produced measurable progress for racial minorities, while making many American women more acutely aware that they too experienced second-class status. It fueled the notion that social change did not have to advance by baby steps. Big strides were possible.

Those are among the reasons Collins cites for the sudden mass movement of American women into fuller citizenship. In Rochester, there was one more potent force: an active chapter of the League of Women Voters. The organization whose vision created this book deserves credit for much more. In Rochester and throughout Minnesota, local League chapters kept alive a flame of women's civic involvement that was originally kindled during the suffrage movement of the late nineteenth and early twentieth centuries. Without the League, that flame might have been snuffed out by the hardships of depression and war and the desire for domesticity that followed them. It's likely no coincidence that the few Minnesota legislative districts that elected women more than once between 1922 and 1972 were places where League chapters flourished.

When doors began to open for women in Rochester, the League of Women Voters was there to propel them across the threshold. It trained them in election law and public policy formation, giving them knowledge, confidence, and a base of support from which to seek elective office. It spurred their interest in public affairs. For example, Dorothy Callahan was a biochemist before moving to Rochester in 1952 and joining the League. Its study committees kindled her interest in water quality, land use planning, and affordable housing, which became a springboard for her appointment as the first chair of the Rochester/Olmsted Community Housing Partnership. Rosemary Ahmann, the first female Olmsted County Commissioner, attests that joining the League changed her life. Working on a League tax policy study gave her a base of knowledge that proved essential when she ran for the county board in 1972. Her League friends gave her practical campaign advice and served as foot soldiers for the campaign's literature ground war.

It's characteristic of the League and of many other women's organizations that they see other pro-female groups not as rivals, but as potential allies. That spirit shines through this book. Credit is given the American Association of University Women for inspiring in Carol Kamper the confidence to run for the Rochester City Council and the base of support that made her the first woman elected to the post. Sue Lemke's AAUW state presidency is duly noted. The preparation for leadership that Sheila Kiscaden gained at Planned Parenthood is acknowledged, as is Jackie Trotter's experience as a founding member of the Rochester chapter of the National Association for the Advancement of Colored People. The story of Ancy Tone Morse, Olmsted County's first female judge, features her long involvement with the Girl Scouts.

The connections women created in those organizations and the networking habits they acquired as a result were crucial to the careers that blossomed after 1970. Rare in this book is a story about a woman who stepped out alone to try a new career in public service, driven only by personal ambition. More typical is the story of Nancy Brataas, a Republican volunteer-cum-paid political campaign operative who said "no" when she was first approached to run for the Minnesota Senate. It took a group of friends to convince her otherwise. Carol Kamper had a master's degree in political science. Yet it took a dare from her AAUW friends to convince her to seek a city council seat. Jean Michaels ran for the county board after sessions with a

YWCA career counselor convinced her that she was indeed prepared for public service. As former state Sen. Sheila Kiscaden said, "My network of colleagues and friends has always been and is an important part of being successful in creating community change and being able to take advantage of personal opportunities."

But the women profiled on the pages that follow also did their own parts to succeed–and, in so doing, they paved the way for the women who followed in their footsteps. Readers will meet women who out-hustled male opponents on the campaign trail, who never showed up unprepared for meetings, who mastered the most complex policy topics, and who overcame shyness to speak out, often on behalf of the young, the old, and the voiceless whom they represented.

Taking the Lead women approached their public work out of a desire to serve, not to make gains for themselves. Some of them drew energy and purpose from a sense that they were part of a national movement for gender justice. Others likely would pooh-pooh any such connection. A few may have scorned as firebrands the feminists who came onto the national stage in the early 1970s to lead the push for change. "I'm no women's libber," some Rochester women might say. "I was just doing my part." But whether or not they embrace the label "feminist," give all of them this: They were lucky enough, clever enough, and connected enough to notice when the part that they could play suddenly grew bigger. They worked hard, singly and together, to fill its new dimensions well. Their contributions are enduring. And their stories are well worth remembering.

Lori Sturdevant
Minneapolis *StarTribune*
December 2012

A "Bug" for Community Corrections

Rosemary Ahmann was the first woman to run for Olmsted County Board

In 1972, Rosemary Ahmann was the first woman to run for the County Board of Commissioners in Olmsted County. She won in November, becoming the first woman to serve as an Olmsted County Commissioner and one of the few female commissioners in the state. She served ten years, from 1973 to 1981, also sitting on numerous state and national taskforces and commissions. Rosemary worked to keep juveniles out of jail, and she helped establish group homes in Olmsted and Dodge Counties. She advocated for a Minnesota community corrections law that provided money to local communities for developing jail alternatives for adult offenders, earning the nickname "Godmother of Community Corrections." According to Dick Devlin, County Administrator, "Rosemary was in the forefront of getting that law passed. Olmsted County was the first to take advantage of it." As chair of the County Board, she established the Family Violence Task Force. She worked on planning issues and improvements to the Olmsted County Hospital. "She was one of the best commissioners I have worked with. She was concerned about human services, especially (services for) kids," said Devlin. While in office, she also dedicated herself to increasing the number of women who ran for local, state, and national offices.

Her mother's example

Rosemary and her brother grew up in Joliet, Illinois, where her father worked for Caterpillar. Rosemary was in fourth grade when her father died, before he could be called up for WW II military service.

1

In 1949, her mother went to work as a secretary at the Joliet Statesville Prison. Among the first women to work at the prison, she rose through the ranks in the state civil service of Illinois. Eventually, she was appointed by the legislature to the post of Superintendent of the women's prison in Dwight, Illinois. All salaries were set by the legislature and, as was custom then, she was awarded lower pay than her male predecessor. Though a single mother raising two children, she was not considered "head of household." At the time, no one considered paying a salary for the position rather than the person. Years later, when Rosemary took office as Olmsted County Commissioner, for every dollar that men were paid, women were paid an average of fifty-nine cents for the same work. Now that she was in a position to make a difference, Rosemary worked for change in salary policies.

Rosemary's brother became a lawyer; she became a nurse. Rosemary wanted to major in liberal arts, but due to a lack of finances, she chose nursing. Her family reinforced her practical choice in case she might later need to support a family of her own, as her mother had. Rosemary won a scholarship to a hospital-based school of nursing in Milwaukee. After finishing, she transferred to Marquette University to study liberal arts. There she met her husband, David, who was studying medicine. They married and moved to Europe for four years while David worked as a military doctor. In 1962 they moved to Rochester for his residency at Mayo Clinic. Rosemary briefly worked as a nurse at Saint Marys Hospital.

When her children were young, she went back to college at Rochester Community College and the University of Minnesota. She joined the League of Women Voters, which she says changed her life. She eventually served as its president, but it was her first assignment that set her on the path to public office: she chaired the League's 1971 study on taxes, which gave her a basic understanding of the roles of all three levels of government and budgets–local, state, and national. For a year, she observed the County Board, attending every meeting and learning how it operated.

The first campaign

The First District Commissioner seat, which covered the Southwest side of Rochester, opened up on the board in 1972. Rosemary decided to run against the two other candidates: Willard Knapp, who had run for several local offices, and Gerald Cunningham, the former sheriff. Because there were three candidates, a primary would be held in August. Rosemary remembers the day she went down to the Auditor's Office to file, her hands shaking as she signed the papers. What was she doing, she wondered. What would the campaign be like? Could she expect to win? Her greatest concern was her uncertainty about speaking in public, but she knew her best asset was public policy knowledge because of her participation in the League of Women Voters.

Most of the people who helped in her first campaign were members of the League and many had never worked on a campaign. They had to learn quickly about bumper stickers, buttons, and brochures; most of all, they had to learn to strategize. Together, they made three crucial decisions, the first of which was not to feature her children in her publicity. Rosemary and David had six children: Mark, Mary, and David in high school, Carla and Greg in junior high, and Chris in kindergarten. The committee ran a formal picture of Rosemary on the front cover of the brochure.

The second decision was to conduct a campaign to educate the voters about the scope of the County Board's responsibilities. If most voters were under the impression that the board only worried about roads and bridges, what could a former nurse know about such things? On the inside of the brochure was a pie chart of the county budget showing that sixty percent of the expenditures were in the area of public health and human services. Her credentials were listed next to the chart. Now a former nurse and President of the League of Women Voters looked qualified.

The third decision was to go door knocking throughout the whole district in order to get the information in the hands of voters. She took kindergartener Chris with her; he was a great helper and companion on those long afternoons. What they had not expected was that door knocking would give Rosemary and her committee an intimate look at the condition of life–particularly housing–in the county. Although county government does not have an interest in housing, several campaign workers went on to promote better housing for Rochester citizens.

Rosemary made it through the primary and faced the former sheriff in the general election in November. She began to attend candidate forums and coffee hours in people's homes. The well-known sheriff often began his speeches with, "Everyone called me to run." Self-conscious about her public speaking capabilities, Rosemary chose to educate the audience about what the County Board did and all the ways in which voters are affected by Board decisions. She is still very grateful for the help from a former commissioner who talked to local fraternal organizations about her attendance at County Board meetings and garnered invitations for her to speak. She won on November 7, 1972.

Getting the job done

Now that she was elected, she dedicated herself to creating effective public policies. The reaction of her new colleagues was mixed. Some were supportive; others were not so welcoming. She realized she needed to learn how to be effective and not respond with pat answers. She learned to compromise and took classes on how to make presentations to hostile audiences. She learned how to generate consensus. "I had to learn how to improve myself in order to do a good job," she recalls. The biggest issue was the reorganization of the county government itself. At the time, there was no administrator and County Board members often handled the finances without a budget.

The Board first decided to hire a County Administrator, eventually choosing Dick Devlin. A full-time administrator ensured good budget planning for the county programs. Rosemary said, "This was one of my best decisions while serving Olmsted County." Secondly, the budget needed streamlining, with accounting standards and efficient processes for expenditures. There were substantive issues, as well, in the areas of public health, corrections, and social services. Olmsted County Hospital's facilities and equipment were deteriorating, according to Devlin. He said that Rosemary led the fundraising effort and helped persuade Mayo Clinic to support the renovations. One of her initial efforts was to improve ground water quality. There was increased demand for new subdivisions in the county. Devlin said that Rosemary worked for new zoning laws on lot size and new codes mandating cased wells (lined with a factory-made pipe, typically steel or plastic.)

Governor Wendell Anderson appointed Rosemary to the Crime Control Planning Board. The Board was in charge of federal funds for the courts, jails, juvenile justice, corrections, police and sheriff's departments, and social services. Before the funds could be released, the Board established goals and standards for each area of the criminal justice system in Minnesota. This was an area in which she felt comfortable. She served for several years and became the chair of the board.

Can't you hear me?

At national meetings, Rosemary felt overlooked because there were so few women. If she sat next to a fellow commissioner, he would be asked if she were his wife. Often the only woman in a committee meeting, when she spoke no one would react–as if she had said nothing at all. Several minutes later, a man might propose the same idea and the others would comment favorably. At other times, in both local and state meetings, commissioners and other officials would interrupt her or condescendingly suggest what she really meant to say. During a discussion at the national level, she spoke out strongly on the need for standards regarding gun use, also called "deadly force." After the meeting one of her male colleagues said, "You're so quiet" and asked why she hadn't said anything. He literally had not heard her. After such exchanges occurred several times at the local County Board meetings, one Commissioner pointedly told the other Board Members to stop doing it. Those experiences prompted Rosemary to support women when they spoke at meetings of all levels. She would second the motion or reinforce the points made by the other women in order to "get the idea heard." Women who had the same experiences sought each other out. Together, they were able to take and offer workshops on improving leadership skills.

Because she was so often the only woman serving on national or state committees, she began to work with other female officials to form an organization of women county officials that worked to support women candidates for county offices. Women in the U.S. House of Representatives and the Senate invited Rosemary and other local officials to discuss the advancement of women in government. She worked locally to encourage women to run for county board, city council, and the school board.

In 1973, Rosemary was appointed to the board of the National Association of County Officials (NACO) as a representative of the Women of the National Association of County Officials. She was instrumental in getting the national board to conduct a survey to determine the percentage of women on appointed boards and commissions in counties. After all, a group that made up more than fifty percent of the population should have more than five percent of the appointed positions.

Rutgers University began to take actions that addressed these inequalities. Scholars at the university started researching women serving in government programs and helping get women elected to national offices. They interviewed people such as Ann Richards, Barbara Mulkulski, and Barbara Boxer, who had also started as a county commissioner. The Rutgers study, completed in 1977, stated that there were 400 women serving in county positions in the United States, less than ten per state. Rutgers invited women from around the country to discuss the future of women in elected office. Elected women met with female journalists to discuss the barriers females faced in seeking higher office, pointing out that there were few women in TV journalism. The group pressured the broadcasters to feature women in newscasts. Very shortly after these efforts, Geraldine Ferraro was selected as Walter Mondale's vice presidential candidate. Rosemary was there when Mondale introduced Geraldine Ferraro as his running mate in his hometown in Minnesota. Rosemary believes that all of this work set the stage for Hillary Clinton's run for the presidential nomination in 2008.

Rosemary wrote a local editorial supporting the open meeting law and explaining that small groups of Rochester officials were gathering for a quorum in private meetings and then voting on resolutions without consulting with their colleagues or the public. Her editorial was reprinted all over the state.

Godmother for community corrections

In the early 1970s, Rosemary was appointed to the National Coalition for Jail Reform. The members represented more than twenty stakeholders, including judges, police officers, prosecutors, defenders, wardens, and state and local governments. They were charged with creating standards. At the time, California was spending more money on jails than on schools, and this was becoming a national trend. The members of the commission reached a consensus and decided that it was inappropriate to jail certain groups of people: no juveniles should be jailed, and neither should mentally ill or mentally retarded people. Women should be housed in separate quarters from men. They failed to reach a consensus on the treatment of women picked up for prostitution. The coalition supported programs like the "Green Door" in Washington, D.C., which helps mentally ill people obtain jobs and housing, even during periods of illness.

All the group homes run by private, non-profit agencies in Olmsted County were initiated during Rosemary's tenure, and the county even bought two group homes. The county board usually sent juveniles away to programs in the western part of the United States or in northern Minnesota, where there was no one to oversee their treatment and difficult for families to visit. She attacked that policy as a budget item and argued that the county could treat young people locally for less money. She wanted a choice model that would support the young people in school where social services could watch over them. Selected adult offenders began to be treated in the community

In 1972 the PORT program (Probation Offenders Rehabilitation and Training) was established under the Community Corrections Act. After leaving the county board, Rosemary worked at PORT preparing training and education programs for other states and counties interested in starting similar projects. Rosemary was named "Minnesota Corrections Person of the Year" in 1983. (Courtesy Post-Bulletin Co.)

rather than jailed. In 1972 the PORT program (Probation Offenders Rehabilitation and Training) was established under the Community Corrections Act. After leaving the county board, Rosemary worked at PORT preparing training and education programs for other states and counties interested in starting similar projects. She was named "Minnesota Corrections Person of the Year" in 1983.

As a result of her work in jail reform, she was appointed to Minnesota's Cameras in the Court Committee. After many hours of deliberation and collecting information from states that allow cameras during testimony, the committee recommended permitting cameras under strict controls. These findings were presented to the court. To date, no action has been taken by the State Supreme Court.

In 1980, Rosemary was appointed to the National Law Enforcement Accreditation Agency, which sets the standards and goals for police and sheriffs. It was a new agency, and she was the first woman to serve. They addressed standards for everything from use of deadly force, to shooting a fleeing suspect, to high speed car chases. These standards were used to accredit law enforcement agencies in the United States. Rosemary made establishment of the Family Violence Task Force her goal while on the county board in the late 1970s. The task force was made of up several committees, each with a special charge: sexual abuse of children, battering of women in marriage, and violence against children. Each committee investigated how these problems were handled in the social service system and in the community. Jean Michaels and Daniel Broughton, M.D. were leading figures in this effort. In some cases, the issues were ignored or thought unimportant. After the committees came to the county board with their findings and recommendations, many steps were taken to implement new services within the County Social Services, Corrections, and Health departments. The creation of new community organizations such as the Women's Shelter and Rapeline was funded by the County.

The county commissioner job is a part-time position. There are official board meetings, other county committee meetings to attend as liaison members from the County Board, phone calls to return, time spent reading background information, and service on state and national boards. Rosemary's husband was once teased at work about why he had let her be a public official, but he and the rest of the family were supportive. One exception was her campaign car, which was decked out as a ladybug. If she had to pick up one of the boys after football practice, he would always ask if she was bringing "the bug." If she was, he found another ride home.

After her service, she continued to live in Rochester until 2000. She worked for PORT and led organizing and training sessions for other communities and states that wished to establish community corrections programs, such as the one in Rochester. She ran for a state legislative seat but lost, helped Sally Martin run for the party nomination for the First District Congressional seat, and continued to be a member of AGOG ("All the Good Old Girls") in Rochester. Rosemary and David had built a lake home in Minocqua, Wisconsin, and moved there when David retired. She continues to encourage women to run for public office and works on campaigns, but she is now also a painter and photographer. In keeping with her natural leadership abilities, she helps organize exhibits for artists and has started a local photography club.

Rosemary believes her greatest achievements were in the areas of corrections and support of women, two issues she championed because of the legacy of her mother's experiences. She promoted alternatives to prison for juveniles and adults and worked on the local and national level for standards for law enforcement agencies, supported policies that ensured equal pay for equal work, and helped bring family violence issues to the attention of the County and the community. To this day, she continues to encourage women to run for public office and let their voices be heard.

From Curb Cuts to Cable

Jane Belau, in 1974, began the longest running cable TV political interview show in the U.S.

Turn on the radio, I want to listen to Jane on Monday Melodies." This comment was made often in the late 1940s in rural northwest Minnesota as people tuned in to hear the thirteen-year-old play the piano, sing duets, and accompany her partner. Years later, listeners (and watchers) are still tuning in to her show, *The Belau Report*, but now to hear her interesting interviews with our national, state, and local political movers and shakers.

Jane was born between the Great Depression and World War II in a small rural community in the northwestern corner of the state. As a child of the Greatest Generation (named by Tom Brokaw), Jane agrees with comments penned by Charles Denny, Jr., former CEO and Chair of ADC Telecommunications, in the January 30, 2012 Minneapolis *StarTribune* article entitled, "What My Fortunate Generation Can Do":

> I am a member of the 'Fortunate Generation,' those born in the 1930s, and who were raised during the Great Depression and World War II . . . Our grade school, high school, and college years we recall as idyllic: a time when we joyfully embraced learning, sports, and development of new social skills. From the national cultures of the Great Depression and the war years, we were raised to be thrifty, patriotic, and communitarian . . .

In school she developed a zest for life that continues to this day. A sampling of her activities included cheerleading (says Jane, "that was women's athletics in those days"), class plays, Girl Scouts, 4-H, and piano and organ accompanist for many community groups

11

and her church. At her father's farm implement company, she helped with bookwork and inventory control. She graduated as her class co-valedictorian while being voted "nicest smile" and "most likely to succeed." Like most girls of her time, Jane felt destined to become a teacher or a nurse. A young woman then was expected to pursue such professions either until married or after her husband died. She attended college on a one-year academic scholarship, and when the scholarship ended, she entered a three-year nursing program ($700 for three years, including training, room, and board). Jane says, "The nursing program combined science education with administration and management. The student nurses provided much of the manpower and learned not only patient care but organizational, management, and communication skills—and especially empathy—all of which served me well through my life." While working after graduation from nurses' training, she met and married her husband, Paul Belau, a medical intern.

The sixties began with Jane happily at home with her three small children, sewing matching outfits for Christmas, getting them started in school, baking cookies, and hosting birthday parties. She was active in the Children's Theatre of Rochester Civic Theater, making costumes out of cardboard, sequins, felt, and wool for performances such as Pinocchio and Goldilocks and The Three Bears. Later, Jane would follow her many artistic talents: from poetry (Rochester's first poet laureate) to painting to piano. Since 2002 she has played a magnificent grand piano in Mayo Clinic's Gonda building. Gifted with a remarkable memory for old songs and the ability to play by ear as patients request songs, Jane, and a dedicated group, the Gonda singers, use their lunch hours to entertain patients, visitors, and employees at Mayo. Randy Chapman, publisher of the *Post-Bulletin*, said of her, "Jane has a marvelous talent of being able to play show tunes and inspirational favorites without reading music, her gaze constantly sweeping the audience, observing the joy, the pain and healing that the popular music brings to Mayo Clinic patients and caregivers . . ."

"You can't have everything happen at once!"

As her three children grew older, in the late sixties, Jane's public service began. The Civil Rights Act of 1964 did much to address racial discrimination, but the fight for civil and equal rights for people with disabilities was just beginning. She began her long and varied career as an active citizen by serving as a member of the board of the Hiawatha Paraplegia Foundation, and in 1966, Governor Harold Levander appointed her to the Governor's Committee on Employment of the Handicapped in Minnesota. This assignment ignited a spark in Jane that has burned brightly her entire life–a passion to help those less fortunate through the political as well as non-profit and corporate sectors.

In 1971, Governor Wendell Anderson appointed her the first chair of the Minnesota Council on Developmental Disabilities. Jane's approach was both statewide and national to remove barriers–architectural and attitudinal–for people with disabilities. As chair of the Minnesota Governor's Council on Developmental Disabilities, she believed that the power of the collective Governor's Councils in all the states would be formidable. The coalition thus formed resulted in landmark legislation, expansion of the definition of developmental disabilities, and the related programs like special education. She called a meeting of all the chairpersons and executive directors of the respective State Planning Councils and went on to organize the National Conference (now Association) on Developmental Disabilities. Her executive director and partner was a young professor at the University of Minnesota named Robert Bruininks, who later became the University's fifteenth president. With the bipartisan support of Senator Walter Mondale and Senator Bob Dole, she was named chairman of the National Advisory Council on Developmental Disabilities.

When Gerald Ford became President in 1974, Jane noticed that he met with representatives of many different groups to learn of their needs. She felt that people with disabilities ought to be represented at meetings like these to discuss unmet needs, barriers to education and employment, and priorities. With the assistance of Ford and her friend, Minnesota First District Congressman Al Quie, she secured a meeting at the White House in October 1974 of people with disabilities and their advocates from across America. They communicated issues important to their needs to the new President, the Secretary of Labor, and the Secretary of Health, Education, and Welfare. Besides recognition of those needs and expression of support for programs meeting those needs, one of the outcomes was legislation for a White House Conference on Handicapped Individuals, similar to the coalition-led conferences in Minnesota. She was appointed to serve on the Planning Council for the Conference on Handicapped Individuals that was held in 1977 under President Jimmy Carter's administration.

During this same period, Jane, along with Cliff Miller of the Minnesota AFL-CIO organized and co-chaired the first Minnesota Coalition of and for Handicapped Persons. Governor Wendell Anderson held Governor's Conferences in 1972 and 1974 on the needs of people with disabilities. Thousands of people were involved in regional conferences leading up to the state sessions. Jane recalls, "We were helped by a great number of people, agencies, and organizations across the state. The recognition of needs is due to the participation of so many in these first-ever conferences."

Barrier-free transportation, working, and living arrangements were deemed critical. Without a barrier- free environment, people with disabilities could not be employed. One of the more visible achievements came from a meeting between Belau, Miller, and staff from the Governor's office and Department of Administration to hammer out changes to the Minnesota State Building Code to require accessibility for people with disabilities. Governor Wendell Anderson, his chief of staff, Tom Kelm, bipartisan legislators, and the legislative leadership, including the Senate Majority Leader Nick Coleman, House Speaker Marty Sabo, and many others, helped support accessible restrooms, apartments, and parking; ramps instead of steps; elevators; and curb cuts enabling people with wheelchairs to navigate sidewalks–all taken for granted today. The first modification enacted was curb cuts and ramps, installed whenever a sidewalk or corner was replaced. Of course, Jane wanted immediate and far-ranging action rather than awaiting replacements. She was patiently counseled: "Mrs. Belau, you can't have everything happen at once." These landmark changes in Minnesota's building code were formally passed into state law in 1975. Today, Minnesota cities continue to replace their corner curbs with gently sloped ramps to allow all people mobility where they live, work, or visit.

"The issues of accessibility, although different, are still with us today," Jane says. "New technologies are available that have not been put in place–for example, to open doors. Even some public buildings are not fully accessible. There are places where ramps aren't shoveled in the icy snows and slush of Minnesota winters that prevent wheelchairs and wheeled vehicles and people with reduced mobility from navigating the sidewalks. There is more to be done with continued vigilance."

The Belau Report

When Belau returned from Washington and the President's Committee on Employment of the Handicapped in May 1974, several who had attended the meeting asked if she would conduct a cable television interview on the needs and barriers issues. In 1972, at the insistence of the FCC Chair, Dean Burch, public access television had been created to fulfill some of the social potential of the newly emerging cable television. First required in top ten cable markets, it then expanded to all markets with more than three thousand subscribers. After her first interview, Jane was deluged with requests for similar programs. Soon, candidates for elections found the one place where they could get a half hour discussion of their issues rather than a thirty- to sixty-second clip on broadcast media. Jane's program, called The Belau Report, started in a small building on East Center Street in downtown Rochester. The recording studio was in the basement. To get there, the national, state, and local public figures trudged down the dimly lit stairs and along a hallway lined with photographs of previous guests. When it rained heavily, water seeped

Jane with Nancy Brataas on *The Belau Report*

into the hallway's carpet, and interviewees could be heard squeaking and squishing their way to the studio. Jane and her assistants thought it ironic that, for a time, they were owned by TelePrompTer Corporation but didn't have one. Sometimes when she went to Washington, her guests would arrange recording in the Senate recording studio, and Jane would bring the tapes back with her on the plane. Besides her continuous cable program, Jane also did programs at various times on KROC TV, KTTC TV, KSMQ, and KAUS (predecessor to KAAL), as well as sharing production with them. Occasionally in later years, programs would also appear on the Internet. Sometimes print media would join them, and many times national media followed national candidates.

There are many people who stand out in the years of *The Belau Report* for Jane. "This book's authors asked for some stories", she said. "So I thought I would mention some that everyone knows."

My first International guest was Ehud Olmert, then the youngest member of the Knesset, later to become Mayor of Jerusalem and Prime Minister of Israel. It was his first trip and we talked mostly about his government. When national figures came to Minnesota, I would frequently get the only personal interview and always the only half hour interview. Both Vice President Nelson Rockefeller and the Ronald Reagan interviews were conducted in cities other than Rochester (because that's where they were), with KTTC TV providing camera and production support. Vice President Nelson Rockefeller entered the room for his interview and, instead of going to meet his interviewer, went immediately to the long row of cameramen lining the back wall greeting each of them and shaking hands. I thought that was really nice and the cameramen were pleased. Shortly after that, I interviewed Ronald Reagan during his effort to gain the Republican nomination for President. He was not successful that year but four years later he was elected president. Gracious and charming, he talked with me about the many different jobs he enjoyed–from the silver screen to Governor of California and how such a diverse background would serve him well as president. Tapes of both those interviews were lost in the Rochester flood of 1978.

The always wonderful Senator, and then Vice President, Walter Mondale was with me all these years, even to a retrospective interview late last year. Whether under the horse chestnut tree on the lawn of the U.S. Capitol or the little studio on East Center Street, he was always honest, candid, and thorough. He told me when he decided he was not going to seek the nomination for President because he "didn't want to spend the next year in Holiday Inns" and then his "where's the beef?" quote in the election cycle when he did run for President–both before those phrases became household words in the mainstream media. He contributed so much to U.S. history and still does as an elder statesman. Vice President Hubert Humphrey was known for his extensive vocabulary and long answers. I would ask one question–what is the most pressing issue you face in–(your committee, the Senate, the country), and twenty-nine minutes later with just a few clarifying questions in between we would wrap up. Warm and friendly, he always brought friends with him to his interviews–breaking in to tell them to either sit down or stop talking—and then resuming where he had left off. The Happy Warrior, he was aptly called.

Senator Ted Kennedy, whom I interviewed on the U.S. Capitol steps, presented a different style. After I introduced myself, he asked, "What is the subject and how much time do we have?"

I said, "Senator, the Developmental Disabilities legislation and we have three minutes" He concisely summarized the bill, status, and prospects, finishing in exactly two minutes and fifty-nine seconds. We talked about that amazing precision several times since. And before long, I was interviewing the next generation: Ted Mondale, Chip Carter, and Skip Humphrey. When Al Franken was running for U.S. Senate, people referred to his Saturday Night Live appearances and his comedy, but as an interviewer, I knew that he, in a similar position with Air America, knew a great deal about public policy, foreign affairs, and economic principles, because as interviewers we learn so much from our guests. The Belau Report became a weekly one-hour class with an expert.

Congressman and then Governor Al Quie was a regular guest, bringing reports from Washington to his constituents in Southern Minnesota, with his most recent interview including Governor Arne Carlson and Governor Wendell Anderson and their perspectives on governance and politics. From Tim Penny's first television interview, all through his Congressional terms, his candidacy for Governor, right up to the present when he reports on the SE Minnesota Initiative Foundation he heads, he still takes time to talk about the National Committee for a Responsible Federal Budget that he co-chairs. Dave Durenberger, in his first winning campaign for U.S. Senate, talked about Washington "fever" where the problems arose when they started "believing their own press releases." After interviewing Governor Rudy Perpich, we went to a pizza place and the Governor made the pizza, twirling the dough over his head to the delight of six of us—four customers and two employees. Governor Tim Pawlenty, both as Governor and as candidate for the Republican presidential nomination, appeared on the program with a good grasp of national problems. Governor Jesse Ventura was a master at one-line answers, while I served as straight man. Senator Rudy Boschwitz with

Jane Belau interviews Senator Ted Kennedy on the U.S. Capitol steps. Before the cameras rolled, Kennedy asked, "What is the subject and how much time do we have?" Jane said, "Senator, the Developmental Disabilities legislation and we have three minutes." He concisely summarized the bill, status, and prospects finishing in exactly two minutes and fifty-nine seconds.

his plaid shirts, Senator Paul Wellstone, who prided himself as the "conscience of the Senate"–such a shock when he died–Senator Amy Klobuchar with her national reputation and bright future, Senator and then Governor Mark Dayton, current Congressman Tim Waltz, four Chief Justices of the Minnesota Supreme Court and five Associate Justices, Senate Majority leaders from Coleman to the remarkable Roger Moe, known for his effective leadership, all the way to current times with Senator Dave Senjem, so accommodating that he would come in at six a.m. for an interview on his way to the Capitol; all those interviewees from Federal, State, and local governments, agencies, spokespeople– more than there is room for here. We had great educational programs–fire prevention week, healthy living interviews with Mayo Clinic, and so on. Still, there is a long list of people I wished I had interviewed because they have such a wealth of history in their experience, like Al Eisele, Minnesota native and national figure, other authors local and national, people I worked with, a photographer whose experience with reclusive and other national figures would yield all kinds of stories–I emphasize there is no way in this chapter for me to acknowledge every interviewee, public servant, or those in the radio/TV world who gave me the most loyal and extensive help. How fortunate I was–and am.

Jane adds it has always been her policy and practice never to seek an interview with any person who was in Rochester for health care at Mayo Clinic. Other media did it, but it just seemed to her it would be inappropriate to do so. Over the past thirty-eight years she has recorded more than 2,100 programs with more than 2,600 guests. Jane has conducted programs with well-known people such as Jesse Jackson, Ralph Nader, sports figures, authors, mayors–Minneapolis, St. Paul, Rochester's: Smekta, Day, Hazama, Canfield, Brede–state and local government officials, higher education presidents, superintendents, school board members, Republicans, Democrats, Independence party candidates, and private sector leaders–winners and losers. Every single one she respected and valued, and all of whom shared remarkable insights, impressions and information with listeners. When asked how she developed the questions to use with the many different figures she interviewed, Jane replied, "I become a part of the audience, asking questions that would answer their questions. I learned so much from each interview, and that often became the basis of interviews for others."

Today Jane continues to host what is considered to be the longest running local origination public affairs program in the country. Her first program award was in 1974 for an interview with Attorney General Warren Spannaus, a best program for public affairs from what became the National Cable Television Association (and the awards became cable ACE awards). *The Belau Report* is recorded now at Rochester Community and Technical College and appears weekly. She preceded C-Span, which was conceived in 1975 by Brian Lamb and launched in March 1979. Her program began four years before the first of Andy Rooney's one thousand commentaries on CBS's *Sixty Minutes*.

An earlier proposed title for this chapter was "Jane Belau: Rochester's Barbara Walters". She did not approve that–she said she had her chance to go to New York in the late seventies but declined because it would mean leaving her home and family. She never envied Walters for getting up at three to four a.m. every day to do the *Today Show*–limousines, hair dressers, and all. Her commitment was, and is, to her home, community, and state. So, if anything, she would like to be "Jane Belau: Rochester's Brian Lamb", because of his conception of C-Span and its commitment to information for the public in a non-commercial environment.

Promoting the interests of Rochester

She was and is a "full-service" interviewer, often meeting the subject at a hotel or even the airport, driving him or her around town for interviews with other media, setting up tours of local businesses and organizations like IBM and Mayo Clinic, and facilitating plans for any other meetings the subject may want. By the 1990s, she was the founder of Government Forums and moderator of the Rochester Chamber of Commerce's very successful Eggs and Issues breakfasts (and lunches) with key political figures, often the same ones she would interview for her TV program. To aid in citizen-speaker interaction, she often asked the attendees to introduce themselves and their issue in a short statement, before the speaker addressed the crowd. What had once been a speech-to-audience format became a conversation between public figures and a community of individuals. Jane has used her knowledge of issues and key political people, as well as superb interviewing skills to provide a rich interaction for Rochester citizens and interests.

Former long-time Majority Leader of the Minnesota State Senate, Roger Moe, who was also a native of northwest Minnesota, describes his friendship with Jane:

Throughout the years I was in office Jane would visit me at the Capitol and was the consummate ambassador for Rochester and for disabilities issues. Everyone in my office knew Jane Belau! She would "stop by" the office, rarely made an appointment, but always had a list of things she needed to brief me on. Those big round glasses and wearing her favorite color, black, coupled with a big smile and gregarious demeanor made her memorable to everyone. She would have me come to Rochester for Chamber meetings on Saturday mornings, for visits to Mayo Clinic, IBM, and other companies, and then I would always do her TV show.

Corporate executive

In 1974, Jane was appointed by the Governor to the Minnesota Parole Board, a full-time, five-member board, one of many local and state boards on which she served. The makeup of the board was described in the enabling legislation to contain a member of the judiciary, one from law enforcement, one from the parole system, a former inmate, and a woman. This job, the only one she ever got simply on the basis that she was a woman, was described to her as requiring about a day a week, but ended up full time with daily commuting to the prisons. The experience, frustrating because services were so limited at the time, both inside the facilities and on the street, expanded her public education and human services background. Jane also served on the newly-created Corrections Ombudsman Commission where she met Norbert Berg, a top official at Control Data. Impressed with her and her work, he asked her to interview for a position at the company, then in the middle of the *Fortune 100* list. As a result, she became the Vice President for Governmental Affairs in 1979 for Control Data when there were only a handful of women in the country holding comparable positions. That fact led her, along with Marilyn Carlson Nelson and others, to co-found an organization patterned after the Detroit Economic Roundtable and a similar New York organization, a high-level women's networking organization that flourishes today.

One of Jane's proudest accomplishments as Vice President resulted from a trip to New York City. Senior Vice President Norbert Berg had been home with a cold, watching a TV Report on New York's City Harvest, which fed surplus restaurant food to the poor. He dispatched Jane to New York to visit the program, learn about it, and bring it home. On her return, Control Data organized a task force to start a similar program in Minnesota, which became Second Harvest Heartland. In 2012, they are in their twenty-ninth year of operation. Jane helped secure passage of necessary legislation to enable and encourage businesses to help. Locally, Joe Powers, owner of the Canadian Honker Restaurant, brought the Community Food Response program to Rochester.

Jane worked for four different Control Data Chief Executive Officers: founder Bill Norris, Bob Price, Ron Turner and Larry Perlman. She learned much from each of them. Norris' active mind and incredible energy led CDC to provide leadership for many programs: business and technology centers, healthy living programs, health data bases, City Ventures and Rural Ventures, and Control Data Education centers, with which Jane had the privilege of working. His seed capital, angel capital, venture capital, and job creation network are still applicable today. That, and working with the city of Bloomington and the state on the construction of a new headquarters in Bloomington, addressing environmental and other sensitive issues, were valuable to Jane when she became the first president of Rochester Area Economic Development, Inc. (RAEDI), in 1985. She was nominated by Bill Boyne, then *Post-Bulletin* publisher and himself active in the founding of RAEDI.

Control Data's business changed dramatically in 1992 to become a more efficient, smaller services business called Ceridian. As Control Data changed, so did Jane's role. She commuted for twenty-two years to the headquarters in Bloomington. She drove to the Twin Cities and back so many times on Highway 52 that she developed a first-name relationship with many of the Minnesota State troopers and was even invited to their retirement parties. The commute began to wear on her. She recalls, "One dark, bitterly cold early morning I was driving to the Cities. South of Cannon Falls I passed a farm. Steam was pouring from barn doors where a farmer milked his cows. The lights were on in the farmhouse kitchen where the mother served breakfast to her family. I wished I were home." Jane left Control Data soon after and started her own consulting business with Ceridian as her major client.

"If that isn't being a good citizen, I don't know what is."

Board, committee, and leadership positions seem to follow her wherever she goes. Success in one endeavor, and the personal connections and relationships developed therein have led to an ever expanding list of accomplishments for Jane in the public and private sectors. Currently, she is President of the University Regent Candidate Advisory Council, a member of the Rochester City Charter Commission, and a Minnesota Supreme Court appointee to the Third District Judicial Selection Commission. Awards must line the shelves of her home because of her successes in a broad range of national, international, state and community public service activities but she will say that her accomplishments, along with her gifts, are due to her blessings of faith, the support of her family of bright and public service-oriented adults and loving little ones, and her many friends.

Her "old fashioned but still good" advice to young women today is:
· "Honesty is the best policy."
· "Be prepared. Opportunities open up but you need to be ready."
· "The Golden Rule: do unto others as you would have them do unto you."
· "Never do, say, or write anything that could not appear in the national or local press or go viral on the internet. And this goes for social media and e-mails. There is a whole new etiquette for texting, use of personal electronic assistants, how to write e-mails, proofing, distribution, etc. (That's another book!)"
· "*Listen* to people: your co-workers, your bosses, your employees."
· "While "dress for success" may be outdated, don't dress for failure. (First impressions always matter.)"
· "Don't forget stewardship of your gifts and 'giving back' by mentoring others."
· "And, doing this chapter reminds me–keep records of what you do, whom you see, what public policies you interact with–someday you may need to recall things you thought you would never forget. And, guess what, they are no longer in your database. Maybe they are but they don't come to mind easily. That also applies to your family activities. A history kept up regularly will make your children happy you did it."

Albert Eisele, editor-at-large and founding editor of *The Hill*, a non-partisan newspaper covering Congress that he helped start in 1994, life-long friend, author and press secretary for Vice President Walter Mondale, worked with Jane at Control Data and served with her on the National Advisory Council of Saint John's University. He provided the following tribute to Jane:

Jane Belau is the personification of the good citizen. She's an amazing combination of energy, brains and heart, all devoted to making life better for all those she comes into contact with, whether it's her neighbors in Rochester, Minnesota, her fellow Minnesotans and her fellow Americans . . . She's demonstrated her leadership skills while promoting civil rights for people with disabilities and encouraging innovative public policy in economic development, higher education and job creation at the local, state and federal levels, especially through coalitions and partnerships in the public and private sectors. All this and she's a wife, mother, grandmother, and great-grandmother, dedicated to faith, family and friends, still active as a public servant, an accomplished musician and poet and still host of the political talk show The Belau Report. *If that isn't a lifetime of being an exemplary citizen, I don't know what is.*

Looking Out for Future Generations

Doris Blinks took the lead on water and zoning issues

The Rochester community has a history of awareness regarding environmental issues. In the spring of 1964, Mayo Clinic invited Rachel Carson to speak in a panel discussion about the conservation of natural resources. Carson was famous for having published the book *Silent Spring* in 1962. She accepted the invitation knowing that she was very sick. Sadly, she died just before the conference. Dorothy Callahan attended the event and remembers that during a moment of silence to remember Carson, insects were heard buzzing around the ceiling of the auditorium. One panelist looked up and said, "I think Dr. Carson is here in spirit."

Doris Blinks is also here in spirit in Olmsted County whenever issues about the environment are discussed. Doris and John Blinks arrived in the area in 1968 and lived here for more than twenty years. John served as Chair of Pharmacology at Mayo Clinic, and during those years Doris brought considerable influence and passion to all matters dealing with water planning and land use. The Environmental Lifetime Achievement Award for Olmsted County is still called the "Doris Blinks Award," and she was the first recipient. She also received awards from the Minnesota Environmental Education Board, the Olmsted County Board of Health, and the Community Citizenship Award from San Juan County, Washington, after she relocated there in 1989.

Doris Chambers Blinks was born in Philadelphia in 1929 and was raised in the countryside near Dover, Massachusetts. Her early interest in science led to a biology degree from Bryn Mawr and a master's degree in biological sciences from Stanford. She married her hus-

Doris Blinks brought considerable influence and passion to all matters dealing with water planning and land use. The Environmental Lifetime Achievement Award for Olmsted County is still called the "Doris Blinks Award," and she was the first recipient. (Courtesy Post-Bulletin Co.)

band, John, in 1953 and moved to Boston, where he was a medical student at Harvard. Doris continued graduate studies in Boston, Bethesda, Maryland, and finally in Milton, Massachusetts, where she and John settled for a time. It was in Milton that Doris first became active in conservation issues by serving on the Warrant Committee of the Town of Milton. That position led her to become a member of the Open Space Committee and advocate for cluster zoning and wetland acquisition.

Many of Doris' personal activities prepared her for work in conserving the natural world. She loved a variety of outdoor activities and was a horsewoman, hiker, cross-country skier, and gardener. She joined both the Sierra Club and the League of Women Voters in the early 1960s and was an active member of both organizations until her death in 2003.

In Rochester, Doris was a member of the Soil Conservation Service Advisory Committee and the Citizens Advisory Committee to the Army Corps of Engineers, both of which dealt with the Flood Control Project. After her three years of experience on the project, she joined the Olmsted County Planning Advisory Commission and served from 1978 until 1985. She was the chair in 1982 and 1983 when the commission revised the existing zoning ordinance based on the Land Use Plan adopted in 1978. Doris has written that the goal pursued in these activities was to direct growth and preserve open space and agricultural land.

Terry Lee, currently the Water Resources Coordinator for Public Works of Olmsted County, remembers Doris as a "remarkably intelligent, active and thoughtful person." She was helpful to the community by coming forward and advocating the right things at the public level. "She helped provide the energy on key problems." Terry calls her a "progressive spirit" who stood up for the things she felt strongly about.

Looking ahead to the future and future generations

Doris also served on the Olmsted County Board of Adjustment from 1981 to 1983 and the Hiawatha Valley Resource Conservation and Development Area Committee of Soil Conservation Service from 1987 to 1990. In 1987 a growing understanding of the importance of water to Olmsted County led to the creation of the Water Policy Advisory Committee, a group charged with developing a water management plan. It was natural for Doris Blinks to become chairman of the new group. In a *Post-Bulletin* article written at the time of her appointment, she was quoted as saying, "[E]nvironmental issues are at a critical point. We don't have a Love Canal situation here, but we must look ahead and avoid it. That's what I try to do–to look ahead to the future and to future generations."

Doris was legendary for her ability to master the details of difficult areas of study and to be completely prepared for her meetings. Dorothy Callahan remembers, "She was so careful. She investigated everything and she knew exactly what she was talking about."

Doris always told the truth and was not one to back down from a confrontation. In later years she wrote to a friend, "But I am involved . . . [despite] all the situations I got into in the past as a matter of principle . . . fear[ing] that I would be sued."

Phil Wheeler, the Planning Director for Rochester and Olmsted County, remembers that Doris worked on the Committee on Urban Environment, which was among the first to come up with the idea for a bike path. On one occasion, during a presentation of the official map for a street widening in the early 1980s, Doris questioned the description of a structure near the right of way that was described as a shed and would have to be removed. Doris asked, "If this is a shed, why are there curtains in the windows?" This level of detailed knowledge was typical of Doris. Dorothy Callahan remembers that when she and Doris drove to an area that was under scrutiny, they always got out and inspected the grounds.

After Doris and John moved to the San Juan Islands near Seattle, Doris continued to be involved in causes related to conservation. She served on the San Juan County Land Bank Commission and on the Advisory Committee for the Comprehensive Land Use Plan for San Juan County. In her application for the Land Bank Commission, she wrote, "I am able to make informed decisions and not be intimidated by short term pressure interests; I am pragmatic and believe that management of land use and growth must and can take into account both environmental values and economic viability; and I am willing and able to spend the time needed to become adequately informed."

Doris' science background helped her to master the intricacies of threats to natural resources and to figure out solutions to those problems. But part of her passion for conservation work came from her love of the outdoors. This appreciation of nature is evident in a letter she wrote after relocating to San Juan. Her closing remark can be read not just as an invitation to a friend to visit. It is also a suggestion to all of us, to get outside and explore the incredible world we live in.

We watch Orca whales passing our land several times a day, sometimes just below our cliff–as close as you would see them at a place like Sea World. They go by in 'pods' of fifteen to twenty and we find them very exciting. Bald eagles pass overhead. On a really clear day we can see three glacier-covered mountains: Mt. Baker in the Cascades, Mt. Rainier behind Seattle, and the Olympic mountains. Come see for yourself.

A Woman's Place is in the House
. . . and the Senate

In 1975 Nancy Brataas became the first woman to be elected to the Minnesota Senate in her own right (Laura Emilia Naplin filled her deceased husband's senate seat from 1927 to 1934)

It was December, 1974. She was in Cleveland, both exhilarated and exhausted, as she worked on the first contract for her new consulting firm, Nancy Brataas Associates, Inc., and her first non-political client, the March of Dimes. She had been hired very late in the process, and the short days of winter were hardly long enough for her to get the work done. One night, her husband phoned from their home in Rochester, Minnesota, with a surprising suggestion: "Why not submit your name for consideration for state senator?" The Republican endorsing convention would be held that week in Rochester. The incumbent senator, Harold Krieger, had resigned following his judicial election, creating the vacancy. This could be Nancy's chance to be a candidate instead of just working for one.

But Nancy couldn't leave her job in Cleveland unfinished. After all, she had a small business loan, as well as the future of her business, to consider. Furthermore, having led Voter ID (Identification of potential supportive voters) and GOTV (Get-Out-The-Vote of those same identified voters) efforts for the 1972 Nixon re-election campaign in the ten key industrial states, she knew she must to be present at the convention to win the endorsement. She declined her husband's suggestion and considered that opportunity closed.

The day after returning home in mid-December, Nancy was invited to lunch by Jan Gallager, a future Olmsted County Republican Chairwoman, and several Republican friends, including Craig Beck, Carl Laumann, and Chub Stewart. To her surprise, Nancy was told that the convention had failed to endorse a candidate. There had been

31

two contenders for the senate seat endorsement–City Alderman Darrell Strain and County Commissioner Bruce Cherland–who both indicated they would run in a primary, but this lunch group wanted Nancy to run.

After a long pause, Nancy responded, "I don't know if I can be elected or not, but if I do run, I will need people to carry out serious responsibilities in a short, intense campaign." Immediately she put on her familiar hat of campaign volunteer organizer par excellence, and continued, "Who is going to chair my campaign? How about you, Carl? And Chub, how about you for finance?" She continued around the table, assigning jobs to the ten who had invited her to lunch. Her campaign for state senator was off and running.

The first campaign

After telling her friends she would undertake the campaign, Nancy decided she'd better set up a final reality check for herself. Her close friends, who happened to be Republican leaders, supported her, but did other "thought leaders" in her community think she could win? For two days she made phone calls, hearing the same message from those phoned: "You are a nice lady, but a woman probably can't win." Her two primary opponents, each a current elected local government official, stopped by her home to urge her not to enter the race. Then her husband, Jerry, intervened as she considered throwing in the towel. "Quit phoning people and run," he said. "You are not a state senator now, so if you don't win, you haven't lost a thing. You know how to do this. Just get to work!" And so she did.

Nancy knew she had to combat voter apathy at a special election scheduled on a snowy Saturday in February. She alone of the candidates realized the importance of purchasing and using a copy of the list of registered voters for personalized mailings. Her campaign letter introduced herself and asked all voters, regardless of party, for support. Her volunteers followed up with an extensive telephone campaign to identify voters "for," "undecided," and "against" Nancy. On Election Day, the volunteers kept calling their list of "for" individuals

with the message, "Have you voted yet?" until they heard, "Yes."
Nancy warned, "There's no phoning going on without daily reporting.
The only people who don't want to report are those who haven't done
their jobs!" Her organizational method attracted enthusiastic volunteers and inspired them to report their progress.

During her campaign she emphasized issues unusual for a
woman: taxes and capital investment. State Senator Bob Stassen, an
investment banker from West St. Paul, tutored her thoroughly so that
she could speak clearly and authoritatively to constituent groups on
these topics. Even though it was sometimes twenty degrees below
zero, she went door-to-door in high voter turn-out areas–even to a
small trailer court, where she surprised the residents who had never
been approached by a political candidate.

Using the techniques she had perfected in campaigns for other
candidates all across the country, and armed with the $20,000 raised
by her finance chair in just two weeks, Nancy committed to a comprehensive campaign. The community, not just the Republicans or the
political elites, responded with an average of $17.22 per donor. This
pattern of soliciting numerous small donations continued throughout
her future elections. She often raised the most money among all Minnesota Senate candidates, but in the smallest denominations.

Nancy won the primary and the general election as well, this
time against Tom Resner, a young man who had been a state representative but had just suffered defeat for re-election in November. The
1974 elections were the first time that Minnesota legislators were required to run with party designation; so Resner's status as Demo-
cratic-Farmer-Labor (DFL) worked against him in Republican
Rochester despite his being well-known. Nancy credited her win in
good part to her previous Republican Party activity and to her husband, who, as a civic leader, had already made "Brataas" a recognized
and respected name in the community. But she also won because of
the desires of women to elect one of their own. For months afterward
while she shopped at the grocery store, women she did not know
came up to her, grabbing her arm or hand, to tell her how glad they
were she had won.

Nancy Brataas, the first woman to be elected to the Minnesota Senate in her own right, is shown with (left to right) Sen. Mel Frederick, Rep. Don Freidrich, Rep. Ken Zubay, Rep. Dick Kaley, and Rep. Warren "Tom" Stowell, all locally elected Republicans circa 1980.

Inquiring minds want to know

Will your main legislative work be on behalf of women's rights?" the newest senator was asked repeatedly, according to an article in the March 21 *Senate Perspective '75*. Nancy is quoted as answering, "My election represents equal rights in action. I represent both men and women in Rochester so it would be a mistake for all other issues to become secondary. Throughout my campaign I said repeatedly that I would not vote to rescind the Equal Rights Amendment"–in spite of the fact that the Republican platform had the opposite position–"but I am really amazed at how many other women's issues there are that I, at least, have not been reading about in the papers."

People wanted to know if one of the men's restrooms in the Capitol would need to be converted to a women's restroom. According to a DFL Majority Leader's aide, John Kaul, Senate Leadership met to decide whether to make such an architectural change. After all, the election of one female senator did not a trend make. Why make permanent changes in a perfectly good men's bathroom?

People also wondered whether the Senate dress code would be applied to a woman. Nancy's conservative dress would be referred to years later in a 1991 *Session Weekly* article. Pat Flahaven, Secretary of the Senate, when asked about the Senate's strict dress code in relation to the more casual House's code, responded, "It could be that the Senate has 'annunciated' its unwritten 'appropriate attire' code, which has meant ties for the men and conservative dress for women, following Senator Nancy Brataas' lead." A former senate page, Mary Beth Davidson, remembers admiring the "beautiful suede suits that Senator Brataas wore to sessions."

Another question on the minds of many was how the all-male Minnesota Senate would receive their newest member. Nancy re-members: "I was unequivocally welcomed from both sides of the aisle. In fact, I was probably the recipient of reverse discrimination, with all sorts of offers for help from both Republican and DFL Senators, and bipartisan reprieves for some parliamentary errors as well." She learned how to be effective as a double minority during her entire career in the Minnesota Senate: as a woman, and as a Republican. Her success came not from "fighting" the majority party and committee chairs, but "from working with them within the bounds of shared core principles."

Majority Leader Nick Coleman assigned Nancy, a University of Minnesota Art History major, to the Labor and Commerce Committee, telling her, "You can do the least damage there." But it was on this committee that she became expert on the details of the workers' compensation law, carrying the Republican reform bills year after year. Actually, she deemed her expertise an "albatross," because no other Republican wanted to remove this issue from around her neck. To escape, they always claimed no one could equal her grasp and organization of detail. Her training bill which she co-authored with the other minority member, Bob Lewis, a black DFL Senator who was a veterinarian, was on the subject of a health-related state licensing board and examining committee for physical therapists.

In very little time Nancy got down to the business of championing key local issues for Rochester. Her campaign organizational skills came to the fore as she maneuvered these bills through the state legislature. She was helped, as she believed all senators were, by using the many receptions held for all legislators by interest groups lobbying for their issues. At these informal gatherings, after listening to the groups' pitches, senators like Nancy Brataas did their real work by lining up support for their bills, developing friendships "across the aisle," looking for allies, feeling out positions of key members, discovering what was important to others, and in her case, relentlessly pursuing votes for Rochester issues.

Ask what you can do for your country . . . and community

Senator Brataas lists as two of her most important legislative victories the passing of the first Rochester local option sales tax (1983) and the positive disposition of the closed Rochester State Hospital (Third Special Session 1982 and later sessions). After the flood of 1978, Rochester city leaders worked tirelessly for legislation to fund a flood control project. Federal money was essential, but a local match of sixteen million dollars was also required. A one percent local option sales tax would raise sixteen million dollars for flood control and sixteen million dollars for a civic center expansion, and that was what the Rochester delegation (Senator Brataas, Representative Dave Bishop, and Representative Gil Gutknecht) was asked to deliver.

Before the city could collect the sales tax, however, the Minnesota Legislature would have to approve it. The legislature had always jealously guarded its taxing authority–having allowed, at that time, a local sales tax for only the three first-class cities in the state. Rochester's top civic leaders visited the Tax Committee members one-by-one, in a full-scale campaign. The bill's authors agreed to add a local referendum to aid passage. Senate Republicans supported the measure, and Senator Doug Johnson, DFL Tax Chair, agreed not to oppose it.

In the House, the DFL leadership demanded two votes from Republicans on the omnibus tax bill as a requirement to include the

Rochester sales tax. One of the Republicans, Gil Gutknecht, refused to vote for the tax bill, but a suburban Rochester Republican, Representative Don Frerichs, agreed to be the other Republican vote. The partnership of Bishop and Brataas delivering major legislation for Rochester was just beginning.

In the 1981 session, facing a recession and a large deficit, the DFL legislature voted to close one state hospital–and it was in Rochester, Governor Quie's former congressional district. Many regarded it as the premier institution in the state, but Governor Quie felt he must acquiesce to this cost-saving measure, given the large deficit facing Minnesota.

Attempting to "pull some chestnuts out of the fire," Nancy convinced the Governor to allow Olmsted County to buy the facility for one dollar, because millions of dollars in annual maintenance would be borne by the county as the "caretaker" of the property. In fact, when she heard that his administration planned to recommend charging the county fourteen million dollars, she left the Senate floor during the Third Special Session in December 1982 and marched down to "discuss" the price directly with the Governor, convincing him that one dollar was indeed the appropriate amount.

During the process of closing the Rochester State Hospital and looking for uses that would bring needed jobs back to the community, Nancy called some of her contacts in the Reagan Administration. One U.S. Bureau of Prisons acquaintance in D.C. told her that the Bureau might be quite interested in this Rochester property. While the idea of selling part of the property for a prison was politically contentious, Nancy Brataas and Dave Bishop passed legislation allowing the county to keep the profit from the sale–profit that otherwise by law would have reverted to the state–in the form of state investments in their community's projects: a waste-to-energy facility, a human services campus, and a Winona State University building on the University Center campus in Rochester. All of these projects helped the community accept a federal prison in the area once occupied by the former Rochester State Hospital.

In the 1985-86 session, Senator Brataas and Representative Bishop won an easement and purchase from the Department of Natural Resources (DNR) to allow Olmsted County to complete East Circle Drive (County 22). Although the DNR had oversight of the former Rochester State Hospital property, including the land needed for this highway, they did not have "ownership." Even so, they were not willing to allow Highway 22 to cut through the property they were using to protect and feed flocks of Canadian geese. Nancy turned for help to Senator Gerald Willet, DFL chair of the Finance Committee, former chair of the Agriculture and Natural Resources Committee, and soon-to-be-appointed to Commissioner of the MPCA (Minnesota Pollution Control Administration) by Governor Perpich. Senator Willet recommended that the county take aerial photos of the area, noting especially the circuitous route garbage trucks must take through residential areas on their way to the newly built waste-to-energy facility. Then he suggested creating a block-long gallery of these photos propped up on the tables lining the semi-private hallway along the side of the Senate Chamber. "You've got the Republicans, Nancy, so you need to invite every DFL Senator, one at a time, to view these pictures as you explain what needs to be done and why," he advised. When the bill was heard in committee, Nancy gave a short introduction, and the affirmative vote was unanimous. "Thanks to Senator Willet, and others like Senator Lessard, that was the miracle of the century," she concluded. DNR staff appeared surprised and miffed, causing Nancy to observe, "No highway has more mitigations than this one. There is hardly one living creature that is not afforded an expensive mode of crossing, except people!"

In 1985 Governor Rudy Perpich had a judicial appointment to make in the Third Judicial District (including Rochester). Nancy joined Sandy Keith (former DFL Senator, Lt. Governor, close friend of the Governor, and ultimately Chief Justice of the Minnesota Supreme Court) in lobbying on behalf of a highly competent Rochester woman attorney, Ancy Morse, who if appointed, would become the first woman judge in the judicial district's history. While Sandy lobbied the Governor, Nancy drafted a letter of support and gained the signatures of every female Minnesota legislator, both DFL and Republican, some of whom she tracked down during their travel in foreign countries. The Governor appointed Ancy Morse as the first woman Third Judicial District Judge.

A woman's work is never done

Being a state senator is a part-time job In Minnesota. When she was not organizing community and senate issues, Nancy was organizing on behalf of other Republican candidates. Her clients included Presidents Nixon, Ford, and Reagan; U.S. Senators Richard Lugar, Phil Gramm, Pete Domenici, Chuck Percy, Rudy Boschwitz, and Dave Durenberger; Governors Arne Carlson, Bill Clements, Dave Treen, Al Quie, and Bill Milliken; more than 200 state legislators; and several corporations and non-profit organizations.

Nancy had amazing success recruiting enthusiastic volunteers to perform Voter ID and GOTV tasks in a highly organized fashion. It was hard and risky work, as one never knew if candidates would ultimately pay their bills in full. "She was a very smart lady and ahead of her time on Voter ID," said former DFL Minnesota Speaker of the House, Bob Vanasek, who once toured her very impressive home-based operation.

One of Nancy's employees in the 1980s was a high school student council president, John Wade (now President of the Rochester Area Chamber of Commerce). Twenty-five years after working for Nancy, John still carried in the inside pocket of his suit coat an enduring lesson from his former employer: a black pen, a blue pen, a red pen, and a highlighter–all at the ready. He remembers marveling at her attention to detail, her command of the facts, and her perseverance. He compliments Nancy by remarking that, since working for her, he has advised others on many campaigns to "Just give in and do it Nancy's way–because you know you will in the end. It'll be right. You might as well get to it."

Wade recalls being told one evening to appear at her home the next day at seven a.m. to drive her to the airport in Minneapolis.

She was preparing a presentation for a client in California. When he arrived, his employer was sitting at the dining room table, just completing an "all-nighter." Nancy looked like anyone would who had been up all night, working on a project. She headed upstairs telling him to "wait there until I whistle." Thirty-five minutes later, a whistle sent him bounding upstairs where he found her packed and "looking like a million dollars." Off he drove with his employer and her luggage and presentation in the station wagon, heeding the suggestion to "gun it" as soon as they passed the highway patrol office on Highway 52, heading for the Twin Cities airport.

Gender or agenda?

As a past State Republican Chairwoman for seven years, responsible for writing, producing and leading statewide Voter ID and GOTV; consultant for campaigns of famous Republicans at the federal level; delegate to several National Republican Conventions; and a sitting state senator, Nancy Brataas had a résumé that revealed a highly qualified candidate for higher office. But again and again, her own state and local parties denied her that opportunity.

In 1978, she was the odds-on favorite to be the nominee for Minnesota Lieutenant Governor. It would have been another first for a woman. But as viewers watched the televised convention, they saw the delegates choose the relatively unknown Lou Wangberg, a school superintendent from Bemidji, instead of Nancy.

In 1984, the year Nancy brought to Rochester the largest ever bonding project in the amount of nineteen million dollars for the expansion of the Rochester Community College, she ran for Republican endorsement for the First District Congressional seat from Minnesota. But newcomer Keith Spicer secured that endorsement.

In 1990, her own senate district refused to endorse Nancy, the sitting senator, forcing her to run and win a highly contested primary election. The evolving Republican Party disagreed with her pro-choice position, which apparently overshadowed her extensive past service to party and community.

Was it "gender or agenda?" wondered David Lebedoff (Minneapolis DFL attorney and University of Minnesota Regent) who wrote an editorial in the Minneapolis *Star* on December 18, 1978, in which he called Nancy "one of the most respected and powerful women in Minnesota politics." He also discussed the recent convention and election.

So there she was, left out in the cold, passed over by the party she had served so well. And what did she do with that rejection? Did she pout? Did she cry? Did she quit? She did not. Instead she redoubled her efforts to serve the Independent Republican (IR) Party. She made up her mind to feed the hand that bit her. What Nancy Brataas did between the IR convention and the November election (managing statewide Voter ID and GOTV) has more to do with her party's landslide victory than the work of any other Republican in the state . . . surely the engineer of the most impressive party comeback in recent political history.

Perform something worthy

Nancy's advice is "young people should jump with both feet into the ocean of public affairs and civic activities. Participate fully in the process. Learn how the system works." She does not tutor those who are thinking about politics; she prefers to call her guidance "sharing experiences." But she doesn't let capable people hang back. After serving seventeen years in the Minnesota State Senate, Nancy finally successfully recruited her successor, Sheila Kiscaden, asking her over and over again to run and finally promising to be her campaign manager.

Nancy's leadership style has turned many "watchers" into "doers" in the political realm. She is unfailingly polite, incredibly organized, purposeful–and persistent, persistent, persistent. One volunteer joked that Nancy "summons, she doesn't invite." That is because she assumes that citizens should want to be involved in the current issues affecting their lives. Most end up agreeing.

Some local women who have inspired Nancy include the "unbelievably courageous" Alcantara Schneider who, as a Catholic nun, defended her pro-choice position as a DFL candidate during a local candidates' forum. Nancy also admires the "extremely competent and tremendously talented" Jane Belau, a successful Control Data executive and highly accomplished pianist, artist, and television issues commentator, who for many years hosted a local interview program on which Nancy appeared countless times.

"We all stand on the shoulders of others," Nancy says. "My mentors were Charlotte Anderson, who invited me to my first Republican meeting, and Betty Grindley, former Olmsted County Republican Chairwoman, who inspired me to become politically active. When Betty ran for school board around 1960 she was, in effect, my 'snowplow,' opening the way for me, as well as for other women to run for public office, even though she herself lost."

The frieze around the top of the wall in the Minnesota Senate chamber contains a quote from Daniel Webster: "Let us develop the resources of our land, call forth its powers, build up its institutions, promote all its great interests, and see whether we also, in our day and generation, may not perform something worthy to be remembered." Nancy Brataas, the first woman Minnesota State Senator elected in her own right, founder of a highly successful consulting firm, and well-known community champion, has indeed lived up to this challenge.

Loaned Executive, Household Manager, Etc.

Dorothy Callahan tackled affordable housing

When Dorothy Callahan moved from Philadelphia to Rochester, Minnesota, in 1952, she was a young biochemist and mother of one. She had always loved science and excelled at Radcliffe, which led to three years as a research scientist in her hometown of Boston at Harvard University and one in Philadelphia at the University of Pennsylvania. Little did she realize that the move to Rochester would in short order turn her thoughts to housing and public policy issues. After living one year in a walk-up apartment, carrying groceries and a baby up two flights, she and her husband, John, moved into the Quonset huts. The huts were old World War II wooden housing units which were being used to house Mayo Clinic medical students and their families. Dorothy estimates that there were more than 300 children under six years old in them. She contributed three of the children herself, finally moving out in 1955. She remembers the huts as "leaking a lot."

Housing as a personal issue

The Quonsets were closed in the early 1960s, and Mayo Clinic developed new housing for its medical students. The new project became Homestead Village in the southeastern part of Rochester. Dorothy, asked to give input from a resident's perspective, had definite opinions on what needed to be done. The high water table in that area meant that these new units could have no basement and, instead, would have a centralized laundry area. In the Quonset huts, Dorothy had used her old downstairs washing machine with the wringer and

43

Dorothy Callahan with her son Mark in front of the Quonset huts. Dorothy advised against a proposed centralized laundry area, saying, "You can't leave babies alone to go do the laundry." She persevered in her arguments, and finally the units were built with laundry facilities off the kitchen area. Her fight for better housing design had just begun.

then had hung out the clothes on lines there, since she had no dryer. The kids would run through the newly hung laundry as she worked. Dorothy advised against the proposed centralized laundry area, saying, "You can't leave babies alone to go do the laundry." She persevered in her arguments, and finally the units were built with laundry facilities off the kitchen area. It would not be the last time she would fight for better housing design.

Eventually Dorothy and her family moved into a house on 16th Street, officially outside the city limits. They joined St. John's parish, the only Catholic church in the southwest quadrant of the Rochester area. The pastor was concerned that some people within his parish had never been visited by the church. Dorothy and a friend volunteered to go door-knocking and see if there were families in the hilly area behind her house who would like to attend St. John's. Dorothy was appalled by some of the conditions she saw. There were houses with no running water and some with no sewer lines and a horrible stench. This was yet another experience which sensitized her to the importance of adequate housing.

Because of her religious upbringing, Dorothy felt a deep calling to help the poor and the needy. She would spend thirty years leading a current-events study hour for the closed psychiatric unit at Saint Marys Hospital. Her work in community corrections to advocate for good treatment of inmates is a story told in another chapter of this book. And her work in the League of Women Voters is legendary. During her early days in the Quonset huts, one neighbor kept insisting that Dorothy should attend the League of Women Voters meeting that met in the housing project. When Dorothy finally did attend, a lifelong interest in government and public affairs was ignited. "It was such a marvelous time!" she recalls. During her years in the League, she would study the United Nations, water quality, land use planning, and waste disposal issues, among others. Her oldest son remembers he would come home from college and all his mother would want to talk about was sewage treatment. In 2004, Dorothy was made a lifetime member of the League after fifty years of active participation.

Dorothy's conscience motivates her into action

In 1985, the Rochester Area Chamber of Commerce and others commissioned a study known as FutureScan 2000 to help plan intelligent policies for the future of the community. Dorothy was on the steering committee of thirty-eight members, listed as representing the Rochester League of Women Voters (LWV). That steering committee requested suggestions for areas to study. The initial four subjects were higher education, job formation, downtown development, and restructuring local government. Each subject became a task force with a chairperson and a "loaned executive" from the area being studied.

Dorothy was worried that the process had not included a large enough cross section of the public. She also worried that there were other issues that were of more immediate importance to the poor. Here was another time that Dorothy's conscience motivated her into action.

The LWV Minnesota had been studying housing, and Dorothy felt certain that the Rochester community had a problem in that area. Following the 1980 census, members of the League of Women Voters had participated in a phone survey that showed a significant percentage of Olmsted County's population was paying too much for housing. Too many people were spending more than the recommended thirty percent of take-home pay on housing. Anecdotal understanding of this also came from the many people volunteering to help immigrants find a place to stay in the community. Houses designed for two families had been split up to accommodate four families, but the arrangements were not reasonable. The consciousness of people was being raised about conditions that the poor had just accepted in the past. That gave Dorothy an opening.

Bill Boyne, the editor of the local daily paper, the *Post-Bulletin*, was also on the FutureScan 2000 steering committee. He, too, felt there needed to be more public input on the issue selection process. He graciously harnessed the power of the local daily paper's circulation. A survey open to the public was published, generating a good return rate. The public's response to the survey was no surprise to Dorothy. One of the main topics of concern was the lack of affordable housing in the Rochester area.

Other factors were about to make the rental market worse. In the 1980s, people owning rental property lost the ability to deduct losses connected with their landlord duties on their income taxes. Additionally, the state of Minnesota was preparing to make property tax rates on rental property three times those of owner-occupied housing.

Armed with these facts, Dorothy and others were able to make the case that there should be a fifth study focused on housing. But the FutureScan people did not want to recruit another "loaned executive," so she was asked to be the loaned executive for the task force. While every other loaned executive was identified as "Attorney" or "Dean," her title was "Loaned Executive–Household Manager, Etc." She wasn't officially representing the League, despite the fact that her husband had always opined, "I regret that I have but one wife to give to the League of Women Voters!" Of course, running a household of two adults, seven children, and nine animals was a very complicated matter. She never challenged the published affiliation.

The chairman of the task force was supposed to be different from the "loaned executive" and fulfill a different role. Unfortunately, the named chairman resigned before the first meeting of the group. Dorothy agreed to chair the task force herself, thus fulfilling both roles. She would not allow this study issue to fail for want of committee membership. She was the only woman to chair one of the task forces and the only person to fulfill the two top roles. The task force did a thorough study of the subject of affordable housing with Dorothy at the helm.

The housing partnership

Based on their study, the task force recommended the formation of a public/private partnership to help create new housing for low-income people. Dorothy became the first acting chair of the partnership until it was legally created in 1989 as the Rochester/Olmsted Community Housing Partnership. She was then named the first chairman of the partnership. That's when the work really began.

The Housing Partnership was successful in finding money to help address the problem of affordable housing. "The groups granting money liked our focus and intentions," she says. The Partnership developed the New Hope (Northgate) Community Project from existing property. It provides twelve units for long-term mentally ill tenants. The Zumbro Valley Mental Health Center was an active partner in this development and continues to provide ongoing guidance and supervision. Another project, The Bandel Hill Townhouses, was opposed by the local community because townhouses were a fairly new concept and not well understood. But the partnership raised the money and lobbied the council carefully, and the project was passed unanimously despite a roomful of worried neighbors. Dorothy notes with pride that these units still operate and more have been built, attesting to the viability of the model. The Partnership has also built low-income housing in Byron, located a few miles west of Rochester.

Marcia Brown moved to Rochester in 1976. The first thing she had learned to do in her many relocations around the country was to join the League of Women Voters. She had been a member in New York, Virginia, and Ohio. She found women like herself in these organizations, and from them she quickly learned about her new community. In Rochester she met and became friends with Dorothy Callahan. (Dorothy was president of the League prior to the forming of the Housing Partnership, and Marcia later became League president.) Marcia became a member of the Housing Partnership and observed Dorothy's leadership during that time. As she remembers, witnesses often reacted with surprise at Dorothy's effective questioning. A member of the committee said, "Oh, don't let her fool you, she can handle anyone!" Marcia remembers that men always listened to Dorothy and gave her their time. "They wouldn't do that for the rest of the women," she recalled.

Dorothy continued to fight for good quality housing with the amenities everyone needs. When she was told, "They don't need a garage" or "You spend too much," Dorothy pointed out that low-income people can't afford to change or fix things; they have to live with what they have.

She became angry when housing units were affordable only "when it got to be unacceptable to most people." The Partnership would obtain bids and pick in the middle cost range for their work. Her group worked to make every square inch usable and to have good designs.

One of the early innovations of the partnership was the creation of classes to help new homeowners understand their responsibilities. These classes are still being used by Habitat for Humanity and other organizations. Local banks often require their new mortgagors to attend the pre-purchase education opportunities provided by the Partnership. "The students knew if they missed a payment, we would be on their doorsteps!" Dorothy remembers.

The success of the Bandel Hill project has had a lasting legacy. Judy Plank, current staff for the Rochester Community Housing Partnership (ROCHP), says, "Today 'for profit' organizations are building properties intended as affordable rental housing. The vision and foresight of the Partnership proved you can have affordable housing existing in harmony with a diverse economic community."

When Dorothy Callahan decided to pursue the need for affordable housing in the Rochester area, she didn't stop to wonder if she had the right college degree or the right kind of employment to be able to make change happen. She relied on her life experience and her own common sense and commitment to the poor. The rightness of her cause was her motivation. When others were surprised at the determination of this five-foot dynamo, she hardly noticed. It seems likely that the person who identified her area of expertise as "Household Manager, Etc." meant the title as a slight. What he didn't realize was just how much power was packed into those three little letters, "etc."

Leading Through Tumultuous Times

Jane Campion chaired a task force on the disposition of the Rochester State Hospital, 1982

Jane Campion clearly remembers the day that Sister Generose Gervais, Administrator of Saint Marys Hospital, asked her to attend a meeting to discuss the closure of the Rochester State Hospital (RSH). Jane had been one of Sister Generose's assistants at Saint Marys since 1976. Sister Generose was well aware of Jane's keen interest in mental health issues and assured Jane in her characteristic matter-of-fact style that Jane was more than up to the task and could contribute. "If she asked, I did it," Jane remembers with a hint of a smile. Thus began Jane's intense involvement and leadership on one of the hottest local issues of the time: the disposition of the former Rochester State Hospital.

As a Sister of St. Francis, Jane trained as a nurse at Saint Marys Hospital. She worked in a variety of supervisory settings in the 1960s, which often meant long hours on the job. With a graduate degree from the University of Minnesota in Nursing and Healthcare Administration, Jane returned to Saint Marys as the Director of Nursing. In the late 1960s, Jane was offered an opportunity to work in nursing education and chemical dependency in the State of Georgia. In 1973, she became Director of Alcohol and Drug Services under then-Governor Jimmy Carter. Jane says her experiences in Georgia opened her eyes to "a bigger world" of service to others throughout the community. She hoped to be able to apply this new worldview of "how to make the town work," as she phrases it, when she returned to Rochester.

Jane was appointed by Sister Generose in 1977 to act as Assistant Administrator at Saint Marys. Sister Generose knew that Jane, described by colleagues as extremely competent, committed, and insightful, was also community connected. Jane was thus the logical choice to represent the Sister when, in 1981, the RSH Task force was formed.

Jane recalls the changes that took place in religious orders and Catholic communities of faith after Vatican II in the late 1960s. It was not an "easy time" for Catholics, and she learned then how people could react to change–not always in positive ways. Jane's empathy and understanding of human nature were good preparation for the reactions in Rochester to the "change" generated by the closing of the local state hospital and its eventual sale to the Federal Bureau of Prisons.

One constant meeting

Jane served on the RHS Task Force, appointed by the Olmsted County Board in July, 1981, with twenty-one other community members. At the first meeting Jane was selected as one of two co-chairs, but after her colleague left for a winter in Florida, Jane shouldered the leadership herself. She was very thankful for the able staff assistance of Sheila Kiscaden, at that time an Olmsted County employee and, later, a Minnesota state senator. Sandy Keith, who later became a Minnesota State Supreme Court Chief Justice, was also a hard worker on the committee, which Jane recalls being "one constant meeting."

The Minnesota Legislature, during its 1981 session, had voted to close the Rochester State Hospital in an economical move during a budget crisis. Some services were to end by July 1, 1981, with full closure by June 30, 1982. Jane knew that this was a tremendous loss of services for some of the state's most vulnerable citizens. Dr. Frank Tyce, Rochester State Hospital Medical Director and Superintendent, ran a widely respected facility and was ahead of his time in the treatment of mental illness. Rochester's State Hospital, the only Joint Commission accredited psychiatric hospital in Minnesota, performed all surgeries for mental hospitals in the state.

"What was tragic," says Jane, "is that an entire system that cared for at-risk, mentally ill people was lost." The Task Force was charged with making preliminary recommendations for the state legislature regarding the impact of the loss of mental health services on individuals and communities in the region. Future use of the facility by December 1981–just prior to the 1982 Minnesota legislative session–was also to be determined.

The eventual sale of the property to the Federal Bureau of Prisons for use as a Federal Medical Center was what caused the most public furor. What weighed heavily on Jane, though, was the displacing of the hospital residents and the need to find ways to ensure appropriate treatment and services. On behalf of the Task Force, she gathered data from throughout the eleven-county catchment area to assess the needs of patients who would be released, identify existing programs that could provide services, and anticipate access barriers that patients and their families might face.

At meeting after meeting, Jane and the Task Force members listened as patients, families, providers, county and state welfare

It took almost two years of monumental work by a task force (chaired by Jane) and community leaders to arrive at a solution for the disposition of the Rochester State Hospital. Jane recalls the time as "one constant meeting." (Courtesy Post-Bulletin Co.)

workers, and elected officials presented testimony. Jane worked diligently to maintain an open and inclusive process.

"As a community we had to decide what to do with the property," says Jane. Building inspection reports were prepared for the 153-acre campus, which included ten main buildings and numerous peripheral structures and staff residences. The Task Force solicited interest from potential local, state, and national buyers of the campus and kept detailed information on the needs of these organizations. Jane and other Task Force members made trip after trip to the State Capitol and scheduled many visits with interested buyers. She provided endless tours for interested parties such as the Veteran's Administration, Ebenezer Society, Good Samaritan Lutheran Society, and even Minnesota's Department of Corrections, which was considering a new site for a women's prison. Unfortunately, "tours killed the interest," she recalls. The complexity of the campus with its many aging buildings presented serious disadvantages for potential occupants. Local realtors who showed an interest in dividing up the land for housing lots resisted when they learned the potential uses for the existing buildings that would remain nearby. In every direction, there were barriers and new challenges to finding a solution. Eventually it became clear that the property was more suitable for a single major tenant, rather than multiple smaller organizations.

Generous . . . or mean-spirited?

In response to the report from Olmsted County's Task Force, Governor Al Quie created a second task force to determine the use and disposition of the Rochester State Hospital site in March 1982. Jane remembers that everyone's frustration was high and time was running out to make a decision and find a buyer. To no one's surprise, Jane Campion was unanimously chosen to lead the fourteen-member group. This Task Force included seven area county commissioners, two area legislators (Senator Nancy Brataas and Representative Don Frerichs), the two legislative chairs of Minnesota State Legislative Health and Human Services Committees, and two other citizens: former County Commissioner Rosemary Ahmann and Robert Roesler from Mayo Clinic. The report this group submitted in December 1982 was incredibly organized, thorough, and inclusive of all viewpoints in the region. It's easy to see Jane Campion's hand in this, although she extends much credit to the staff and commissioners from Olmsted County who provided aid at every turn. In the end, surrounding counties voted to suggest that the state hospital property be given to Olmsted County to manage and to find buyers/users.

It took almost two years of monumental work by the task force and community leaders to arrive at a solution. The final report addressed future mental health services in the region and the disposition of the campus. Part of the state hospital campus would be sold to the Federal Bureau of Prisons as a Federal Medical Center, with patient care coordinated through Mayo Clinic and Olmsted Medical Center. The remainder of the property would be retained and managed by Olmsted County for human services, correctional needs, and space for a future waste-to-energy facility. The rest would become City of Rochester park land for youth soccer fields and other recreational uses. Jane remembers that the decision was wildly unpopular with some in the community–at least the medical prison part. Many Task Force members were vilified for the end result. Looking back, Jane reflects that "it was wrenching and mean spirited for a community that sees itself as generous. We did not look very good."

Despite the furor, a representative from the Justice Department stepped into negotiations with the County, which by now had taken ownership of the campus. According to Jane, his aunt lived in Madonna Towers, a local facility for older adults; he had always loved Rochester; and he really wanted to locate a facility in Rochester. A very favorable deal–fourteen million dollars in early 1984–was negotiated, and when the first warden, Joe Brogan arrived, he quickly became a true part of the Rochester community. Unfortunately, the hostility and fear toward this solution continued to fester, in spite of assurances from Minnesota's Department of Corrections Commissioner, Frank Wood, that a federal medical prison housed primarily nonviolent offenders. Jane believes that residents who opposed the prison did not appreciate the nuance, nor did they recognize that hosting a prison is another way to serve our country.

During this difficult time Jane was interviewed on a local TV program called *The Belau Report*. Included in the interview was an opponent of the Federal Medical Prison and Mayo Clinic physician. He pointedly asked her, "If you are from Saint Marys Hospital and you promote it [the federal prison], can I assume that Saint Marys supports it?" Jane, refusing to be put on the spot, assured him that she was acting as a citizen, not a spokesperson for her employer. Then she went on to ask if the converse were true. Since he was a Mayo Clinic physician and he opposed the prison, could she assume that Mayo Clinic opposed? His response was the same as Jane's; he admitted that he, too, represented only himself, not his employer.

For a one dollar investment, a twenty-eight million dollar development

In a Rochester *Post-Bulletin* article published October 17, 1987, staff writer James Walsh wrote:

> *On Wall Street it would be called "making a killing."* . . . *But whatever you call it, a $1 investment in southeast Rochester resulted in the multi-million dollar development of an area that once was only used by ducks and doctors. In the four years since Olmsted County bought the former Rochester State Hospital campus from the state for a buck, the entire surrounding area has seen more than $28 million in development, renovation, and expansion.*
>
> *"It was tumultuous, without any question," Huss (Human Services Campus Administrator) recalls. They didn't want a prison here in Rochester and they didn't want a prison town. People were concerned about appearance, too. They were expecting walls and gun towers, and it didn't turn out that way." Huus says that commotion has died away. Part of the reason has been that the prison has kept a low profile, he said. Another is because the FMC has pumped money into the local economy.*

Jane's happiest memory of the two-year drama–and perhaps some vindication for being in a leadership role during an unpopular public decision–occurred the day that the Human Resources office opened at the new federal prison. To her pleasant surprise, 700 to 800 people stood in line waiting to apply for jobs. At that moment it became even clearer to her that there had been a significant lack of diversity in job opportunities in the community, and the new Federal Prison would be an economic boost to the region. The unintended but very positive consequence of opening a Federal Medical Center in Rochester was the creation of additional jobs in the community and an expansion of the economic base.

Sisters are "doers"

Unlike other women, Jane has never felt patronized in the public sphere. This may be because, in the past, the general public has treated nuns somewhat differently from other women when encountering them in non-traditional female roles. Jane acknowledges that she was given significant latitude in her work for Saint Marys, as well.

Describing Jane as a "doer" is a grand understatement for Jane's level of work commitment. While she tirelessly worked as chair and chief "doer" on the two state hospital committees, her "day job" included serving on the leadership team that oversaw the building and opening of the Mary Brigh wing at Saint Marys Hospital. She later worked with the integration of Saint Marys with Mayo Clinic, a major milestone in the history of both organizations.

Even though she left the Franciscan Community in the late 1970s, her commitment to her "faith that is lived" has never wavered. Over the years, she has continued to maintain a close relationship with Sister Generose and the Sisters at Saint Marys and Assisi Heights.

In 1986, Jane was named Mayo Clinic Equal Opportunity Administrator, where inclusion became her mission and her priority. She understood that an institutional appreciation for diversity was the

Jane credits her loving parents for impressing upon their children a shared responsibility for one another—especially those in their midst who were less fortunate.

first step toward economic success in the twenty-first century, so she
set about collecting data and raising awareness. In her usual under-
stated way, she admits that people seem to respond to her personally,
and she is not easily discouraged when they don't.

In 1990, looking for a new outlet for her energy and community commitment, Jane went to John Herrell, whose grandfather had
initiated the Rochester Foundation, and requested to join the Foundation's Board. She said that while she knew she could not be Mayo
Clinic's official representative, she could bring information back about
the community's needs. On the Board she found women she describes as "phenomenal," such as Ann Ferguson and Isabel Huizenga.
Their knowledge of the community and their commitment to others
were traits Jane shared and admired. During this period, the
Rochester Area Foundation Board hired a director and received its
first Bush Foundation grant. Jane continues to serve as an Emeritus
Board Member on the Rochester Area Foundation Board of Directors
and Emeritus Staff at Mayo Clinic.

As Jane looks back on her childhood she describes loving parents who impressed upon their children a shared responsibility for one another–especially those in their midst who were less fortunate. As a young girl, Jane remembers the box her father kept in his office that was filled and refilled over the years with money collected for the Salvation Army. Her parents always seemed to know who in the community needed help, and Jane and her sister Mary were often called upon to dip into the box to buy bus tickets or other items for people in need.

Like most good leaders, Jane shares the credit for success, believes that blame is vastly overrated, and happily avoids the limelight. She has found herself at the center of many important and often tumultuous events, but the clear consensus among those who have known her is that she is a role model for many, a mentor to the lucky ones, and a gift to the Rochester community.

A Neighborhood Recipe

Cynthia Daube was the first female Chair of the Rochester Planning and Zoning Commission

Cynthia Daube was busy raising her children in 1975 when local developers filed a request with the Rochester Planning and Zoning Commission to change the zoning on a piece of property in her neighborhood in order to accommodate the building of a condominium complex. As president of the Neighborhood Association, she led the Association in opposing the complex. She and her neighbors appeared before the city council, arguing that the development was "the camel's nose under the tent" and that the neighborhood density would become too high. She learned from this experience how to work with city officials and present arguments respectfully.

The Association lost the case in front of the city council and in the courts, but a member of the planning department thought Cynthia and her team had accomplished a moral victory. He told Cynthia, "No one else would try that in your neighborhood." Soon after, Saint Marys Hospital planned to build a new road that emptied into the neighborhood; once again, the association swung back into gear. Although they lost again, this time they were included in the planning–the hospital landscaped the property to shield the neighbors from the road.

Calm, effective leadership on the Planning Commission

These experiences led Cynthia to apply for the Rochester Planning and Zoning Commission in 1979, and she was appointed on a 4-3 vote. Though not the first woman appointed to the Commission, Cynthia may have been the most controversial up to that time. Previous women appointed to the Commission were: Mrs. Russell Ewert

61

(1960), Mrs. Ray B. Wheeler (1966), Mrs. Donald (Marilyn) Wick (1972), Margaret Brimijoin (1975), and Roberta Herrell (1978). These names are written as they appeared in the public record, and it is interesting to note how that has changed over time–"Mrs." followed by her husband's name, then the woman's first name in parentheses, finally the woman's first and last name. Phil Wheeler, Director of Rochester-Olmsted Planning Department, said that Cynthia once told him that she thought of herself as Mayor Alex Smekta's "swan song," because he did not run for re-election the following year. Cynthia served on the commission for nine years (1979-1987). In 1981, she was the commission's first woman president.

Cynthia, the first female chair of the Rochester Planning and Zoning Commission, believed that often people fear what they don't know. "They will be more willing to accept change if they know what it is going to be."

There is a lot of drama at public hearings of any planning and zoning commission, especially in communities that are experiencing rapid growth or change, as Rochester was in the 1970s and 1980s. Next to their children's education, average citizens are probably more personally and emotionally involved with local government over their biggest investment–their homes–than anything else. So one can imagine the fear, anger, and angst displayed by a large group of neighbors who have been informed by postcard (as the law requires) that there will be a public hearing on an issue affecting the area where they live. They show up ready to protest and make statements such as, "Who does that developer think he is to locate a business on my corner?" "How dare a land owner propose a home-based business across the street!" "I bought my home next to the cornfields on pur-pose–why are you letting someone buy that land and develop it as apartments?" "I am worried about the extra traffic. How safe will my children be?" and "How can I be sure that what is developed won't look awful, affect my neighborhood's lifestyle, or decrease my prop-erty value?"

Developers typically couch their proposals in words and ac-tual pictures of what is good for the future of the City of Rochester–enhancing the beauty, economy, and livability of the entire community. Aware of Cynthia's relationship with her neighborhood association, many developers promised that they would work closely with the neighborhood as their project rolled out. Most were also aware that Cynthia believed in quality and beauty of design; therefore they displayed pictures depicting fencing and landscape elements.

Cynthia's comments recorded in the December 4, 1980, meeting minutes, directed to staff as they accepted input into the pro-posed zoning ordinance, summarized her views on how to receive calm, non-political, and helpful citizen involvement: "President Daube stated that 'presently a project will be presented as a zone change or plat, without a specific plan shown. Many times people fear what they don't know. They will be more willing to accept it if they know what it is going to be. Neighborhoods won't have to accept a project blind, and developers will be able to go to a neighborhood with a compatible use. The final decision goes to the City Council. The Zoning Ordinance can only deal with planning issues, not the issue of politics.'"

During her two-year presidency, Cynthia presided, calmly and effectively, on the second and fourth Wednesday evenings over a nine-member board including James Ward, Robert Gill, Roberta Herrell, Paul Zollman, Michael Fogarty, Richard Binns, Donald Peterson, Harland Walker, Bob McIntosh, Jack Dale, Gordie Bluhm, and Christopher Colby. The first Land Use Plan for Olmsted County and the City of Rochester had just been completed, and the staff, county commission, and council–through numerous hearings and presentations—were laboring over the Zoning Ordinance update. While these issues would have the most long-lasting impact on the community, and while Cynthia Daube was highly interested in them, the day-to-day response to request for changes by property owners and developers took most of the time at meetings.

Community standards, urban design, and downtown development

Planned Unit Developments (PUDs) were often proposed by developers who could not quite fit what they wanted to do within the strictures of existing zones. For added building density, they were willing to offer some enhanced aesthetics and design. From 1981 to 1982, PUDs were proposed, but denied, for Old Stone Barn, Resurrection Lutheran Church, and Riverview West. Cynthia voted to oppose these projects based on issues brought up by neighbors and planning staff. In response to one of these proposals, the April 23, 1980, minutes noted, "President Daube stated that the commissioners are responsible for setting community standards and should not set them just because something is selling . . . President Daube stated that she is concerned about what is going to happen twenty years down the line."

PUDs were approved for Broadstreet Café, Hiawatha Adult Home, Woodhaven, and the former Seventh-Day Adventist Church. Preliminary plats were approved for Homestead Acres, Woodlake Industrial Park, Northern Slopes, Innsbruck 6, and numerous residential subdivisions on the north and west fringes of town. Zone changes were approved along North Broadway, Valley High Drive, and Thirty-seventh Street Northwest. Some were controversial, meaning that meetings lasted until nearly midnight; some were *pro forma*.

Cynthia initiated the discussion of aesthetics and overall planning for the Second Street corridor, although the City Council could not be persuaded to follow through. She addressed the "look" of a flood control project through a new subcommittee—the Committee on Urban Environment (CUE). She also responded to the request from the Council to develop an overall plan for former churches' use criteria. She proposed many measures to streamline the process of zoning ordinance development and was always searching for better ways to enhance communication with the city council. She summarized goals and achievements from 1981 as she stepped down from the presidency. The January 11, 1982, minutes read: "She stated that a few goals for last year were the zoning ordinance and the Second Street Study. The zoning ordinance has not progressed as quickly as the commission thought, and the Second Street Study has not been adopted. Nothing happens very quickly when it comes to planning . . . She stated that a CUE committee has been formed to look at urban problems. She would like to meet with them occasionally to give them support. The Commission could meet the last Wednesday of the month or take one meeting out of four to meet for planning purposes, such as updating the Land Use Plan. There are so many issues to be looked at."

Besides representing neighborhoods throughout the city on traffic issues, Cynthia was also particularly interested in preserving downtown neighborhoods, promoting infill rather than urban sprawl, and preventing urban housing rot near downtown. She served on the Downtown Development District Advisory Board, first as a liaison from the Planning Commission and later in her own right as a downtown business owner of a bakery and two restaurants. She felt that all successful downtowns have an urban housing component, and she pushed for more housing in the downtown. She says, "It has taken a long time, but we are getting there."

Of the eleven members on the Downtown Development District Advisory Board, six were downtown business people. Most of the few women who made it on this board represented the three local governments, except for Cynthia. Doug Knott, staff to the board, said, "Cynthia was dedicated and took her task to heart. She had an interest in historic preservation." During her tenure, the advisory board approved many projects including: Broadway Plaza, Ferris Alexander properties, and parking ramps and skyways. They also approved the Chateau Theater and Old City Hall preservations.

From Detroit to Rochester by way of Japan

Cynthia Sokol, her brother, and sister were born and raised in Detroit. Her parents had known each other as children in Detroit's Polish neighborhood where Cynthia's grandmother was a local caterer and proprietress of a blind pig (speakeasy), selling liquor out the back of her candy store in order to support her family. Cynthia's father had to quit school to support his brother and sister but later earned his General Education Diploma (GED) in the Air Force during WW II. He worked at General Motors as a foreman and later sold insurance part-time. He became a full-time State Farm insurance agent, believing in the importance of insurance. Rosa Parks was one of his policy holders while she lived in Detroit. Cynthia's mother was a nurse's aide and a hairdresser who later helped in her father's office after the children were grown.

After graduating from high school, Cynthia wanted to go to nursing school and was accepted at the University of Michigan. However, she was unable to attend because it was too expensive. She graduated instead in 1963 from Henry Ford Hospital School of Nursing as a Registered Nurse (RN) and went to work at Henry Ford Hospital. Army recruiters offered her the chance to go overseas to a place of her choice if she would sign up for two years. She chose Japan, where she met her future husband, Jasper Daube. He was a neurologist who had published a paper on the problem "rucksack paralysis," common among American soldiers carrying loads that were too heavy and unbalanced–a problem doctors see today in students and our troops in Afghanistan. Their son, Chris, was born in Japan and their daughter, Lizzie, was born in Rochester after Jasper became a consultant at Mayo Clinic. For many years, she stayed home raising her children while finishing a liberal arts degree in food history.

Culinary dreams come true

Although she was interested in planning and briefly worked for the 1980 Census, Cynthia's primary passion has always been food. She had grown up in a neighborhood of ethnic bakeries and loved to watch Julia Child's television show on cooking. Her husband's father had run his own bakery in Chicago and later worked as a baker for General Telephone. In the mid 1980s, she pursued a liberal arts degree in food history at the University of Minnesota, dreaming of owning a bakery or a restaurant. Afterward she worked as a lunch cook at Rochester's Broadstreet Restaurant for a year, to see what it was like. There she learned how to manage people and to handle the challenges of maintaining consistently good food standards in spite of staff turnover, humidity, equipment failures, and changes in ingredient supplies.

Devoted to her growing family, she thought that a bakery would take less time to manage than a restaurant. In February 1987, she and her husband borrowed against their house to finance the purchase of what is now called Daube's Cakes and Bakery on Civic Center Drive. In October 1987, they remodeled downtown space on Third Street Southwest and opened the restaurant now called Jasper's. Later, they opened Daube's Down Under in the Mayo Clinic subway. At this point, she returned to the Downtown Development Board as a local business owner and stayed on the board until the sunset of the Tax Increment Financing District, which the city used to provide financial incentives for businesses to improve. Shortly after Cynthia moved to Rochester, most of the major downtown shops relocated to the new Apache Mall on the city's south edge, and downtown looked deserted. She was on the board while the downtown became revitalized with the development of downtown skyways and the Galleria Mall Centerplace, an enclosed, multi-level shopping complex with a variety of specialty shops and restaurants. Cynthia remains enthusiastic about the downtown revitalization that continues today–for example, 318 Commons is a new housing community for students and health professionals located a short walk from the center of the University of Minnesota Rochester and Mayo Clinic.

Cynthia believes that her greatest contribution to public policy was the inclusion of voices from neighborhoods and neighborhood associations in city discussions of building projects and streets.

While serving on the Rochester Planning Commission and the Downtown Development Board, she brought the citizens' points of view to the business community. For instance, when the Chamber of Commerce voted to oppose school bonding, she addressed members on the importance of school funding in providing well-trained future employees and in making Rochester a desirable place for families moving in the city. She believes there is currently more respect and more dialogue among citizens and policy makers and that the city does a better job of informing people of changes. She says, "If citizens are honest and respectful in presenting their points on view to the City Council or as members of local boards and commissions, they will be heard and their views taken into account."

Transforming the System from the Inside Out

Donna Dunn, activist and feminist, helped move victim advocacy into the criminal justice system's response to violence against women

Donna Dunn was shaped for work as a social change activist early in her lifetime. Born and raised in Minnesota, Donna graduated from Robbinsdale High School in 1964. Her mother worked as a secretary to the principal of her high school, and her father worked for a company that manufactured items such as missile launchers. Donna remembers her parents as highly engaged in the community and helping neighbors and others in need. "I was raised in a family that placed high value on civic engagement and giving back," she recalls. "We were lucky and we owed something to the world. It wasn't necessarily something that we talked about; it was just how people acted. The idea you wouldn't be a joiner just never occurred to us." One volunteer role her father held was as driver for the Society for the Blind. Donna recalls riding along with her father when she was a child and witnessing the enjoyment his passengers found in his companionship and humor. "When one woman offered Dad chicken manure for our rhubarb he responded that he preferred sugar and cream!–no end to the laughter."

Following her high school graduation, Donna attended and graduated from Gustavus Adolphus College in 1968, with a major in German and a minor in Russian. She attended graduate school at Vanderbilt University and received a Master of Arts in Teaching. Thereafter, Donna taught German, Russian, and English at the junior high, high school and college levels for five years in Nashville, Tennessee.

In 1976, Donna accompanied her then-husband to Riyadh, Saudi Arabia, for his two-year work engagement at the King Faisal Specialist Hospital and Research Center. While in Saudi Arabia

Donna gave birth to two sons. She reflects that her time in Saudi Arabia provided her with a context for the role of women in two very different countries and societies. Donna remarks, "I saw a lot of similarities between the constraints on women in Saudi Arabia and here in the U.S.–in fact, ultimately there were more similarities than differences. It was like a veil was lifted and I understood just how women's lives were restricted all over the world."

Donna arrived in Rochester in 1979 as a young mother of two sons, then eight months and two years. The family came to Rochester because of her now ex-husband's employment at Mayo Clinic. Donna anticipated that she would find a teaching job and pick up where she left off prior to the move to Saudi Arabia, but was unsuccessful. Instead, Donna immersed herself in movements that mattered to her. She volunteered on local and statewide women's campaigns for Rochester women Sally Martin and Joy Fogarty. She worked on pro-choice and ERA-support efforts. Through her political network and connections with feminist activities, Donna stumbled upon the battered women's and anti-sexual violence movements. Her understanding of the dynamics of battering, the abuse of power and control, and the underlying oppression of women in society became a powerful force in her life.

When Donna accepted the position of Community Education Coordinator at the Rochester Women's Shelter in 1982, her understanding of battering was through a political lens. However, she soon learned about the harsh realities. "When I saw the women and children, it provided an entirely different understanding of women's lives. It was overwhelming to me that women lived there because it wasn't safe to live in their homes. "

Political sea changes

In the early 1980s, violence against women became acknowledged as a legitimate and serious issue on the political scene. The battered women's movement gained visibility, and it was a time of increased collaboration between advocates for battered women and the criminal justice system. Intervention projects were developed and grants made available to fund the work. The Duluth (Minnesota) model, now used across the U.S. and in more than seventeen countries, was created by the Duluth Abuse Intervention Project as an interagency collaborative response to domestic abuses. Because of the Duluth Model, mandatory arrest policies for police departments became the norm. Women could now file for an order for protection from an abusive husband.

In Rochester the law enforcement community and elected officials were largely supportive, although resistance was also present. Donna recalls one high-ranking police department official stating in frustration, "I'd like to put a big chain on the women's shelter and drag it out of the city and into the county." Retired Rochester Police Department Captain Jim Pittenger explains that during this time, law enforcement often became tangled up in building cases that held offenders accountable to state laws. "That wasn't a bad thing," he says, "but that focus didn't always allow for much victim input and participation. We found cases suffered for that. It was necessary for somebody to focus on victim needs and expectations. Women's Shelter advocates and others were able to provide that focus. Our outcomes improved and we learned the value of having somebody maintain victim involvement in cases."

Representative Dave Bishop, a strong supporter of shelter funds, authored a bill to provide dedicated funds from marriage licenses to women's shelters. Donna recalls one day while working at the shelter there was a knock on the door. The advocate on duty opened the door to find a man asking to be let in. Advocates were trained not to admit visitors–particularly male visitors–for the residents' safety and privacy. The advocate summoned Donna, who greeted the man. He said, "I'm your Representative, Dave Bishop. I just got you a whole bunch of money, and I should be able to come in." Donna ushered Representative Bishop into her office. He asked, "How much new money have you received?" She answered that the new money had been funneled into the general fund and therefore had not translated to an increase for the shelter. Bishop promptly used Donna's phone to call the Department of Corrections, the office in charge of distributing the funds. He demanded to know what had happened with the funding. "Dave Bishop was really impassioned for this issue," says Donna, remembering that his loud and angry conversation with the official made some of the shelter residents uneasy. Ultimately, he was successful in realizing an increase in funding for the shelter.

Learning from the victims

With funding from Continuing Education, Donna partnered with Marlise Riffel of the Sociology Department at Rochester Community College. The two began talking about teen dating violence—an issue that hadn't yet been acknowledged. Donna had regularly conducted presentations in high school classrooms about women in marriage relationships who were being battered by their spouses. Girls in the classrooms had asked questions about their boyfriends. One day following a presentation, Donna found a shelter brochure left behind with the "If you need help" section torn out. It dawned on her that teen dating violence was an unaddressed issue with scant resources. Donna and Marlise worked on a slide show presentation for the schools. The presentation was embraced by schools locally and sold to schools around the country.

In 1985, the year Donna became Associate Director of the Rochester Women's Shelter, activist Andrea Dworkin in Minneapolis was working with Catherine MacKinnon, University of Minnesota professor and lawyer, to draft an anti-pornography civil rights ordinance as an amendment to the Minneapolis city civil rights ordinance. The amendment would define pornography as a civil rights violation against women and allow women who claimed harm from pornography to sue the producers and distributors for damages in civil court. Dworkin and MacKinnon put a call out to shelter advocates to ask shelter residents about their abusers' use of pornography. The question was, "Did pornography play a role in your battering?"

Women at the Rochester shelter began sharing their experiences, revealing situations where their partner increased acts of vio-

Donna speaks at the 1987 Take Back the Night vigil, where citizens gathered to support the end of domestic violence.

lence towards them after viewing pornography. Donna summarized their stories and agreed to provide testimony to the Minneapolis City Council. A snow storm interfered with her giving the testimony in person, so she dictated it over the phone so her words could be read into the record. The law was passed twice by the Minneapolis City council but vetoed by Mayor Don Fraser, who considered the wording of the ordinance too vague. Ultimately, Donna and the stories she collected were cited in a 1997 book edited by McKinnon and Dworkin called *In Harm's Way: The Pornography Civil Rights Hearings*. Donna remarks, "We don't always realize the power of the stories from the field."

The power of collaboration

In the mid 1970s, the State Legislature had approved funding for the Minnesota Program for Victims of Sexual Assault within the Department of Corrections. At that time the only sexual assault programs were in the metro area. In 1975, International Women's Year, four women came together through the Women's Resource Center and the Rochester Area Family Y and organized a grassroots effort to reach out to victims of rape and sexual abuse. Joy Fogarty, a volunteer police reservist; Cindy Hunstiger, an emergency room nurse at Saint Marys Hospital; Ilona Westwood, a counselor; and Connie Fossen-Anderson, a social worker who later became the first Director of Rapeline, called an informational meeting. They were stunned at the attendance of nearly fifty people. The group's immediate goals were to provide crisis intervention for victims, develop an information and resources network, and educate the community about sexual assault. On May 1, 1976, the Rapeline crisis line became operational, taking calls at 507-289-0636–the same number as today, thirty-five years later.

Connie Fossen-Anderson made the following remarks at the occasion of the twenty-fifth anniversary of the Rapeline (Victim Services) program:

Perhaps what gave us the most energy were those first phone calls. More than one woman said, 'I never thought I could talk about this.' A sixty-four-year-old woman told me that once, just once, before she died, she wanted to say out loud what happened to her fifty years ago. One survivor hugged me so hard after four hours in the emergency room. Anger, disappointment, sadness–all created a powerful spirit in this group of women–a spirit to keep on helping, to keep organizing, to keep educating, to keep talking, explaining what it was really like for survivors in our community. This was the most important work of my life. I am grateful for every individual, volunteer, survivor, agency staff who supported our important work twenty [now thirty-five] years ago and I am with you in spirit, those of you who continue this work today.

The program had embraced survivors, providing a safe place for them to verbalize their pain and to begin focusing on healing. There were also disappointments and frustrations along the way, recalls Donna. At times the system seemed to re-victimize the victim. While the rape crisis-center movement was developing strong and reliable advocacy programs for survivors of rape, the movement was slower to embrace the systemic change occurring in the battered women's movement to transform the system of response from re-victimizing to victim-centered.

In 1989, Donna shifted from the Rochester Women's Shelter to serve as Director of Rapeline. She sought immediately to incorporate the system change work she was so familiar with from her days at the Women's Shelter into the goals and objects of the programming at Rapeline. At that time, the federal Office of Victims of Crime was looking for sample protocols for responding to sexual violence. With the support of Mark Carey, Director of Dodge, Fillmore, and Olmsted County Community Corrections, Donna applied for and received a national grant to develop a model protocol for the state of Minnesota. She made contact with authors Anita Boles and John Patterson, who had written a book entitled *Improving Community Response to Crime Victims: An Eight Step Model for Developing Protocol*. The premise of the book was that professionals should respond in a way that was consistent and predictable–in other words, following a protocol. Otherwise, rape victims relied on luck, such as having an investigator assigned who responded in a victim-centered way, or living in a part of the county with access to services, or having a county attorney who reviewed the case without passing judgment about a victim's behavior. Ray Schmitz, then Olmsted County Attorney, Mark Carey, and Donna embarked on an uncharted journey to test the eight-step protocol development process described in the book. The excitement was high. "I really started believing in the power of collaboration and buy-in to transform the response to sexual assault," said Donna.

About this time, Olmsted County was experiencing the ongoing challenge of paying for rape exams. Some victims were receiving bills for the evidence collection examination, even though the state statute directed the county as responsible for payment of exams. Donna interceded on the behalf of victims. Rochester Police Department investigator Roger Peterson, now Chief, aided the effort by reasoning that the cost of the exam should be paid whether the victim reported the assault to police or not. Some sexual assault victims, uncertain about whether to report to police, did not seek out the critical evidence collection because they couldn't afford the visit to the emergency room. Donna and Roger were in fact ahead of what is now a federal law mandating that in order to receive Violence Against Women Act (VAWA) funds, counties must fund the payment of the rape exam regardless of whether the victim chooses to report to law enforcement.

During Donna's tenure at Rapeline, the name of the organization was changed to Victim Services. "We found that it was hard for some people who were victims of some forms of sexual violence to identify that their experience was rape," she explains. "Victims of sexual harassment and attempted sexual assault felt they weren't eligible to receive services." Changing the name of the program, however, was challenging, as Donna also wanted to be sensitive to the early founders and the general loyalty to the name. Some saw Victim Services as a vague name that sanitized the underlying act of violence. Dropping the word "rape" also seemed to move the organization away from that activist point of view. Donna understood and appreciated all points of view: "Rape is a much more evocative term, and in dropping it I fear we may have lost something," she reflects.

Reaching out to male survivors of sexual violence became more common in the 1990s. In Donna's opinion, acknowledging that boys and men are victims of sexual violence was an important development toward a comprehensive understanding of sexual violence. "As a society we have a total misunderstanding of how sex can be used as a tool to harm and abuse. Sexual violence is more than just a misunderstanding or communication problem between people."

Donna Dunn

You can't go back

Ultimately, Donna's vision for the creation of the Model Sexual Assault Response Protocol Project was tested in four counties. Based on those experiences, in 2001 the project became a program of the Minnesota Coalition Against Sexual Assault (MNCASA). Donna became Executive Director of MNCASA in 2006, a position she still holds today. The Model Sexual Assault Response Protocol Project has become known as the Sexual Violence Justice Institute (SVJI) and is still a program of MNCASA. SVJI provides technical assistance to multi-disciplinary teams in twelve counties in Minnesota and four other states in the U.S. The model is considered a best practice by the Office for Violence Against Women.

The impact of Donna's life's work on her own life has been profound. "I learned early on that once your consciousness is raised you can't go back. You learn as much about yourself and who you are as you learn about survivors and the system. Working with survivors is the easiest part; to watch the loss of the sweetness of healthy sexuality—to see it get hijacked and devalued for all of us—is the hardest part. The work has forced me to get clear about how power and privilege work. It changed me in how I raise children and in what I expect of myself and others."

She Would do Anything For You

Ann Ferguson changed lives for people with disabilities

It appeared to be a typical day in 1956. A young couple from Texas, stationed at a U.S. Air Force based in Germany, had just given birth to a baby boy. However, Ann and Dick Ferguson's lives would never again be typical. Their son, Douglas, was born with forty-seven chromosomes instead of the usual forty-six. He had Down Syndrome, a genetic condition causing intellectual and physical delays in his development.

Ann Northcutt was born in Dallas, Texas, the youngest of five children. She and a brother were raised by an aunt who taught Ann that the only "proper career for a young lady" was teaching, so she attended Southern Methodist University and majored in elementary education. Armed with her new teaching degree, Ann joined the working world–as a clerk typist for a construction firm. She married Dick Ferguson in 1948, shortly after he finished medical school. They spent the next several years moving around the country, first to Ann Arbor, Michigan, where Dick interned. Dick entered the Navy and they moved to Washington, D.C., where Ann worked for an Air Force general and Dick transferred from the Navy to the Air Force. In 1951, they made their first move to Rochester, where Dick served a fellowship at Mayo Clinic and Ann worked for the chair of medical statistics. In 1954, the military sent the Fergusons to Wiesbaden, Germany. Dick served as a major in the medical corps of the U.S. Air Force Hospital.

In 1958, the Fergusons made their last move–back to Rochester. This time, however, was very different from the first because of Douglas, their young son with Down Syndrome.

The bad old days

In the 1950s and earlier, aside from large state institutions there really were no publicly funded programs for people with developmental disabilities. This meant no mandatory public education, no recreation opportunities, no employment opportunities, and no places to live that weren't isolated from the rest of society. In fact, when a child with a disability was born, families were frequently told to institutionalize their baby immediately and not even take the baby home from the hospital. They were counseled to forget they had given birth to that child and get on with their lives.

That thinking didn't sit well with many families. In the early 1950s, a small group of parents in Rochester banded together and started their own school for their children with disabilities. This "school" was held in a Sunday school room at Trinity Lutheran Church. On September 23, 1955, they incorporated as the Olmsted Association for the Mentally Retarded. (After several name changes over the years, it is now called The Arc Southeastern Minnesota.) In addition to the school of five students and a teacher they paid for themselves, the parents began contacting local and state elected officials about supporting legislation to mandate public education for "trainable mentally retarded" children. They received very little encouragement or support.

By 1957, public education classes for "educable mentally retarded" children were mandatory, but classes for "trainable" children were merely permissible. "Educable mentally retarded" were those children whose IQs were in the 50-75 range. It was expected they would make academic progress to the late elementary level. "Trainable mentally retarded" were those children whose IQs were below 50. At that time, little academic progress was expected. Many years later, experts realized those expectations were often inaccurate.

A guru in the making

The Fergusons, new to Rochester, were referred by a local physician to the group of Rochester parents for information and support. Thus began Ann's foray into the world of public policy. The Fergusons joined the Association in 1959. It became a major part of both of their lives. By spring of 1960, Ann was nominated for Vice President of the Olmsted Association for the Mentally Retarded Board and would represent the organization as a delegate at the state convention. She also became the chair, or "guru," as she jokingly referred to herself, of the Legislative Committee, which worked successfully on several significant issues.

A major success was the passage of legislation to allow for a new service called a "day activity center," a program for those children with disabilities who were not served by the public schools. Ann and others from the Association helped draft the legislation and testified at the state legislature in support of it. Then state Senator A.M. (Sandy) Keith worked with the group for passage. Olmsted County became a location for one of the first six pilot sites in the state.

Olmsted Day Activity Center (DAC) operated out of old Bamber Valley School. According to Ann, it began with the most "advanced" equipment–a sand pile, an auto harp, and a water table. The state of Minnesota provided half of the operating costs; the Association provided the remainder. The Ferguson's son Douglas was one of the first children to attend this program. As a result of this legislation, the parent-operated and funded school was no longer needed, and so was discontinued.

One thing Ann learned while working on legislative initiatives was the importance of having elected officials who supported new ideas. She was also good at convincing people that they had skills they had not yet identified. She knew if children with disabilities were ever going to be truly included in public education, the Rochester School Board needed members who would support the idea. In 1967, she convinced Dave Dunn, an Association member and volunteer, to run for the school board. He won and became a change-maker for children with disabilities.

During this time Ann worked as Fashion Coordinator for style shows at Dayton's Department Store. She was aware that the American Association of University Women (AAUW) held a style show each fall. She worked with Dayton's and the AAUW to sponsor a Spring Style Show that would benefit the Olmsted DAC. The first show was held in 1962 and continued for more than twenty-five years. The Association also held its first Holiday Bazaar during the same time period. This fundraising event would continue for more than thirty years. Many families are still today making lasagna and caramels with Ann's recipes made famous by that event.

By the late 1960s, the Association continued to identify unmet needs of people with disabilities. Recreation was one of those. A monthly program for adults was begun. Two other system-changing goals were identified–creating a home for people being released from state institutions and obtaining legislation to require public education for all students with disabilities. Success was reached with both of these in the 1970s.

The overage housewife, sub-minimum-wage Executive Director

With more and more identified gaps in the service system for people with disabilities, in 1976 the Association's Board of Directors felt it was time to hire a part-time executive director to help them accomplish their goals. Ann was the logical choice for this position. According to Ann, the screening committee demanded the best qualified and most professional candidate but instead hired "an overage housewife for fifteen hours per week at sub-minimum wage, working from her kitchen counter." This decision proved to have a greater impact on people with developmental disabilities and their families than anyone could have predicted. Under Ann's leadership the organization flourished, but more importantly, the quality of life for people with disabilities reached levels previously not even imagined. Certainly not all of this was Ann's doing alone, but her leadership helped make it happen. A longtime friend and parent of a son with a disability, Marilyn Fryer, once said of Ann, "She made things happen for people with developmental disabilities in Rochester and elsewhere. She thinks up the projects, gets people to do them, then steps back and lets them get the credit. I'm not saying these people don't work hard, but she's always the person behind it."

Under Ann's leadership in the 1970s, massive changes continued to happen for people with disabilities. The Association commissioned a survey done by Mankato State University on the recreation needs of people with developmental disabilities. The results were presented to the Rochester City Council with testimony given by a variety of people, including Ann. The result was that the City of Rochester agreed to hire a Director of Adaptive Recreation Programs, and after a year the Association was able to discontinue its own program. Ann always believed that people with disabilities deserved the same kinds of opportunities as others in their communities. The city sponsored recreation programs for people without disabilities; why shouldn't people with disabilities deserve that same opportunity?

Ann also believed that people with disabilities should live in small homes within typical neighborhoods and not be forced to live in large institutions with fenced-in grounds. They would benefit, as would everyone else by having people with disabilities included in their communities. Ann's beliefs led to years of work developing the first typical-size homes in Rochester for people with disabilities. Between 1976 and 1980, the Association opened four group homes in Rochester. Each home had six adults with developmental disabilities living in it–quite a difference from living in an institution with hundreds! At that same time, Hiawatha Children's Home (now Hiawatha Homes) opened for children with physical disabilities and mental retardation. Not yet satisfied, Ann worked to recruit additional providers of service to open small homes in Rochester so people with disabilities would no longer be forced to move away from their home communities. In 1976, the Ferguson's son moved into the first group home, Sixth Street House. He was nineteen. Ann said of the move, "Douglas was thrilled to death. We were heartbroken. But I'd been saying for years it was every eighteen-year-old's constitutional right to have his parents off his back."

Ann was also active in the area of education. Following years of public policy advocacy, in 1973 the federal government passed a law then known as PL 94-142, or The Individual with Disabilities Education Act (IDEA). This law required public school districts to provide free and appropriate education to all children, no matter their disability or functioning level. The Rochester School District began serving students with varying disabilities, but most of the classrooms were in lower levels away from typical students. To more effectively use resources, the district decided to consolidate all "trainable" students into one building, Horace Mann, in southeast Rochester. Every student in the building had a disability. In 1979 and 1980, Ann led a group of parents and school personnel from Rochester to Madison, Wisconsin, to observe a school system where students with disabilities were integrated into neighborhood schools, often attending classes with "typical" peers. The vision was clearly to "maximize the potential of each individual and prepare them for life after school." The inclusion model was designed not only to provide greater opportunities for students with disabilities, but also to provide opportunities for "typical" students to get to know students with disabilities–not only their needs, but more importantly, their abilities.

As a result of these visits to Madison, in the summer of 1980 under Ann's leadership the Association filed a complaint with the Minnesota Department of Education and the U.S. Regional Office of Civil Rights in Chicago. The complaint charged that the district was discriminating against students with disabilities by not providing a continuum of services and requiring them to attend a segregated school without the opportunity to learn in the least restrictive environment as required by law. At least thirty parents of students in the Rochester District signed the complaint. That complaint resulted in a three-year plan to move all students out of Horace Mann into regular education buildings throughout the district. Within two years, students of all abilities and disabilities were given the opportunity to be educated together.

From advocacy to administration

In late 1980, the Association's Board of Directors made another life-changing decision for Ann. With a primary mission of advocacy, the

Under Ann's leadership in the 1970s, massive changes continued to happen for people with disabilities. She always believed that they deserve the same kinds of opportunities as others in their communities. She is pictured here in 1981 at the recognition event that ARC held for her. (Courtesy Post-Bulletin Co.)

Association had a history of identifying gaps in the service system, starting programs to close those gaps, and then spinning off those programs to get back to the work of advocacy without conflicts of interest. The Association determined it was time to form the four group homes into a new entity. Olmsted ARC Homes was formed. Ann left her position as Executive Director of Olmsted ARC and became the first Executive Director of Olmsted ARC Homes. That role provided her with many new opportunities. While she had provided support and mentoring to many families in her previous position, now she had the opportunity to mentor employees, often new professionals with little experience or exposure to people with developmental disabilities. She took staff under her wing and often into her home, giving them the opportunity to learn from the best. She continued to work with other providers as well as county and state officials. She taught people how to make life better for others. She held that position for only a year, retiring at the end of 1981.

The ultimate volunteer and mentor

Retirement did not slow Ann down; it simply gave her an opportunity to go back to her roots as a volunteer. She served on a variety of boards of directors of non-profit organizations and as a parent representative on the Olmsted County Mental Retardation Providers Cooperative (a loosely formed network of providers, parents, and advocates to ensure communication and cooperation among various stakeholders). Ann served on Olmsted County task forces that impacted the service system design for people with disabilities, and she served on statewide committees. She led and taught others to lead. She gave her time, money, and expertise freely and humbly, always with a sense of humor and a sense of purpose.

Ann died in November 1998. Late in her life when asked about her accomplishments, she said, "I have made a lot of lasagna. I have made a lot of caramels, and I have made a lot of friends among the retarded people I have worked with–which I consider to be the most worthwhile result of my activities." While being honored as a "longtime guiding force," she was interviewed by Janice McFarland of the Rochester *Post-Bulletin*:

> *Ferguson speaks of her early and continuing involvement as something she needed to do. "I think in the early years, when I worked as a volunteer, I felt very incompetent to deal with Douglas' social behavior and education problems because I didn't know how to do it. I could program him professionally, but I sort of felt like a failure as a mother. But I did find I was able to make up for that a lot by doing something for retarded people in a broad sense and this made me feel I accomplished something for Douglas in the long sense."*

Ann's son Douglas retired in 2010, after working for many years in the cafeteria at Rochester Community and Technical College.

Though Ann didn't live to see all the fruits of her efforts–her own son having a job where he interacted daily with college students, living for years with close friends, and being an integral part of his community–Douglas has been able to live the life she dreamed for him.

Mickey Prince, long time The Arc Southeastern Minnesota member and volunteer, once said, "Ann was a catalyst for change. She turned people into leaders without them even realizing it. I became President of the Minnesota Arc. I would never have done that without Ann pushing me, believing in me."

Dave and Sonja Dunn agreed. Because of Ann's encouragement, Dave not only served on the Rochester School Board but was president of both the state and national chapters of the Association. Sonja chaired events and worked on things she would never have considered without Ann. They recall, "Ann made you feel important. She became a true friend. She would do anything for you. We jokingly said if Ann asked us to jump off the Plummer Building, we would simply ask, 'Which direction?'"

Ann Ferguson left her footprint and her fingerprints all over Rochester and the state of Minnesota, making it a better place to live not only for people with developmental disabilities and their families, but also for all of us.

A Supreme Test

In the 1970s, Joy Fogarty challenged a rule that prohibited her from becoming a police officer for the Rochester Police Department

Joy Fogarty's ambitions were more in line with those of a woman in today's world. What she tried to do should not have been a story at all; what makes it so is her timing. In the early 1970s, Joy wanted to become a police officer with the Rochester Police Department. She was not allowed to take the test because she was a year past the cut-off age of thirty-two. Joy didn't realize her attempt to become a police officer would turn into a five-year struggle and court battle that would eventually end up in the Minnesota Supreme Court. In the end she lost the court case; still, Joy was a winner who raised a consciousness for equal rights in the workplace. She also worked effectively for many organizations in the Rochester community.

In the late 1970s, Joy met Diane Fass, who invited her to attend the first convening meeting for a local chapter of the National Organization for Women (NOW). "Something just clicked for me that night," Joy recalls. "Things were just not right for a lot of women. We became a very tight group, and when I look back now, I realize that we accomplished a great deal."

With Joy as a founding member, the NOW chapter helped to start Rapeline in Rochester. The program's mission was to provide support and information to victims of sexual assault in the community. In the beginning, volunteers from the NOW Chapter took shifts in answering the Help Line and assisting callers. Joy's group of four advocates was the first trained to accompany victims throughout the process of reporting the crime, obtaining medical care, and prosecuting the offender when possible.

Joy also joined the Rochester Police Reserve, a volunteer organization of citizens trained as backups to regular police officers. The volunteers rode eight-hour shifts as second officers in the squad cars on weekends, accompanying the regular officers on all their calls during the course of that shift. The calls could include traffic control, bar fights, alarm calls, sexual assaults, and domestic violence reports. Members of the Reserve carried weapons and were required to qualify with those weapons. Prior to the initiation of the Rapeline, Joy would often be called by the department to accompany officers sent on sexual assault calls.

"Domestic calls were always more dangerous than a bar fight," Joy recalls. She counseled the female victims, giving them guidance and directing them to services that could help. "I wore a uniform, had the training, carried a gun, and walked into the same situation as the regular officers. The problem came when I wanted to be paid for my work as a regular police officer."

Too old at thirty-three?

Shortly after her thirty-third birthday, she inquired about taking the test to become an official police officer. She was told that the cut-off age to take the test was thirty-two years, except for veterans. This rule eliminated most women, as there was a quota attached to the number of women allowed to serve in the military at the time while for men, having veteran status was very common. "I naïvely thought I would just waltz right in there and say, 'Hey, we all know this rule is unfair, so just give me the test,'" Joy recalls. Her request was denied and Joy had no idea what she had just started.

"The first Civil Service Commission meeting I attended was held behind locked doors in a small room inside the police department. The first time, it was just me. Very quickly the meetings grew to include me, many members of the police department, a few city leaders, and a huge crowd of reporters."

There wasn't coverage for age discrimination under the state Human Rights Law, so it was easy to have a loophole citing veteran's

A rape victim with Police Captain William Anton and Joy Fogarty. (Courtesy Post-Bulletin Co.)

preference. This allowed men far older than Joy to take the test, join the police force, and receive pay for their services.

"It was up to the Police Civil Service Commission at the time. They were the local authority and had the power to change the rule." They weren't interested in changing the rule, however. The Chief of Police agreed with them and told her, "You could come to work as a secretary for the police department." Joy wasn't interested. "I remained on the Police Reserves and continued to do the same job as the police officers, just without the pay."

Joy then hired an attorney, Bob Suk. It was very clear the case wouldn't go anywhere, so they started the appeal process. The reaction from the public, the police department, and even from friends and family ranged widely. Many in the police department didn't want a woman on the force, while others were very supportive, including one of the two assistant police chiefs. Some people never said a word to her, acting as if nothing was going on.

Her husband, Mike, didn't want her to take on the fight in the beginning. Once it gained momentum, he became very supportive, even though his business suffered. He worked at an insurance agency and some people pulled their business because he "couldn't control his wife." He also received anonymous phone calls at work, telling him she was having an affair.

"Through it all my family was supportive," Joy recalls. Her children, four and seven years old when the ordeal began, said, "Mommy, we'll go with you to see the judge and tell him to let you take the test." Joy said, "Never once did my family say, 'Don't do this. You're embarrassing us.'"

Some friends and acquaintances offered words and notes of encouragement, while others were not so supportive. She remembered being in the restroom at a local restaurant when she was cornered by the wife of a Rochester police officer. The woman warned, "Don't let me ever hear you were riding in a car with my husband!"

The entire process dragged on from 1972 to 1977. Early on, Joy filed a complaint with the Minnesota State Department of Human Rights, alleging sex discrimination by the City of Rochester and the Rochester Police Civil Service Commission. The complaint cited the Veteran's Preference Waiver as one proof of discrimination. The State Department of Human Rights found in favor of Joy and took the case on from that point. The fight ultimately made it to the State Supreme Court and is still in the record books today as *The State of Minnesota vs. The City of Rochester and the Rochester Police Civil Service Commission*. Ultimately, it was decided that although the policy was discriminatory, the remedy was to change The Veteran's Preference law.

Joy was now thirty-six years old. "I felt really old by then and I was tired of the fight," she remembers. She and her attorneys agreed they weren't about to take on the Veterans of the United States "because that is how the opposition would have framed it."

Joy says, "It was a wild time personally. The police department's response seemed so out of step with the way society was moving. I never would have imagined that I would have taken on this fight. I think it was a compilation of events in my life that took me to that point; the point where my only option was to fight."

Men telling women what they should and shouldn't do

It may have begun with an experience in high school that called into question Joy's "naïve assumption" that she could step into a man's world. She and another girl wanted to go to college, but unfortunately, money wasn't available. Joy was the child of a widowed mother and funds were tight. She and her friend explored their options and decided that joining the Air Force could be their ticket to a college education.

Their high school principal learned they had been to visit the Air Force recruiter. He called them to his office and much to her surprise, was quite angry. They received an earful. "You girls will not go into the military! You will just be whores for the officers!"

"He scared us so badly, we abandoned the idea," Joy recalled and then paused a second before adding, "Ironically, if I had joined the Air Force it would have given me the veteran's preference I needed to skirt the age rule for the police test."

After high school, Joy took a job in a bank. She worked as a bookkeeper and remembered being thrilled when she was promoted to teller, where she sat on a stool up front and helped people with their transactions. She was very proud to be the youngest person promoted to the position of bank teller, until a few days later. A young man was hired and, with no more training and far less experience than Joy, was sent to bank officer's training. "At that point I realized I would never move any further than the stool I was currently sitting on."

Shortly afterward, Joy applied for a position with Braniff Airways as a flight hostess. She was hired and excited to get away from the limitations of her hometown and travel the world. Shortly after her announcement, a local priest come up to her teller window at the bank and admonished her in the same way her principal had a few years earlier. "You will just become a whore for the pilots. You should stay here and do what you're expected to do." This was to get married.

"The men in those days thought nothing of telling a woman what she should do. I didn't listen to him, of course."

Joy joined Braniff Airways in March 1960 and signed a contract that, by today's standards, would horrify any human resources

Texas Tech All-American center and linebacker E.J. Holub hoists Braniff Airways Hostess Joy (Phillips) Fogarty.

department. It stated that her weight must remain in proportion to her height. "I was five-foot-four so my maximum weight was 122 pounds when I was hired. Shortly after, they lowered the maximum weight for my height to 116 pounds. We lived on cigarettes and diet pills that the doctors prescribed at the drop of a hat." They were subjected to monthly weigh-ins in front of their supervisors. If they weighed too much, they were furloughed without pay for two weeks and given a chance to lose the weight or they would lose their job. Marriage and outside employment were also prohibited, according to the Braniff contract. Women who got married were immediately let go. And the capper: when she turned thirty-two, her employment would be terminated. "Men were hired to perform duties as Flight Hostesses but they were given the title of Pursers. This way they didn't have to adhere to the same rules that we did. It was automatically assumed that they were our supervisors, even if it was their first day on the job and their female co-workers had years of experience under their belts." Joy wanted to quit several times but her options for other employment were limited. Ultimately, though, Joy did have to resign when she made plans to marry Mike.

Volunteering for change

While in Rochester, one of Joy's proudest accomplishments was serving for many years on the Board of Probationed Offenders Rehabilitation and Training (PORT), a Community Correction's local alternative to jail. PORT acquired a national reputation and was very successful. The program was used as a model across the country.

Today the Rapeline program which the NOW Chapter began operates under a different name and has become a part of Rochester's victim services system. Joy acknowledges she may have been so passionate about Rapeline out of guilt. Years earlier when she worked for Braniff Airways, she shared an apartment with three other women. Joy came home from a flight to learn that one of her roommates had been beaten and raped by a professional football player. Joy and a few other friends consoled her. "We were young and advised her not to go to the police," she recalls. "In those days you almost had to have a witness to the act to get a conviction, even though the physical evidence was there. We felt no one would have believed our roommate and no one would convict a well-liked professional athlete." Because the memory had always haunted her, it felt cathartic to work for Rapeline, to do something to help rape victims.

In addition to her work with Rapeline and as a reserve officer, Joy was a founding member of Omnia Family Services, an organization designed to provide unconditional care to troubled children, and a founding member of AGOG (All the Good Old Girls). She has served as a board member for many organizations, including the Rochester Police Civil Service Commission, Minnesota State Board of Education, State of Minnesota POST Board (Peace Officer's Standards and Training), Rochester Area Foundation, Rochester Community College Foundation, Legal Assistance of Olmsted County and several times president of the Rochester NOW Chapter. Ironically, Joy was Chairperson of the Police Civil Service Commission at the time of the hiring of Police Chief Roger Petersen.

Joy may have lost her fight and never earned her chance to become a Rochester police officer but her fight alone and her contributions to helping women made a tremendous difference. Joy Fogarty earns the right to be named an outstanding woman whose contributions in public affairs helped advance women's rights in Rochester during the 1970s and early 1980s.

The Opportunities of Obedience

Sister Generose Gervais, a humble hospital administrator, was the first woman to serve on the Minneapolis Federal Reserve Board of Directors

When asked what drew her to hospital administration as a career, Sister Generose Gervais, OSF, a small, finely boned woman with keenly intelligent eyes that look directly at you smiles and replies: "Obedience."

"When I first entered the convent, I took a vow of obedience and knew that whatever was asked of me I would do to the best of my ability," says Sister Generose, who today, at age ninety-three, still keeps regular working hours in her office at the hospital. That vow, taken in 1941, when she was nearly twenty-two years old, led the young nun on an amazing life journey.

Jeanne Rose Gervais was born and grew up on a small farm near Currie, a village in southwestern Minnesota. She was the third of seven children–two boys and five girls–and has clear memories of the dust storms and the Great Depression of the 1920s and 1930s. Sometimes, she says, the blowing dust was so thick, "we couldn't see the barn from the house, and you could write your name on the table just a few minutes after wiping it clean."

"We didn't have much money, and we grew most of the food we ate, but we knew absolutely that our parents loved us. They taught us we could be anything we wanted to be when we grew up." The family was active in their local parish church, and the children all went to a Catholic school where they were taught by Franciscan Sisters from Rochester.

A winning loaf of bread

Everyone in the family worked hard on the farm. Sister Generose worked in the fields and in the house helping both her father and mother. At age ten, a time when most girls today are playing with toys or electronic games, Sister Generose's bread baking efforts for a 4-H Achievement Day earned her a trip to the Minnesota State Fair.

"I was so short I could hardly reach the table, and the people around me were surprised that I really could make the bread by myself. But early on Mother taught my sister and me to bake, so in the summer my sister and I did all the baking for the nine people in our family. And, we packed six or seven lunches every day of the school year."

The Gervais children all were active in 4-H, and their mother was one of the adult leaders. "I was always interested in doing a variety of projects and did several each year. Generally there was a point when I wanted to set aside one or two of them because I was tired of writing the achievement story for each project, but Mother simply said: 'You agreed to all of these projects, now you must finish them all.'" It was a good lesson in obedience to a promise made, and one that would forever stay with the young Jeanne Rose. As she grew up, she learned to do the hard work of the farm as well as how to cook, bake, can, garden, and sew–all skills that would serve her well in adult life.

Choosing life in a convent

I always knew I wanted to go to the convent," she recalls. "One night Daddy was mending a tire in the kitchen, and my sister and I were fooling around. I said that I was going to be a Sister when I grew up–my sister said she was going to get married and have twin daughters right away. Daddy said, 'it would suit me fine if all my girls went to a convent.' There was no money to hire a man to help on the farm, so I helped at home for a year after high school and then went to Rochester to enter the convent of the Sisters of Saint Francis.

"The postulants went to the College of Saint Teresa in Winona, Minnesota. They received their habits and entered the Novitiate, a two-year program where they studied religion and continued college, which prepared them with a teaching certificate. After completing the Novitiate program, they took their first vows."

Sister Generose was assigned to teach eighth grade at Cathedral School in Winona. During her first year of teaching, 1941, the Japanese attacked Pearl Harbor, and the United States entered World War II.

"I was correcting papers and the radio was on when they announced that Pearl Harbor had been attacked. At first nobody believed me because it was such a shocking thing," she recalls.

"When the war began, my students wanted to make an afghan for the soldiers. They would knit squares and some of the mothers agreed to crochet them together to make the blanket. That meant I needed to teach my students to knit even though I didn't really know how myself. I could only cast on and cast off, so if any students had problems while knitting their squares, I would take their work home and another Sister would sort out the problem. We finally got it all finished and the students felt very good about making a contribution to the war effort. I still don't know any more about knitting than I did then, but we got the job done."

After two years of teaching eighth grade in Winona, Sister Generose's new mission was to return to school and pursue a bachelor's degree in home economics education. She enrolled at Stout State University in Menomonie, Wisconsin (now the University of Wisconsin at Stout), which had a highly recognized program in home economics. After finishing her degree she attended the College of Saint Teresa in Winona for a year, where she took classes in chemistry and physics, thinking she would have a career as a home economics teacher. Three of her four sisters were students at Saint Teresa's at the time, and for one year all of them were on the same campus. Sister Generose had an opportunity to get to know better her two younger sisters who had been very young when she entered the convent. This was an enjoyable year of academic challenges and sibling interactions.

From the classroom to the hospital kitchen

Her willingness to try new things and her ability to learn quickly were important traits that fit her vow of obedience to do whatever she was asked as a member of her religious congregation. As she proceeded on the path toward her degree, she met with Mother Alcuin, who had been elected General Superior that summer, 1946. At their first meeting, Mother Alcuin asked Sister Generose if she would like to be a dietitian. "I told her I didn't know what a dietitian did," recalls Sister Generose, "but I said, if you need one, I'm willing to try." The next week found her at Saint Marys Hospital in Rochester.

While she was a novice, Sister Generose had said that she would die if she were ever missioned to the hospital. "But, I found out that you don't die that easily." So it was back to school for a semester to take the required courses for a dietetic internship.

After completing her course work and an internship, she graduated in the spring of 1948, then became an administrative dietitian at Saint Marys Hospital. Her duties included ordering food and overseeing food preparation and its delivery to patients and to the employees' dining room. At the time, Saint Marys Hospital had a dairy farm to provide milk for the patients, and the hospital pasteurized the milk to ensure it was safe.

New opportunities

About the time Sister Generose finished the dietetic internship, Sister Domitilla, the hospital consultant, asked her if she would become the director of the newly proposed Rochester School of Practical Nursing at Saint Marys Hospital.

"I said I thought that job should be done by a nurse, but I also said I would be willing to help however I could," says Sister Generose. "So, we decided that I would become a co-director with Rose Peterka, who was a graduate of Saint Marys Hospital School of Nursing (an RN program) and, at that time, was working with practical nurses in New York. I agreed to teach the non-nursing classes.

"A little later, we [the Sisters of Saint Francis] were reorganizing the dietary department in an addition to Mercy Hospital in Portsmouth, Ohio. I was assigned there for what was to be a period of three months, but it was seven or eight months before I returned to Rochester." While Sister Generose was in Portsmouth, Sister Domitilla asked if she would study hospital administration. "I said 'It looks like an awfully high mountain,' but I was willing to try."

Upon her return to Rochester, in preparation for hospital administration, Sister Generose took the pre-clinical course in nursing and had some experiences in various hospital departments. At the conclusion of that year, she enrolled in a graduate program for hospital administration, a two-year program at the University of Minnesota.

It quickly became clear that hospital administration was a good match for Sister Generose's skills and talents. She was one of only two women in the program and did extremely well academically. This was 1952, eleven years after her first assignment as a teacher in Winona. During those intervening years, her life had been filled with a variety of experiences, most of them related to health care.

"My only hospital experience had been at Saint Marys in Rochester. It was at the university that I discovered not all hospitals are organized the way we are."

Saint Marys Hospital was built by the Sisters of Saint Francis in Rochester and opened in 1889. The first staff was composed of five Sisters. "Our Franciscan heritage of integrity, compassion, and respect for the needs of others is a major focus of our hospital," observes Sister Generose. "It always comes down to what is the right way to treat the patient and what is the right way to treat each other. Our relationship with the doctors at Mayo Clinic ensures that the medical care our patients receive is second to none."

The education begins

In 1954, Sister Generose graduated from the University of Minnesota with a master's degree in hospital administration and returned to Saint Marys Hospital. She was thirty-five years old and carried the title Assistant Administrator, working directly with Sister Mary Brigh, a dynamic and talented woman who had become the hospital administrator in 1949. A superb businesswoman and administrator, Sister Mary Brigh was a powerful role model for the young Sister Generose.

"She was an amazing woman," says Sister Generose. "She knew everything about the workings of the hospital and was willing to take on anything that needed to be done. For many years there had been major construction projects–some structures were torn down because they were not up to code and older buildings were remodeled, adding air conditioning. Other buildings got new additions and some new buildings were put up. This continued through the fifties, sixties and seventies, so understanding construction was an important part of heading up the hospital. I had finished my schooling, but now it was time for me to get a hands-on education–and Sister Mary Brigh taught me as much by example as anything else."

Sister Generose realized that doing a variety of jobs throughout the hospital would give her a sense of all that went on in the course of a day. "For a time I was even in charge of the lost and found," she says, smiling. "I do believe that to be the administrator of a hospital means being out of your office and interacting with all the people who work in the hospital, as well as the patients and their families."

The first major administrative project Sister Generose was part of was the construction of the Domitilla Building. She found the entire process "fascinating–I loved reading the blueprints and thinking about what the final product would be. How would it look? How would it feel? Most importantly, how would we use the space to care for patients? I always involved the department heads in the planning because they knew what they needed to care for the patients and make their units efficient."

After being promoted to Associate Administrator in the 1960s, the next step for Sister Generose was to assume full responsibility for Saint Marys Hospital. When Sister Mary Brigh retired in 1971, she became the fifth administrator and, as it turned out, the last Franciscan Sister to hold the post. In 1981, she was named Executive Director; Michael Myers became the first layperson to hold the title Hospital Administrator. Sister Generose retired in 1985, but still maintains an office in the hospital and oversees the Poverello Foundation.

A Century of Caring, a book published by Saint Marys Hospital on the occasion of its 100th anniversary in 1989, tells us:

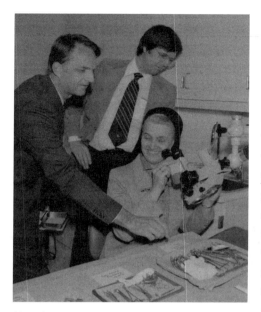

Sister Generose gets an introduction to research equipment. "I do believe that to be the administrator of a hospital means being out of your office and interacting with all the people who work in the hospital." (Courtesy Mayo Clinic)

In 1975, Sister Generose Gervais, who has succeeded Sister Mary Brigh as administrator, announced that Saint Marys Hospital would construct an addition that would cost $55 million; it would be the largest single hospital building project in Minnesota history. The building opened in 1980, and was named the Sister Mary Brigh Cassidy Building. It was a remarkable structure. With almost 100,000 square feet on one floor, it was larger than two football fields and contained forty-three operating rooms ... That Sister Generose was administrator during this era was fortunate, for she possessed an immense knowledge of buildings and [with her department leaders] excelled at making the departments within them more efficient.

"We needed to borrow fifty-five million dollars for the construction," Sister Generose says. "When we met with the bankers, their lawyers wanted to see a copy of the contract we had with Mayo Clinic. We told them we didn't have a contract–we always worked with Mayo in an atmosphere of trust, and a handshake was good enough to arrange any deal." She smiles as she tells this story. "In 1975, nobody did business with just a handshake, especially if it involved millions of dollars. So finally we agreed to a memorandum of understanding and moved ahead with the project. One of the lawyers remarked, 'this has to be the greatest living example of trust in the world.' And so it is."

Sister Generose with Sister Mary Brigh and William Cribbs from Facilities. Sister Generose notes, "I loved reading the blueprints and thinking about what the final product would be. How would it look? How would it feel? Most importantly, how would we use the space to care for patients?" (Courtesy Mayo Clinic)

As the years passed, Sister Generose became increasingly respected for her administrative skills, and other hospitals sought her counsel. Mayo Clinic continued to grow and added many new physicians, which in turn created a need for more hospital space, as well as room for clinical research. Some of the construction during the sixties and seventies was for research laboratories as well as operating rooms. Finally there came the realization that another building was needed to meet the demand for surgical space, which was the driving force for the new construction. Having learned how to manage large construction projects while working with Sister Mary Brigh on the Domitilla Building (1956) and the Alfred Building (1967), Sister Generose was prepared to oversee construction of what is now the Mary Brigh Building (1980).

Sister Generose's administrative skill was not lost on people outside the hospital. In 1975, she became a director of the First National Bank in Rochester, and in 1978, was nominated to serve on the board of the Federal Reserve Bank of Minneapolis. In both instances she was the first woman to hold these positions. The Federal Reserve board consisted of nine directors: three bankers and six non-bankers representing all six states in the district. When Sister Generose joined, there were eight men and one woman.

Sister Ellen Whelan, OSF, in her 2007 work *The Sisters' Story, Part Two*, asked Sister Generose what it was like to be the first woman in her graduate school course and in some business settings that, at the time, were mostly dominated by men. "Being in class around men didn't bother me because anywhere I was working I had to work with men. I never thought I was an outcast or looked down on as an inferior . . . I think they always respected me as a woman and a Sister. I didn't expect any privileges because I was a woman, and I didn't get any."

There was one time while she was serving on the Federal Reserve board that unexpectedly revealed Sister Generose to be different from the others. "Several board members were out of town for a meeting, and the hotel clerk asked for my credit card. I had money to pay for my room, but he said all he could take was a credit card. Another board member was behind me and said, 'I'll pay her bill.' So he gave his credit card to the hotel, and I gave him the money. We laughed because I was the only person in the group who didn't have a credit card."

Help for patients in need

Sister Generose was always interested in helping patients who were poor and unable to pay for their hospital care. Sister Ellen writes of a particular effort by Sister Generose on behalf these patients. "One of Sister Generose's memorable contributions, and probably among the most rewarding, is the Poverello Foundation. The Foundation has as its purpose 'to ease the burden for patients who need financial support for the care they receive at Saint Marys Hospital.' Named for St. Francis of Assisi, referred to as 'Il Poverello' or 'the little poor man,' the Foundation helps about 600 to 700 people each year. Donations abound from former patients as well as employees." In 2011, the Foundation helped 642 patients with a total of $1,198,000.

A major source of financial support for the Poverello Foundation comes from another of Sister Generose's favorite projects. Each autumn the Sisters have a very popular fundraising bazaar. Sister Lauren began the bazaar many years ago; all year long she keeps an eye out for things, large and small, that can be part of the sale, including furniture, glassware, and crafts. Among the best and most well known items are Sister Generose's jam and pickles. She personally makes individual batches of fruit jams and jellies in the Saint Marys kitchen. Other Sisters and volunteers help clean the jars, prepare the fruit, and assist with the canning. Sister Generose makes between three and four thousand jars of jams, jellies, and pickles each year, and all the profit from the bazaar–running between $20,000 and $25,000 annually–goes to the Poverello Foundation of which Sister Generose is the president. During the year, the Sisters hold periodic rummage sales where clothing, furniture, and knick-knacks are the major sources of money for the Foundation.

The Senator and the Sister

On August 7, 1992, Minnesota Senator David Durenberger read into the Congressional Record of the 102nd Congress his statement honoring the work of Sister Generose. In part he said:

Mr. President, life often takes us down unexpected paths. We set our sights on goals we believe we can reach, and begin our journey. So it was with Sister Generose Gervais, who, seeking a life of austerity in service to God, set out from the small farm community of Currie, Minnesota, and went on to become a leading hospital administrator in my home state.

I met Sister Generose in 1977, during my campaign for Governor, and I have sustained a dialog with her in my acquisition of wisdom about what works well in Minnesota medical care.

Her childhood familiarity with common tasks served her well at Saint Marys. As administrator, it was not unusual for her to work a twelve-hour day and then continue until midnight, with the assistance of Sister Lucas Chavez, canning pickles, jams, and jellies to be sold at the Sisters' Annual Bazaar for the benefit of the Poverello Fund.

Milestones of her career include many firsts for women administrators: She was the first woman to serve as a member of the board of directors of the Federal Reserve Bank of Minneapolis, the Rochester Chamber of Commerce, and the First National Bank of Rochester. She received Alumni Distinguished Service Awards from both the University of Wisconsin–Stout and the University of Minnesota. In 1980, the College of Saint Teresa awarded her the Teresa of Avila Award, and in 1985, she received the Pro Ecclesiase et Pontifice *Medal from Pope John Paul II. [Pro Ecclesiase et Pontifice, for which the English translation is "For Church and Pope", is also known as the Cross of Honor. The highest medal that can be awarded to the laity by the Papacy, it is currently given to both lay people and clergy for distinguished service to the church.]*

She continues to serve the hospital as a consultant and as president of the Poverello Foundation. Recently the Mayo Foundation honored her in a ceremony at the site of Saint Marys newest building, which will bear her name: Generose Building.

Mr. President, it is with great pride that I recognize the tremendous contributions of Sister Generose Gervais. In the words of those who know her best, 'She is a strong and gentle witness of who a woman is and can be in our world, in our time.'

When asked about any recent recognition, Sister Generose reveals that in 2011, the Catholic Health Association of the United States presented her the Lifetime Achievement Award for her contributions to the ministry.

Throughout her career, Sister Generose Gervais has followed her vows of poverty, chastity, and obedience and has dedicated her service to God, her Franciscan congregation, the patients and staff of Saint Marys Hospital, and the community at large.

A Wise Student of Politics and Political Issues

In 1971, Carol Kamper became the first woman to be elected to the Rochester City Council

I dare you!" said one of the members of the discussion group to her friend, Carol Kamper. The date was November 1970. The "dare" was for Carol to submit her name for appointment to the recently vacated Sixth Ward City Council seat. The American Association of University Women's (AAUW) "Human Uses of Urban Space" local study group had paused from consideration of the study topic to convince Carol to apply for the opening. There had never been a female member of the Rochester City Council in its 113-year history. The group thought Carol would be perfect for the job.

Carol Kamper was certainly well qualified for the position. She had a master's degree in political science, along with experience as a researcher for the Council of State and Local Governments. She had participated in many study groups in the local AAUW branch. She was active in her community, having been a leading voice in her church in the development of the newly opened Meadow Park Day Care Center. And it just so happened that she lived in the Sixth Ward with her husband Reuben–an IBMer–and her young son.

Carol knew a thing or two about being "qualified." When she and Reuben first moved to Rochester in the mid-1960s, she applied for a job at Methodist Hospital. The administration wanted someone to research the productivity and adequacy of response between two different designs of nursing stations. Carol had worked as a researcher in Chicago, but during her interview at Methodist she was informed she was "over-qualified" for this job. Consequently, she focused her energies where women have traditionally worked: in her home, in her church, and in community groups.

Taking the dare

With the dare fresh in her mind, she applied, along with two men, for the vacant Sixth Ward seat. The six remaining members of the City Council would select a person to fill the remainder of the term of Bruce Cherland, who had been elected to the Olmsted County Board in November. Down in Room 104, in the basement of the old City Hall, the Committee of the Whole held informal interviews. There were the usual questions about qualifications and reason for wanting the job. At the end of the session, Alderman Paul Ludowese reminded the Council that there had never been a female member. He announced to all in the room that it would be inappropriate to appoint one, when one had never been elected. Carol left the session fairly sure that another candidate–the "good old boy"–would be chosen.

Other women whom Carol did not know heard about her application and phoned her with the promise of support for the appointment as well as the upcoming local election in March. Louise Hill, a long-time activist on historical preservation issues, sought out Carol to inform her of her support. Louise told Carol that she had marched into the office of Charley Withers, Editor of the Rochester *Post-Bulletin*, and told him that it was time for him to support the appointment of a woman to the City Council. Louise was successful. On December 10, 1970, the lead editorial, with six paragraphs of arguments, was titled: "Why Not a Woman on City Council?"

As Carol predicted, at the December 14 Committee of the Whole meeting, James Novak, Vice President of Vogel Outdoor Advertising, was selected for official appointment at the next city council meeting. The *Post-Bulletin* reported in a December 15, 1970, story: "Aldermen Monday agreed that, as in the past, the vote on appointment January 4 will be unanimous–although in initial secret balloting at an informal meeting the vote split among the three applicants, the *Post-Bulletin* learned."

In 1971 Carol Kamper (shown with then-mayor Alex Smekta) became the first woman to be elected to the Rochester City Council. For her, leadership is all about relationships with people. "To work through issues, you need to know where people come from, and then you can go on from there." (Courtesy Post-Bulletin Co.)

Shoestring operation

Carol felt obligated to run for the seat in the March election because so many people, including some she did not personally know, supported her candidacy. Dave Griffin and Dr. Charles Kennedy, members from the Elton Hills Covenant Church in the Sixth Ward, offered their help. Frank Klauda, a Sixth Ward resident and Carol's husband's manager, offered his support. A group of IBMers in Reuben's area designed a unique piece of campaign literature for her, and of course there had been the *Post-Bulletin* endorsement. She called her campaign "a shoestring operation of innocence."

With little money to invest in the campaign, Carol knew she had to use the door-to-door approach, even though it was a snowy March. Every afternoon after her husband came home from work, she knocked on doors to introduce herself to voters. One resident, new at the time, remembers being surprised by the visit at suppertime from the woman in the long coat and snow boots. She wondered, "Who would dare oppose such a well educated and prepared candidate?"

Carol had fifty yard signs which she pounded into snow banks when she found willing supporters–even though she was running against a man with a sign company. It was hard not to be discouraged the day that her opponent erected what seemed to be 500 yard signs!

Despite these disadvantages, on March 9, 1971, she won the Sixth Ward race, 711-556. History was made in Rochester. In the next day's editorial, the *Post-Bulletin* wrote:

> [T]he willingness of Sixth Ward voters to entrust a woman to council duties for the first time in the city's 113-year history is especially noteworthy. Mrs. Kamper showed in her campaigning that she is willing to face up to the issues without flinching, without fear that she might have an adverse effect on potential voters. With a rich background in education and quasi-governmental experience, she should be a definite asset to the Council. The fact she is a woman, as well, is a bonus, for she will be able to provide the feminine perspective to a number of subjects.

Life goes on

A memorable picture of Carol and her family appeared in the same issue of the *Post-Bulletin* with the caption, "BREAKFAST AS USUAL–The city's first 'alderwoman,' Carol Kamper, was pretty collected about her election today as she poured coffee for her husband Reuben, a human factors engineer at IBM. He holds their son Donald." The accompanying story noted, "Life goes on as usual at 2204 Valkyrie DR NW (her home) today. Mrs. Carol Kamper drove her husband to IBM where colleagues had, however, reported him acting 'a little like a new father.'" Unreported by the *Post-Bulletin* was the lovely strawberry pie brought to her in honor of her victory by Sharon Barsness, one of the members of the AAUW study group who had "dared" her to seek the post.

A year later, when Carol announced she was pregnant with her second child, the *Post-Bulletin* ran a cartoon of a baby's highchair pushed up to the City Council Chamber's meeting table. Reuben maintained that he received more comments about that picture than about any campaigns or votes taken by his wife. "Do you really want your wife on public display like that?" some asked. His answer: "Wouldn't you rather have a wife who is active?" And what became of that baby, born while her mother was the lone female on the

Rochester City Council? Kim Kamper Therres followed her mother's lead into local government service; she is currently Assistant City Administrator and Human Resources Director for the City of Crystal, Minnesota.

A year after her election to the Rochester City Council, Carol became pregnant with her second child. The Post-Bulletin ran a cartoon showing a baby's highchair pushed up to the City Council Chamber's meeting table and captioned "New furniture for city council chambers?" (Courtesy Post-Bulletin Co.)

Dealmaking

It took more than a week for the City Council President, Dick Postier–whom Carol later counted as a good friend–to call her with a welcome and a schedule of meetings. She felt that she developed good working relationships with other council members, even those who had opposed her appointment. She joined the rest of the Council: Darrell Strain, James McNary, Joe Mayer, Robert Willmarth (replaced later that year by Jim Powers), Bob Larson, Dick Postier, and Mayor Dewey Day for the first Monday of the month Council dinner. She had hoped that she would be included, because that is where relationships were formed, points of view shared, and some decisions made. She was. She remembers Mayor Alex Smekta, whose terms bracketed Mayor Dewey Day's, as "the smoothest politician" she ever saw. "He worked it out behind the scenes and then skipped the controversial votes," she notes. Carol feels that her own style of leadership, emphasizing mediation and compromise, was honed by exposure to these more senior political figures in both formal and informal settings.

Other work of the council was also done outside council chambers or City Hall room 104. She voted "not" when the council chose not to hire then Assistant City Administrator, Stephen Kvenvold, to replace City Administrator Jim Andre, who was resigning to take a job in Roseville. Council members Powers and Larson both had come to her home to lobby her to vote for Steve, whom Carol maintained was too young for the job. Another candidate was chosen. After a short, disastrous tenure, that administrator left, and the Council, including Carol, enthusiastically supported Mr. Kvenvold, who has remained in the job to this day.

Carol learned valuable lessons about how public-private partnerships were developed in Rochester in the 1970s. Soon after her election, the Council was in the final negotiations with Mayo Clinic on moving the public library from the site that would become Mayo Medical School Student Center, to the former J. C. Penney's building on Broadway. The Mayor said, "We'll just have to ask Mayo for more money," when Carol and other Council members complained about the need to make the new site more attractive. They did, and Mayo Clinic paid.

Lonely votes

There were several 6-1 votes, which Carol lost, to change R-1 zoning in the Sixth Ward to R-3 or R-4 to accommodate apartment developments like the Candlewood complex. Carol recalls meeting with Ken Allsen and a large group of homeowners in his house on Forty-first Street NW to hear of their concerns about the zone change and to take their message to the rest of the council. Her neighbors' message "fell on deaf ears." Southeast Rochester could not expand so densely until a new sewer interceptor was built; no one at that time could imagine new apartments in the southwest part of town; and there was an underutilized sewer pipe, originally constructed to accommodate the needs of IBM in northwest Rochester, which included the Sixth Ward, that could easily handle a more dense population than R-1 housing. Thus the lonely votes continued, including one to move the sewage treatment plant out of the Sixth Ward into a township, as Carol represented her constituents and the other aldermen let the growth occur in her ward.

Carol also recalls a 4-3 vote when she was on the winning side. A party wanted to build a Ground Round restaurant in Rochester and needed a liquor license. She and other Council members had recently eaten in one of the franchise's operations when they attended a League of Minnesota Cities meeting in Saint Cloud. She enjoyed the relaxed atmosphere and thought it would be appreciated by many in Rochester. However, Carol recalls, one alderman thought "liquor should be served on white table cloths, and definitely not where food was served in a basket!" Robert Short, prominent Minnesota business-man, wanted the franchise in Rochester and Milt Rosenblad was his local advocate at the Council hearing. Carol's perception of the chang-ing desires of Rochester residents won the day, and one of Rochester's limited liquor licenses was awarded to the Ground Round.

Carol remembers when she was newly elected, she and Sister Generose Gervais, Administrator of Saint Marys Hospital, were the only women invited to the Chamber of Commerce events on local and political issues. That began to change as a growing number of women were elected to other offices in Rochester. Rosemary Ahmann, elected to the Olmsted County Board in 1972, interested Carol in the new field of community corrections. Janet Kneale, newly elected Rochester School Board member, accompanied Carol and city engineer Jack Dolan to Saint Paul to lobby for reduced speed limits along Elton Hills Drive where two public schools in the Sixth Ward were located.

New and Different

It was September, 1976, and once again Bruce Cherland was vacating an elected post, this time as Olmsted County Second District Commissioner. "Why do you want to do rural roads?" some of her acquaintances asked her when they heard she was interested in running for the position. "It's not just roads," she told them. "I want to explore new and different issues." In the mid 1970s, county government in Minnesota was changing with the advent of community corrections, community social services, and community health services. Olmsted County government also appealed to her because she wanted to decide the merits of an issue and not have to follow what a political party determined, as would have been required of a state legislator, a goal that might have been another logical progression. "I wanted to bring people and governments together," Carol says.

After winning a primary and a close election against Bob De-Witz, Carol was ready to get to work.

She did indeed face "new and different issues"–but not the ones she planned. From 1977 through the 1980s, while traveling frequently both to lobby and learn, she was a steady, calm, and determined leader of the county on key issues: flood control, waste management (including building a waste-to-energy incinerator), and surely the most divisive issue of all, the disposition of the old state hospital partially sold to the Federal Bureau of Prisons.

"Downest" day

The Rochester State Hospital was closed, partially in 1981, and completely in 1982, by the Minnesota State Legislature in a budget cutting measure, and the property was awarded to Olmsted County for one dollar the following year. Initially, the County was interested in the property as an in-city site for a much needed waste incinerator. Soon, though, finding the best community use for the entire property, as well as replacement jobs for the economic hole caused by the hospital shutdown, became the broader goal of the County Board of Commissioners. Everyone in the community had suggestions, including the long and deeply held hope for a four-year college. Unfortunately, there were no buyers.

Richard Devlin, County Administrator, called Carol, the County Board Chair, to tell her that State Senator Nancy Brataas had a contact in the Federal Bureau of Prisons. Innocently, Commissioner Kamper told him, "Let's explore that." The Bureau of Prisons did indeed want to purchase a portion of the property, and they were ready to answer questions put forward by the community. Carol still remembers the large and emotional public meeting that she conducted at Mayo Civic Center to introduce the merits of the idea to the public and gather feedback. The auditorium was packed with "not-in-my-town" citizens, including the angriest of all, Carol's former colleague and friend, Dick Postier, Rochester City Council President. "Over my dead body!" his voice rang out.

Quietly, Chair Kamper and several other County Commissioners met with Mayo Clinic administrators. Although Mayo Clinic would not publicly join the fray on this issue, they reiterated that they thought the community needed a third large employer and that a Federal Medical Center operated by the Federal Bureau of Prisons could aid their psychiatric practice and training. Similar meetings were quietly arranged with other private sector leaders in the community to be sure of their support. As Carol said later, "You don't rock the community without support from the big players."

There were four "rock solid" votes on the five-member Olmsted County Board in support of selling a portion of the property to the Federal Bureau of Prisons: Joan Sass and Jim Daley, who were outspoken supporters, Harley Boettcher, and Carol herself. The other board members understood that Commissioner Doug Krueger, given the opposition in his district, could not support this.

The day the organized opponents rented buses to hold a "referendum" to oppose the federal prison was her "downest day" on this issue or any issue. Carol told her family that she was going to lose the next election. She had police protection, and her phone rang with angry citizens who wished to vent. One woman told Carol's middle school-aged daughter who answered the phone, "I hope your Mom goes to Russia, where she belongs." Her daughter answered, "That would be exciting. She'd like to do that." (In fact, later, Carol did lead a group of a dozen teens in a "People to People" program to the Soviet Union.)

Would the negative news never stop? The Rochester City Council scheduled a vote to sue Olmsted County over the sale to the Bureau of Prisons. Mayor Hazama could be counted on for a veto, because he had been moved to the County's position during a visit to other federal prisons with local leaders. Still, one more "no" vote was needed. Carol remembers that the Chamber of Commerce "got to Fifth Ward Alderman Bluhm, who changed his mind and voted against the motion." The proposition failed. County Administrator Richard Devlin recalls asking his uncle if there had ever been a "hotter" issue in Rochester's history. His uncle recollected only one in his lifetime: The accusation, during the McCarthy Era, that the superintendent of schools was a communist.

Final disposition

The final decision by the County Board came in the spring, ending this very intense political issue. The former state hospital campus would be partitioned so that only a part would be sold to the Bureau of Prisons, which promised to maintain aesthetic berms and plantings, to hire a larger number of local employees than usual, and to maintain the facility as a medium-security prison, housing no more than 600 to 700 inmates. The unsold campus buildings would be used or rented out by the County for office space. Open areas would be used for soccer fields and a park, later deeded to the City for one dollar. And the Minnesota Legislature, in return for receiving the profit from this sale according to state law passed funding in a bonding bill for two items that the community wanted and the County needed. One was a new classroom building at the Rochester Community College Campus, across the road from the state hospital property, to house both Winona State and RCC classes. The other was a portion of a new waste incinerator to provide steam heat to many local public buildings.

A host of rewards was thus provided for a reticent community. Carol Kamper considers this her greatest accomplishment as an elected official: the development of the eastern side of Rochester, including the state hospital property, and the assurance that the community would get what had been promised.

Higher education for Rochester

Besides being an elected official at both the City and County levels, Carol Kamper served as a member of the state's Higher Education Coordinating Board, appointed by both Governors Al Quie and Rudy Perpich. She enjoyed the opportunity of working with so many highly qualified female staff at the Coordinating Board, since her work at Olmsted County chiefly involved male department heads. The Board researched Rochester's need for a four-year college and other higher education issues, such as combining state technical and community colleges. Unfortunately, the Higher Education Coordinating Board devolved into managing only student loans, dropping its independent research function. Carol believed that the Legislature did not always appreciate the results of their independent research.

Carol's interest in higher education not only reflected her community's long held desire for a four-year college; she taught government classes for eighteen years at Rochester Community College (RCC). She was a popular teacher, providing theory supported by examples from real-life experiences for her students. RCC President Geri Evans became a close friend when she supported Carol and the County during the state hospital/prison issue; and the feeling was certainly reciprocal, especially after Commissioner Kamper engineered the funding of the "2+2" building on the RCC Campus. The "2+2" concept envisioned a four-year college degree provided in Rochester combining offerings from RCC and Winona State University (WSU). In fact, President Evans called upon Carol as an intermediary at times when she dealt with the "other half" of the "2+2" equation, WSU. Relationships were so strained between Rochester and Winona that Dr. Mary Rieder of WSU held meetings in Saint Charles, half-way between the two cities. Carol recalls getting a call to attend one such meeting while she was cleaning her oven. She immediately stopped what she was doing, cleaned up, and attended the meeting, doing what she could to find a middle ground.

Relationship theory of governing

For Carol Kamper, leadership is all about relationships with people. "To work through issues, you need to know where people come from, and then you can go on from there," she says. As County Board Chair, Carol always encouraged lunches and other informal gatherings of the Board, according to Olmsted County Administrator Richard Devlin. These informal meetings, at which families and other non-county issues were discussed, tended "to take the tension out" of the relationship among board members and helped "hot" issues stay calm during board meetings.

Carol also thought that gathering facts from all viewpoints was important to wise decision-making. During her tenure she took many fact-gathering and lobbying trips with other community members. Mr. Devlin remembers sitting with her and Chief Justice Warren Burger in the magnificent retiring chamber of the Supreme Court, discussing the possibility of bringing the National Institute of Corrections to Rochester as an additional sweetener to the new federal prison. Devlin recalled that as a County Commissioner, "Carol was a real student of government–a statesman. She took the hard votes. She was matter-of-fact, quiet, and well-prepared. She spent a lot of time developing relationships and taught us all a lot."

One of those "taught a lot" by Commissioner Kamper was the late Olmsted County Commissioner, Mike Podulke. He thought that commissioners Kamper and Boettcher, the only incumbents on the Olmsted County Board when the board increased membership from five to seven in 1986, must have been quite concerned about how the new commissioners would work out. "They needn't have worried. We all took our cue from Carol," he said.

After Commissioner Kamper retired, Jean Michaels said upon her own retirement from the County Board that she didn't realize how much she counted on Carol's presence until she was gone. Part of the problem was being the only female left on the Board, she suggested. But a greater factor was the loss of Carol's wise counsel.

Theodore Roosevelt said, "Far and away the best prize that life offers is the chance to work hard at work worth doing." Luckily for the citizens of Rochester and Olmsted County, Carol Kamper found local issues "work worth doing" and has been active on the behalf of many citizens for over three decades.

The Policy Wonk

Sheila Kiscaden was Olmsted County's first female Legislative Liaison

The new mother sat quietly in the rocking chair nursing her month-old baby. Her dreams and musing about her first-born child were interrupted by a phone call from her employer, Richard Devlin, Olmsted County Administrator. "Sheila," he said, "we have to have you back! Carl Maeder has just died, and you know he was our lead staff on the state hospital closing. This is going to be an incredibly difficult issue for our community. Incredibly difficult. Believe me, I will do whatever it takes, including babysitting, if you come back from maternity leave and help us out."

For the previous eleven years, Carl Maeder had been Olmsted County's Welfare Director. In May of 1981, the Minnesota State Legislature determined that the Rochester State Hospital (RSH) was to be closed beginning July 1 of that year. Because of his knowledge of the RHS situation and his familiarity with federal and state regulations, Carl had been appointed the County's first Director of Intergovernmental Relations. He was assigned to work with a community task force to develop options for the displaced patients' and for uses of the campus that could then be taken to the legislature. A month later, Carl unexpectedly died.

Sheila Kiscaden, Olmsted County Human Services Planner, said "Yes" to Richard Devlin and was hired on special contract by the County Board the same day they selected the community members for the RSH Task Force. Those 300 hours of the special contract would not only be the first step in resolving a contentious issue; they would also change Sheila's career path.

Citizen empowerment

In the public mind, phrases like "efficiency and effectiveness, coordination of services for clients, interagency collaboration, non-duplication between public and private agencies, valuing citizen input, and volunteer efforts" are not always associated with government activities. Sheila's multiple careers in Olmsted County, various private organizations, and even later in the Minnesota State Senate, are underpinned by a belief in all of these values, as well as a work ethic to accomplish them all. Key to accomplishing all of these "good government" goals, in Sheila's view, is empowerment of the community.

"I have always been attracted to public policy issues and believe that citizens can have an impact on the outcome," she says. "Olmsted County, more than other places at the time, sought public input, and empowered those who provided it. And this led to better policy. For me, working for Olmsted County was a good fit."

Sheila's first job with the county was as Coordinator for the Justice System Volunteer Project (JSVP) in the mid 1970s. After leaving her position as the Regional Director for Planned Parenthood in Rochester, she came to JSVP considering it an interim position before attending law school. She had been the first Regional Coordinator for Planned Parenthood of Minnesota. When Planned Parenthood's clinical services first opened in Rochester, they were housed in rented space from the county health department. Sheila formed strong professional and personal relationships with many of the public health nurses, including Barb Huus. Barb's husband, Pete, worked for Olmsted County's new Community Corrections Department.

When Sheila resigned her position with Planned Parenthood, Pete contacted her to see if she would be interested in reorganizing and managing the corrections volunteer program. Sheila took the position because it gave her the opportunity to observe and be part of the criminal justice system before starting law school. Ironically, the experience led her to conclude that a legal career was probably not the right choice for her. She discovered that helping empower citizens to create better government and better public services was something she enjoyed and at which she excelled. Through JSVP, countless individuals, non-profits, and businesses participated with offenders by providing work opportunities, counseling, and probation services. One-on-one tutoring was also initiated in the jail after a local study's finding of wide-spread dyslexia among incarcerated individuals. JSVP became very successful under Sheila's watch.

Following a massive needs assessment in 1978, Olmsted County determined that the number one issue of concern was child abuse and services related to ameliorating this problem. When Jean Michaels, volunteer extraordinaire, took on the chairmanship of a fifteen-month effort called the Family Violence Task Force, Sheila Kiscaden was assigned by Community Corrections to be the staff and study coordinator. There were more than thirty citizen and professional members. Scores of other professionals were consulted. An inquiry was made into what was currently available versus best practices. Discussions ranged from an exact definition of child abuse to how to better coordinate between current service providers. A forty-five-point five-year plan was developed and presented in April 1980 to the Olmsted County Board. "It was at the height of the Jordan, Minnesota, child sex scandal" Sheila recalls, "and it was the only plan of which I am aware that resulted in all provisions being implemented." (The scandal in Jordan involved several children making allegations of sexual abuse against parents and one other man. Twenty-four adults were charged and thirty-seven children were placed in foster homes.)

Based on the successful outcome of the Family Violence Task Force, Sheila was appointed to the position of Olmsted County Human Services Planner. In that position, Sheila worked on a series of projects and developed her skills in policy formation as well as citizen empowerment. "I was the convener/facilitator for many different community projects," she explains. One notable project, which was completed after her work on the state hospital closure, was the development of a Community Action Program (CAP), a new program with funding and initiatives for low income people. Sheila designed a program format that complimented County Social Services and prevented the negative reactions from area citizens that were beginning to occur in other locales.

"It was very tricky to get a county-sponsored program rather than an independent agency through state and federal regulations," says Olmsted County Administrator Richard Devlin. "But she did it. Sheila was an extremely hard worker and politically perceptive and savvy." Sheila adds that she was able to get county administrative backing for the CAP project because her work on the state hospital issue had gone so well. By the time Sheila received that phone call from Richard Devlin, she was well prepared to coordinate the Citizen's Task Force on the closing of the Rochester State Hospital, which became the most contentious issue to face the community in a generation.

A passion for improving lives

Sheila had originally planned to be a high school Spanish teacher. Not only did she prepare for this in college, but she spent one undergraduate year in Chile and even received a Fulbright scholarship to study in South America after her first year of teaching. However, she turned that opportunity down to marry and move to Rochester where her husband had a job at IBM.

In the 1970s, employees were hired to come to Rochester, but it was much harder for females to find professional work if they lived in Rochester and were married. She had followed her career plan and had taught Spanish for a year, but found that teaching a foreign language seemed to be too "static;" she wanted greater involvement than that in her world. Her experience in Chile had opened her eyes to the plight of women and children in developing countries. She recalls awakening one morning, looking out her bedroom window. Just a few feet away, a little girl of about eight, balancing a baby on her hip and trailed by a number of younger boys, was going through the garbage cans at the curb. Sheila learned that in the hospitals, forty percent of the beds were filled by women with complications from illegal abortions. She visited communities that had one tap of running water for hundreds of homes. It was clear to Sheila that controlling population growth was vital to improving people's lives worldwide.

For that reason, when Planned Parenthood announced that it was opening a regional office in Rochester, Sheila went into action. "I actively lobbied for, and got that job, even though I had no experience, just passion," She says. A year or so later as Sheila was having a breakfast meeting at Rochester's Kahler Hotel with Mary Margaret DuShane, the Chair of the Regional Planned Parenthood Advisory Committee, they encountered Supreme Court Justice Harry Blackmun. Ms. DuShane, who knew Justice Blackmun, introduced Sheila, and the two women responded to some of his questions about abortion. Sheila later discovered that the justice was in town, using the Mayo research library, to write his famous Roe v. Wade decision. While she passionately believed in family planning, Sheila left her position with Planned Parenthood once they began providing abortions because she felt the politics of abortion would consume too much of the organization's focus and energy. At that point, her career moved to the county.

"Tracking" at the Capitol

The first legislative issue she worked on was the closing of the Rochester State Hospital, which began its shut down in July of 1981, with a full and permanent closure to be completed in 1982. The Olmsted County Board had created a task force to study the issues and options. Sheila staffed this undertaking with the chair, Jane Campion. And then, she says, "We did it all over again on the Governor's Task Force." Since the State Hospital was a state and regional resource and all of the people on the original Olmsted County Task force had been from the immediate Rochester area, it was felt a second task force with broader representation was needed to assure that the state's interests were considered. "While we had a little more detail in this second task force, thanks to state agency help, the group came to basically the same recommendations and conclusions," she notes.

Sheila Kiscaden, Olmsted County's first female legislative liaison, is the only Minnesota State Senator to serve as a member of three different parties: Republican, Independence, and DFL (Democrat).

What a body of work the task force had created: detailed facts about the needs of mental health clients and potential clients; detailed information on the status of the buildings and real estate involved; detailed examination of potential users of portions of the property; and numerous suggestions on how to move forward gleaned from interviews, discussions, and hearings with every possible stakeholder. This gave Sheila and the Olmsted County legislative delegation a solid foundation as they sought to let the local community control the destiny of the former state hospital campus.

The work of the task force led to Sheila becoming a "legislative liaison" at the state capitol. "The County Board realized they needed someone on staff who could track and inform them of legislative issues at the Capitol, and who could also support our area legislators in their work on our behalf," says Sheila. "Following the state hospital closure issue at the Legislature was the beginning. Becoming a lobbyist for the county was an incremental development for me and for the county."

"Sheila Kiscaden was such an outstanding lobbyist," comments former State Senator Nancy Brataas as she remembers how they worked together at the Capitol. "It was a wonderful service for the county to provide her voice—a true breakthrough. I welcomed that the county cared enough to contribute a person of Sheila's standing to the effort."

After the Rochester State Hospital closed, a small task force of social services professionals, including Sheila and Stan Groff, Social

Services Director from Steele County, was asked to recommend alternatives for those with mental illness or chemical dependency who lived in the counties in the region. The Community Social Services Act, which had recently been enacted in Minnesota, charged counties with developing and supervising local services based on a plan approved by the state. According to Stan, this group came up with the idea to have state funds allocated directly in block grants to counties for services for individual clients with mental illness or chemical dependency. Counties would then use county case managers to act as brokers and advocates on behalf of these individuals. This idea was drafted as legislation.

"Sheila was simply outstanding to work with," said Stan. "She had provided much of the staff help to area commissioners during the proposed shut-down debate and so understood all of the issues from the ground up. As we met, her sparkling intelligence, knowledge, good humor, and practicality made it like working with a friend, and not just a colleague. Deeply respectful of others' ideas and opinions, Sheila was the glue that provided the integration of concepts and ideas that finally resulted in recommendations to counties, DHS (Department of Human Services), and the legislature."

Sheila recalls this first bill was carried by freshman Senator Linda Berglin, who later became a giant in the Minnesota Senate in the field of health and human services. Senator Berglin often referred to this as "the dollars follow the client bill," when she later worked with Sheila as a colleague in the Senate. After several years of effort, the concrete result was the creation of the consolidated chemical dependency fund to be used by all Minnesota counties for clients needing this service. Sheila remembers working in a coalition of people on this bill, including: Stan Groff; Tom Bounds, Northland Mental Health Center in Grand Rapids, MN; and Bob Zabel, Director of Zumbro Valley Mental Health in Rochester. The coalition and work at the Capitol resulted in the creation or enhanced financing of many other local services related to the state hospital closure in Rochester: the Thomas House, for those with mental illness, and the detox center and mental health crisis unit at Zumbro Valley Mental Health.

The Olmsted County 1983 Legislative Agenda, developed by Sheila in November 1982, was the first document of its type for Olmsted County. It is an incredibly detailed, yet concise, list of positions, chiefly in the area of health and human services. Among the five "highest priority" issues in the document for Olmsted County are support for the recommendations of the Governor's Task Force for the Disposition of the Rochester State Hospital, and creation of block grants for mental health for community alternatives to the state hospital system, both of which Sheila had helped develop.

Most telling is the number one priority that Sheila laid before area legislators: maintenance of existing state aids and payments for county delivered state services. Her rationale for this position has continued to remain accurate for a generation of state-county relations in Minnesota, never quite being solved:

[T]he state of Minnesota is facing difficult choices in resolving the state's fiscal problems. Area legislators must be alert, however, to the consequences to local government services of the transfer or reduction of state funds. The 1983 Olmsted County budget and local tax levy, which already call for staff and service reductions, have been set. Reductions in state funds will consequently necessitate further reductions in services.

What's a mother to do?

For a person who came to be known as incredibly organized and "planful," Sheila's career trajectory was almost serendipitous. And while younger readers may not be aware, women in Sheila's age group will recall how many career compromises were made during this era to work around husbands' vocations, motherhood, and other vicissitudes of life that impact women. In 1981, when Sheila returned early from maternity leave to help the County on the state hospital closing issue, she had to make ad hoc arrangements for child care. Jean Michael's daughter, Annie, a high school student, could babysit during the remainder of the summer, but that was a temporary solution. The early 1980s were not a time of many child care choices for working parents, especially those with the odd hours of a lobbyist. Sheila was able to call upon her county network to find coverage for the three to four days per week that she worked. One of her area's secretaries suggested her mother, who had raised six children. Luella Schieck agreed to be a housekeeper and "paid grandma" at the Kiscaden household, according to Sheila, after saying, "I thought about it and prayed about it, and I will do it because I think you and I will get along." Sheila wondered at that comment, but came to realize Luella's wisdom; after all, they were raising her son Michael together.

Those who are working parents of young children will realize that every child care arrangement has holes when it comes to responding to changing work requirements. There were times that Sheila had to be at the Capitol in Saint Paul when she had no planned child care. In those instances she packed up her son and then later, her son and daughter, and took them with her, either to stay with her parents in Maplewood or with her sister-in-law, who also had small children, in Vadnais Heights, both suburbs of Saint Paul. She recalls the long drives back to Rochester with her toddler in his car seat, nodding off, and she herself incredibly tired from the early months of another pregnancy–not to mention long hours lobbying. At times she would pull into a parking lot at some halfway point in Hampton or Cannon Falls and nap in the car along with her son.

While still nursing her second baby, she occasionally found she needed to attend out of town meetings with baby in tow. Sheila remembers the arrangements she made for her baby while she attended a meeting of the National Association of Counties (NACO). Little Karen slept in an emptied soft-sided suitcase in the hotel room and had a babysitter provided by hotel management during the day. Another county lobbyist used to tell the story of Sheila attending strategizing events at the Association of Minnesota Counties offices and pulling open a convenient drawer in which to lay her sleeping baby during discussions.

At some point, child care options were destined to improve, partly due to the work of individuals like Tutti Sherlock, whom Sheila greatly admired and who founded Child Care Resource and Referral

The early 1980s were not a time of many child care choices for working parents, especially those with the odd hours of a lobbyist. When Sheila attended a meeting of the National Association of Counties (NACO) in March 1985, she brought her daughter Karen along. Little Karen slept in an emptied soft-sided suitcase in the hotel room and had a babysitter provided by hotel management during the day.

(CCRR) in Rochester. At the same time, many more women with young children were entering the Minnesota workforce in the 1970s and 1980s. Sheila tells the story of identifying herself on a note to a legislator asking him to meet her outside a hearing room: "I'm the one in the gray wool maternity dress," she wrote. After sending the note in to the legislator, she looked around the meeting room and observed that there were three women in gray wool maternity dresses among the crowd.

The year was 1992, and Sheila and her husband had returned to Rochester a few years earlier after his IBM assignment in New York. Sheila was approached by State Senator Nancy Brataas, who wanted to retire from the Minnesota Senate and wanted Sheila run for her seat. "Nancy ran an intense three-week campaign to get me to run," says Sheila. "She met with me, had people calling me, sent me documents, and called me daily, sometimes multiple times a day. Nancy is a force to be reckoned with, and I was the focus of an intense effort."

Sheila finally consented, but her husband was the one to convince her. "You have always looked for the right role for yourself in this community. This is probably a once in a lifetime opportunity," he told her. She recalls asking him, "Rick, are you ready to be the primary parent?" He had to think about that for a day or two before responding, "Yes. This is your turn." Sheila also recalls consulting female Winona County Commissioner Lee Luebbe, whom she had met during her work on the state hospital task forces, and who had six children and still held elective office. "My younger children have a different and closer relationship with their father, due to my being gone so much," Lee told her. And while Sheila's husband indeed sacrificed much to become the "primary parent," Sheila believes that he, too, was rewarded with a closer relationship with his children.

Sheila Kiscaden had just been elected State Senator, after surviving a very close primary. "Honey, I'm coming back; you need me," said Luella Schieck, the Kiscaden family's former "paid grandma." Sheila and her family would definitely need help while she lived in Saint Paul during legislative sessions. State legislators can come home weekends during the session, but while "the body comes home; the mind does not," says Sheila. Parenting and other home responsibilities cannot so easily be resumed. Some parenting responsibilities followed Sheila to the floor of the Senate, even though she thought she was not the "primary parent." She recalls receiving an emergency phone call from her daughter's school during her first week in the Minnesota Senate. Her daughter had been hit in the eye with a ball and needed to be picked up, and her husband could not be reached. Sheila agonized; should she leave the Senate floor and rush home to take her daughter to the doctor, or was this an incident that could be handled by the babysitter? Recalling that a parent involved with her son's cub scout troop was an ophthalmologist, she called him, took his advice, and passed on his information to the babysitter about how to care for her daughter's eye and watch for complications. She stayed on the Senate floor.

Sheila served in the Minnesota Senate for fourteen years. Her years of experience with health and human services issues at the county level quickly made her one of the Senate's policy leaders on health care reform, child protection, and civil rights issues–despite serving as a Republican, the minority party at the time. Sheila was known for her ability to get issues resolved, for her focus on policy, and for her voice of reason. However, during these years, the Republican Party's social agenda became ever more conservative and increasingly prominent. She found herself at odds with her party and, as more social conservatives were elected, at odds with many in her caucus.

In 2002, when the local Republican Party did not endorse her, Sheila ran for re-election under the banner of the new Independence Party. Hers was that party's only electoral victory that year. She still chose to caucus with the Senate Republicans until 2004, when she was driven from that caucus, and literally had her furniture moved into the hall while she was in a conference room championing her local county in a fight with the Department of Corrections over payment issues. She returned to find the janitors moving her desk and filing cabinets out of her office on orders of the Senate Minority Leader, Dick Day. She immediately received a call from the Senate Majority leader, Dean Johnson, inviting her to join the Democratic caucus, which she did. Sheila brought her voice of reason and concentration on policy to her new assignment as the Chair of the State Government Finance Committee. The following year, with the legislature and governor locked in a budget confrontation, Sheila and the House Committee Chair, Republican Marty Seifert, had the only conference committee that worked through their considerable differences and finished their budget bill on time.

In 2006, Sheila ran for Lieutenant Governor as the running mate of a Democratic candidate for governor, Kelly Doran. When Doran withdrew from the race, she decided it was time to return to private life and the consulting practice she had established in 1987. Along the way, commuting from Rochester, Sheila earned two master's degrees: one from the University of Southern California in Public Administration (1986) and one, as a Bush Fellow, from the University of Sussex, in Britain, in International Development (2006). Sheila thought that when she left the legislature she would achieve her long-held dream of working in international development. However, her commitment to family and community made that impossible. She continues to do organizational development and strategic planning with many Minnesota organizations and is an active community organizer developing such community initiatives as the Yellow Ribbon volunteer support organization for families of deployed military members and the first Citizen's League chapter in Rochester. As we go to press, Sheila has been elected to the Olmsted County Board (2012 election) where she surely will continue to make contributions to her community.

Sheila sees proof in her life that individual and community achievements come from more than one person's efforts and abilities, no matter their position or skills. She concludes, "Working with colleagues and members of the community has always been and still is the most important part of being successful in creating community change for the greater good." Sheila Kiscaden is the only Minnesota State Senator to serve as a member of three different parties: Republican, Independence, and DFL (Democrat). For her, the policy and the needs of her community, which she championed in so many ways, came first, no matter the party label or the arena of activity.

"Do You Have an Interest in Flowers?"

Susan Lemke was the first woman to have a long-term impact on the Rochester Park Board

Susan Lemke received a phone call in 1973 that would have an enormous impact on her life and on the City of Rochester. Mayor Alex Smekta had been working on a program at the Graham Arena. Susan was asked to show up and help with the set up as a representative of the American Association of University Women (AAUW). In her usual way, she started making comments and improvements wherever she could. Smekta was impressed by Susan's initiative, insight, and diplomatic manner. He wanted to encourage a woman to become part of the Park Board, one of the most powerful boards in city government. Uncertain as to whether she would want to join what was then a male bastion, the Mayor began the phone conversation saying, "Susan, do you have an interest in flowers?"

What followed was a career of twenty-six years of devoted service on the Park Board and seventy other local boards. Susan's work culminated with being named the 1994 recipient of the Minnesota Recreation and Park Association Award for "Minnesota Park Commissioner of the Year." This singular honor joins many others that Sue has received. In fact, her life story makes it obvious that she would be a leader in whatever field she decided to participate.

Determined to be a professional volunteer

Sue grew up in Maple Grove, Minnesota, and attended a one-room school house until the third grade. She remembers it as a great place to be a child and fondly remembers fishing on Eagle Lake with her dad. Her mother, Irma LeTendre Bergquist, raised the three children and then became the executive secretary for a vice president of General Mills. Her father, George Bergquist, was a marble mason, as his father had been. Interestingly, her father and grandfather had both installed marble in the Plummer Building in Rochester. "My Dad was an artist," she says. It was fun for Sue when her father came to install marble in the new Methodist Hospital while she was living in the city. Making Rochester beautiful seems to run in the family.

Sue Lemke during her teenage years on Dayton's Teen Board. When Alex Smekta recruited her for the Rochester Park Board he asked, "You do like flowers, don't you?"

Osseo High School provided Sue with some of her first leadership opportunities. She was the president of the student body, which was unusual for a female at the time. She was active in 4H, often exhibiting in the Hennepin County Fair in nearby Hopkins. She also began an association with the Girl Scouts that would span thirty-five years. Sue happily remembers being a member of the Dayton's Teen Board, where the students participated in fashion shows but also learned a great deal about business.

Sue entered Gustavus Adolphus College feeling empowered by her high school experience. She would become the Vice President of the Women's Government, which was kept separate from the men's government. She had the rare pleasure of being the student hostess for the Countess Bernadotte, who visited from Sweden to dedicate a library. She remembers her as being "royal, but a real person."

Her academic interests were wide-ranging, reflecting her ability to do many things at the same time—an attribute that would be noticed throughout her life. She majored in French—no doubt influenced by her French-Canadian mother–and English. She minored in speech, religion, and dramatic production. Sue also had an interest in history, but she was told she could not major in history because those spots were reserved for men who would be coaches. She graduated in 1963 and taught in the Little Falls school system for two years before marrying her high school sweetheart, Tom Lemke. Tom had been hired by IBM in Rochester and so in 1965, Sue moved to this community. She served as a substitute teacher–and would remain active in education activities–and had two daughters. She joined AAUW in 1965, and has held many important positions for that organization, including statewide president. Even at this early time, she had decided, "I owed it to Mom and Dad to use my education" and she thus would "become the professional volunteer."

A broad scope and variety of accomplishments

Although the call from the mayor came out of the blue, Sue was ready to take on this role and perform her civic duties in an exemplary way. It was big news that a woman would want to participate in local government. In the Rochester *Post-Bulletin* article that announced Sue's appointment, the three people mentioned are pictured. Under the two men's pictures are their last names. Under Sue's picture is the title "Mrs. Lemke." In 1984, when Sue was named President of the Minnesota State Division of the American Association of University Women, she was identified in the paper as "a Rochester homemaker and volunteer."

By the time Sue left the Park Board in 1999, however, the name under her picture was merely "Lemke." She had served as secretary of the Park Board, chaired numerous subcommittees and special projects, and was well-known and accepted as a leader in the community. Some of the projects completed by the Park Board during her tenure include the Rochester Olmsted Recreation Center, Civic Center Expansions, Northern Hills Golf Course, and Essex Park.

Essex Park was created out of land donated by the Essex family and became a wonderful space where organizations could have picnics for hundreds of people. Sue also worked on the Soldiers Field Pool project. The changing house at Soldiers Field was an architectural gem, but despite many efforts, the original building could not be saved. The new structure kept the style and feeling of the original and the improvements to the pool made it into a festive water park.

Other projects included new tennis courts, the Flood Control Project, a Youth Sports Complex, and Foster-Arend Park. The Flood Control Project used federal monies made available after the record flood of 1978. The effort widened the banks of the Zumbro River while keeping the area scenic and providing for biking and hiking trails. Since Olmsted County is the only county in the state of Minnesota without a natural lake, the Foster-Arend Park was particularly popular as it created a "lake" out of an old gravel pit, complete with sandy beaches.

During her years on the park board, Sue also served on the Rochester Committee on Urban Design and Environment from 1974 to 1999. She was the first woman to serve as chairman of that group. This committee reviewed new building projects in an effort to create a coherent look to the public spaces of the city. They literally created the "look" of Rochester. It is hard to trace all of Sue's firsts because she has served on so many local boards and commissions. In the article commemorating her career, Roy Sutherland, the superintendent of parks and recreations, was quoted as saying, "No one has been more involved in the community than Sue. I don't think words can describe what she has meant to the parks, to the commission, and to the community."

Some of the projects she is most proud of include the Parkland Dedication Program, which requires each new development to provide a neighborhood park; adaptive playground improvements for special needs children; the acquisition of the Plummer House; and the Heritage House project.

The Plummer House was built by Henry Plummer, one of the earliest physicians at Mayo Clinic. He personally designed and built the structure between 1917 and 1924. Many of the innovations used in the forty-nine-room house were later used in the Plummer Building, which Dr. Plummer was instrumental in building with the Ellerbe Architectural firm in 1927. The Plummer Building was the main Mayo Clinic building for many years and was a model for future clinic buildings throughout the country. The Plummer House is preserved by the Rochester Park Board and the eleven-acre estate, complete with gardens, can be used for weddings and other celebratory occasions. Looking at the scope and variety of efforts Susan has been involved in, it is obvious that she has always been interested in more than flowers!

Be prepared, be organized, be bold

Sue is famous for her competence. She modestly says, "I always read the material and prepared for the vote." One of the nominating documents for her many awards reads, "As a teacher and mother, she perfected her organizational skills and can accomplish more, in less time, than anyone I know." In another nominating letter, it appears she was able to impress a male colleague who wrote in 1987, "She has been a respected participant in the meetings of the Park Board over these years and has brought to us the viewpoint of a modern woman. Her opinions are well-stated and direct and well-based on facts. She is not given to petulance or anger but speaks well in defense of her point of view and is not to be bullied."

Sue feels that she has accomplished so much in part due to excellent mentorship. Curtis Taylor, Rochester Park and Recreation Superintendent, is the person she names first when reminiscing about her many colleagues. She watched him bring people together to find common ground during a controversy. He was happy to put her in the limelight and wanted her to be successful. "He moved me along to what I became," she recalls.

Sue has a strong feeling for the preservation of park land in Rochester. She is an advocate for retaining what the city has while adding new green spaces. She says, "Once we give up park land, we will never get it back. My years working in this area have instilled in me the principle that if it's park land, it should remain park land." Central Park has been a special place to protect. The deed for that land, dated 1856, was very specific and has allowed it to be preserved as a park despite the interest of many developers. Since this area, the original Town Square, was close to the downtown area, it was considered a prime piece of real estate. But today, instead of being filled with buildings, it remains an oasis of green, complete with a bubbling fountain and an old-fashioned gazebo. It is a favorite spot for people picnicking on their noon hour in nice weather. Without the devotion and fortitude of Sue and the other Park Board members, it would look very different.

Sue continues to be active in the Heritage House Associates; she is one of the leading forces of that organization. It is remarkable that the Whiting House, built in 1875, was saved from demolition and moved to Central Park in 1972 to become the Heritage House. "We need to leave something for future generations; we don't want to lose our history," she says. Sue fondly remembers Louise Hill who, through great personal effort, saved the house. It had survived the famous tornado of 1883 that led to the creation of Saint Marys Hospital.

Most of the "lower town" of Rochester had been totally destroyed by the tornado. But the Whiting House lost only its roof. The family came up from the basement after the storm to find their meal untouched on the table where they left it, but blue sky overhead! The structure has been restored with pieces of other grand old Victorian homes that could not be saved, but most of it is original. This house represented the upper middle class lifestyle of the 1870s. Some of the furniture is original and all of the furniture is true to the period. It preserves some of the pieces from the earliest waiting room in Saint Marys Hospital and other wonderful artifacts of Rochester's past donated by its citizens. Sue still enjoys leading tours at the house in the summers.

Susan has received the Rochester Mayor's Medal, the Valiant Woman Award for her church work, and the Governor's "Acts of Kindness" Volunteer Award. The AAUW has endowed a fellowship in her honor. But the many awards are not what motivate her to be so involved. In a 1998 *Post-Bulletin* article, she is quoted as saying, "I don't volunteer to get recognition, I volunteer because there are needs to be met. That's what I do for a living."

A Stick of Dynamite

Sally Martin was the first Rochester woman to hold a cabinet position in Minnesota State Government

It was another long day at Rochester's Soldiers Field Park for Sally Martin and her four children. Summer was the worst time to adapt to a new community with school-aged kids who could have more easily made friends if the school year had begun. It would have been easier for her, too. The family had moved nearly every two years, as was IBM promotion policy, and they had lived most recently in Chappaqua, New York. Here they were in Rochester, Minnesota, in the summer of 1973, her husband the new General Manager of IBM's Manufacturing and Development Facility and she without a friend or contact in her new home.

But that was about to change for Sally Martin, who that day met Rosemary Ahmann, an Olmsted County Commissioner, and through her Joy Fogarty, Lyla Bendsen, and other like-minded women. The Martins were to remain in Rochester eight years, until Sally's husband Hal tragically died at Christmastime, 1980, and Sally soon after moved to Minneapolis for employment. During that period, Sally Martin had an enormous impact on public policy, both partisan and non-partisan, and the public's perception of how women should act as citizens. She was one of a small group of active, forthright women who changed the community forever.

More than the 3 Rs: work on the school board

Within one year of her arrival in Rochester, Sally Martin had been elected to the Rochester School Board. In an August 10, 1974 *Post-Bulletin* editorial, Bettie Gibson wrote:

There's no other way to describe new Rochester School Board member Sally Martin except to say that she's been like a stick of dynamite under the rest of the board from the moment she took her seat on June 26. In little more than a month's time, she has probably done more talking than some board members combined have done in a year. If you think women are meek and mild, Mrs. Martin will change your mind . . . She is strong and forceful . . . She's direct—maybe more direct than some would like her to be. It's apparent from what she says that she knows what she is talking about—she's done her homework. If she believes in something, she supports it strongly; if she doesn't, she opposes it strongly.

These were not easy years to be on a school board in Minnesota with the deluge of changes required by new laws: the Minnesota Miracle (new statewide funding formulas), open meeting law for local governments, the advent of special education requirements, implementation of Title IX (equality for girls in sports), equal pay for equal work impacts on employment policy, and declining enrollment leading to closure of some schools.

Rochester's school board also faced wrenching decisions on whether to replace an existing junior high school, despite current declining enrollments, and if and how to dispose of the old property. A citizens' committee was formed by the school board to make recommendations on the replacement of Central Junior High, with Jim Hartfield and Nedra Wicks as co-chairs. Nedra was specifically recruited by Sally Martin for this post because Sally thought that a woman should share this leadership responsibility. "And a year or so later I joined her on the school board," Nedra recalls.

Sally had four children in the public schools, and she had the experience of her children's schooling in other communities. As the *Post-Bulletin* editorialist noted, she was not one to keep silent if she had an opinion or idea. She had a special interest in girls' equality in sports, fueled by the new Title IX requirements at the Federal level. When first elected, she requested information from Superintendent Dr. Harry Vakos on the number of sports offerings in secondary schools, as well as the amount spent on girls' sports compared to boys' sports. "I was shocked. It was a horrifying difference, somewhat due to the cost of hockey rinks, the difference in locker facilities, and the few number of sports open to girls," she recalls. "My son was in junior high at the time, and I wanted his younger sisters to have the same opportunities he had for sports involvement. I started talking about this right away; I didn't want to wait three to four years."

Sally worked to change other "unequal opportunities" for students, as well. She was always puzzled about why more girls did not go into science and math, as she had done. She took a special interest in promoting science and technical course work for girls. During her school board tenure, the previously sex-differentiated home economics and industrial arts offerings in the junior high schools became required courses for both boys and girls. "I thought more exposure to these technical, hands-on classes would help girls become more interested in high tech, math, and engineering as they grew older," she says.

"Equal pay for equal work was a big issue at the time," Sally adds, "and the Feds were checking us out, particularly with how we paid coaches and janitors." She shares a letter sent May 4, 1977, by Woodrow Nelson, Director of Personnel of the Rochester Public Schools, to Janice Wheat, Compliance Specialist of the U.S. Department of Labor Wage and Hour Division. The letter states, "We are continuing to work on the two items which you have outlined in custodian (male/female) pay, and coaches salaries (male/female) . . . It will be some time, however, before a formula will be worked out at our high school level regarding coaches' salaries."

When first elected in 1974, she became the third female member on the seven-member school board; this was the first time in history that three women had served at the same time. Sally fondly remembers working with Karen Ricklefs, Frank Whelan, and especially Nedra Wicks, all fellow school board members. Although she was certainly a champion for issues of equality, her filing statement for re-election in 1977, when she served as Board Chair, reflected a concern for every student, especially the "average" ones, and a practical understanding of needing to pull together, "as we try to do more with less funding."

The "natural" campaigner

Who would imagine that a woman who had majored in mathematics at Smith College and who once urged college friends to take a course in logic "because it was so easy and interesting" would also excel at the "meet and greet" and speechmaking that is central to a political career? But Sally Martin was a natural.

Her first campaign for school board included many coffee parties in supporters' homes. Neighbors and friends were invited to hear the candidate's views and to ask questions. One hostess clearly remembers Sally's ability to focus intensely on a questioner, validating the person as well as the question. Attendees with very different views on issues facing the schools all left that particular gathering clearly intending to vote for Sally Martin. This candidate really cared about what each of them thought and left the impression that she would listen to their advice as she worked to make the schools even better.

Sally was passionate about what she wanted to accomplish and saw government as a way to make things happen for the better as long as citizens had access. "I always thought it was important to be involved," she says. And involved she was. While on the school board she embraced other leadership opportunities to broaden her knowledge and make herself a more effective elected official. She served on Rochester's Downtown Development Advisory Board, the Rochester-Olmsted Council of Governments, the Intergovernmental Committee, and the Minnesota School Boards Association Delegate Assembly. She was an alternate delegate to the Representative Assembly of the Minnesota State High School League and chair of the Education Committee for Olmsted County's Probation Offenders Rehabilitation and Training Program (PORT).

In late 1977, Alice Keller, First Congressional District Chair for the DFL (Democratic Party in Minnesota), came calling. She wanted Sally Martin, Chair of the Rochester School Board, to consider being a candidate for the DFL endorsement for the congressional seat being vacated by long-time Republican Congressman Al Quie. "She was very persuasive," Sally remembers. Sally talked it over with her family members, who saw it as an exciting opportunity. The First District had been solidly Republican with a long-time incumbent, but an open seat looked possible. "Rochester was financially conservative but open-minded on other issues. There was a strong desire by the citizens for good and responsible government," Sally recalls.

"When you are running for Congress, you are out in front, telling the public what you think," Sally says. "But you need others to do the very necessary detail work. Lyla (Bendsen) chaired the campaign committee, and Joy Fogarty, Rosemary Ahmann, and many other committed people helped keep me on track." She visited every county in the congressional district several times for citizen input on local problems and to promote her candidacy to likely delegates at the DFL Congressional District Convention. "Especially in the southern part of the district, the people were very friendly and willing to listen," says Sally. She received endorsements from women's and liberal groups, but also from those who supported local control and local government. Winona City Council member Sue Edel, the *Red Wing Republican Eagle*, the *Faribault Daily News*, and the Rochester *Post-Bulletin* publicly supported her positions on local control.

But despite her organization, her zest for campaigning, and her willingness to broaden her understanding on a broad range of issues of importance to the district, she lost the convention vote to State Senator Gerry Sikorski from Stillwater, who had the support of both the northern parts of the district and the very strong "pro-life" delegates. A *Post-Bulletin* story (May 1, 1978) immediately following the convention quoted Sally Martin as saying, "I'm going to rest up for a while, it's been a very tiring experience." The article went on to state that between November and late April she had attended "scores of meetings throughout the wide ranging First District, made countless telephone calls, and met thousands of people. She had taken great pride in the fact that while raising $11,000 in her campaign, more than 200 had contributed. She had also been one of a handful of women who have become serious Congressional candidates."

Invited to the wrong party

It was out of the bag: Sally Martin was a Democrat! While she never hid her party affiliation, and even local Republican leaders had discovered it "about a week before my first school board election in 1974," according to Sally, by the spring of 1978, everyone in Rochester knew this fact due to her campaign for the DFL Congressional endorsement. It turned out to matter to quite a few of her erstwhile supporters, even the non-partisan ones, who liked to think they lived in a Republican town represented by Republican elected officials. From now on, this fact would cloud electoral decisions for Sally Martin despite all she had to offer in leadership energy, ability, and intelligence.

Sally certainly knew that there were very few admitted Democrats in Rochester at the time. After all, when Lt. Governor Rudy Perpich had come to town, she had attended several luncheons in his honor with local Democratic leaders. It was a small table, she recalls.

Should she turn her sights back to school issues, after the unsuccessful run for Congress, or should she put her skills and newfound knowledge to use in another area of public service? As 1978 wore on, it became clear that there would be another open seat up for election in spring, 1979–this time a non-partisan one. Long-time incumbent Mayor of Rochester, Alex Smekta, was retiring. Two years before he had narrowly won re-election against Jesse Howard, a woman and political newcomer. Sally began to think about this position and the campaign it would entail. Perhaps Rochester could use "a stick of dynamite" in the Mayor's office!

Her filing statement of March 20, 1979, began by nipping in the bud several rumors she had heard about her candidacy:

I am not running to establish a political base from which to run for higher office . . . [and] I am not running so that IBM can take over Rochester. My husband works for IBM–I do not. In my past five years in elective office, I have avoided even the appearance of a conflict of interest by abstaining from discussion or votes on any matter directly involving IBM. I would continue to do so as Mayor.

Her statement continued with what she was running for, what issues she wanted to address, and what she was hearing from the voters as she had listened to them over the past several months: "that our city government is not open and accessible, that the average citizen does not have a voice in community decisions, that our neighborhoods are not being protected from overdevelopment and congestion, that our city leadership operates by inaction and reaction."

She followed up these comments, which may have seemed like platitudes to some, with specific leadership suggestions for a new, more open, citizen board appointment policy, and a commitment to make the necessary hard decisions to forward downtown development progress. She definitely would have been an activist leader should she have been able to implement these ideas.

She was joined in the race by Richard Postier, City Council President, and Chuck Hazama, YMCA Director. While the Rochester *Post-Bulletin* notes in an April 12, 1979, article that the three candidates had few policy differences, at least on paper, "the background and general political philosophy of the three differ substantially . . . Postier . . . prides himself on a 'conservative' image; . . . Martin . . . has been an active Democrat and is regarded as liberal; . . . Hazama . . . holds to a 'middle-of-the-road' philosophy in politics." Sally Martin, the only one of the three with a public party label, was defeated in the primary.

In 1980, she lost her school board re-election bid, as well. A May 21, 1980, article in the *Post-Bulletin* commented, "While both candidates took strong positions on educational issues, the determining factors in the outcome appeared to have more to do with partisan politics and issues other than the learning experiences of children." Another article from the same issue included these comments:

I think Sally has established herself as a liberal and that doesn't sit too well with a lot of Rochester voters," said Carl Laumann, an active Independent Republican (name of Minnesota's Republican Party) who attended Carroll's victory party . . . Laumann was active in Martin's first successful bid for public office . . . "I didn't appreciate we were that far apart politically." Asked whether the Carroll effort was an attempt to "dump" Martin once and for all, Michael Klampe, a DFLer who co-chaired Martin's campaign replied: "That's it. That's exactly it. Feelings ran very high in the other camp. The decision was made to do that even before the race began.

Rosemary Ahmann, Olmsted County Board Chair and close friend of Martin's, refused to say that this marks the end of the line for Martin's political career. "She's tenacious and I'm sure that she'll continue to be active as she has in the past. I wouldn't count her out."

The Governor calls

Of course Sally wasn't to be counted out. Despite the tragic death of her husband at the end of that year, which necessitated a move to Minneapolis for employment, she was to continue in public service. While working for the University of Minnesota as a consultant on project activities for the Institute of Technology and the College of Education, she was asked, in late 1982, to help with DFL Governor-Elect Perpich's transition team, interviewing candidates for appointment. The Governor considered Sally for Commissioner of Education, based on her school board service, but she lacked a Ph.D. Instead, the new Governor appointed Sally Martin to be Director of the Minnesota Department of Public Service. Sally recalls that some of the highest paid state employees (economists) and some of the lowest paid (weights & measures auditors, such as for gas pumps) worked in this department, which also acted as a public advocate on utility rate cases before the Public Utilities Commission.

Barely two months into that position, the new Governor offered her another opportunity. Rudy Perpich was creating something new and forward looking: an Office of Science and Technology. According to an AP news article on March 3, 1983, "One of the new office's prime goals will be to attract high-technology companies to expand in Minnesota . . . Martin will also supervise efforts to improve

Sally Martin was the first Rochester woman to hold a cabinet position in State Government. Here she addresses a division of the state House Appropriations Committee. (Courtesy Post-Bulletin Co.)

the elementary and secondary schools' teaching of science and mathematics, and will try to foster closer ties between high-tech firms and state universities."

In her new position, Sally traveled to Florida, North Carolina, and Massachusetts–all states with active programs designed to encourage high tech companies to locate there. She also chaired a committee of "gold star" corporations, as she calls them, that were interested in improving science and technology in the schools so that they would have a better pool from which to draw employees. "I was a department of one," she laughs. Reflecting on Governor Perpich, she comments, "Rudy was ahead of his time on so many key issues including water and, of course, education."

Following her work with Governor Perpich, Sally decided to move to the east coast to be closer to things dear to her heart–her four children and the ocean. She looked for programs in the area where she could meet others who shared her interest in government and found the one-year Masters of Public Administration Program in Harvard's Kennedy School of Government. She applied, was accepted, and moved to Cambridge, Massachusetts, in 1985. After graduating in 1986 with a Master's of Public Administration, she was hired as the Executive Director of International Health Programs at the Harvard School of Public Health and became involved in the start-up of a new International Commission on Health Research in developing countries. Sally recruited and directed the secretarial staff, organized international meetings, and negotiated project funding. When the program moved to Geneva, Switzerland, she went to work for ten years at the Consumer Credit Counseling Service of Massachusetts. Following retirement from that job, Sally became a member of the Harvard Institute for Learning in Retirement (HILR), to which she still belongs. Today she volunteers at Boston's Museum of Science and has served for six years as Treasurer of the Board of Directors of its Volunteer Service League. Sally also travels frequently to visit her children.

Just do it

What is Sally's advice for young women today? "Just do it; just try it; and work your way up," she says. Regarding her last three campaigns in Rochester, she reflects, "It's the way things go. Sometimes you lose." She is a forthright woman of great leadership ability and high energy, who "needed something to sink her teeth into," as Nedra Wicks, fellow school board member, observed about Sally after first meeting her. She found many opportunities in public service, and she hasn't let defeat deter her from finding even more.

Editorial comments about Sally Martin in area newspapers in the spring of 1978, during her campaign for DFL endorsement for Congress, provide a good summary of her style of public service. The *Faribault Daily News* wrote, "We like a candidate who's willing to go out on a limb; it demonstrates the sort of political courage that marks a responsible, responsive politician." The *Red Wing Republican Eagle* praised Sally Martin as "an earnest citizen who genuinely wants to do something for her district, state, and nation." And she has.

Making the World A Better Place

Jean and Frank Michaels were the first wife/husband duo in local elected office

It was 1985, and Jean Michaels found herself sitting across the table from a career counselor at the YWCA Women's Resource Center. The Center had been established during the Midwestern farm crisis in the mid 1970s when scores of farmers were displaced due to the foreclosure and loss of their farms. Many farm women were forced to look for work off the farm and did not have the skills or education to find jobs that paid enough to support their families. The YWCA received a United States Bicentennial grant in 1976 to fund the Women's Resource Center–a counseling service that provided workplace training and placement assistance. Eventually this was broadened to include support for victims of family violence and women's mental health counseling.

Jean had just retired from a career in early childhood education at Aldrich Memorial Nursery School, and she needed help figuring out where she could put her energy and talents to good use. Never daunted by change or the challenge of charting a new course for herself, Jean talked with her counselor mostly about her future, but they began with a quick look at where she had been and how she had arrived at this crossroads.

A glance into the rearview mirror

The daughter of a physician, Jean Rynearson Michaels grew up when Midwestern culture and Mayo Clinic values guided much of community life in Rochester. Her father was a great admirer of the Sisters of St. Francis who had built Saint Marys Hospital, and Jean remembers frequent visits from the Sisters to their southwest Rochester home–they especially enjoyed those long hot summer days in the family's backyard swimming pool. Jean's parents were both active community volunteers–her dad with the Boy Scouts, and her mother as one of the founding members of Aldrich Memorial Nursery School. Dr. Rynearson was a big believer in the benefits of physical activity, so rain or shine, a sizzling ninety degrees or a frigid twenty-five below zero, their daily commute to work and school was made on foot rather than in the family car. Jean's good friend, Wintie Gray, lived in the neighborhood, and Wintie's dad drove his daughter to school each morning. "Sissies" is what Jean remembers her dad muttering as they trudged through the snow watching the Grays wave as they drove by. Eventually Jean screwed up her courage and declared that the Grays were now going to stop at the Rynearson home to pick Jean up when the temperatures were sub-zero.

After school Jean walked to her dad's office and did her homework while he finished seeing patients for the day. Often she used Doctor William Plummer's office to do her homework. Dr. Plummer was a founding member of Mayo Clinic, but to Jean he was simply a family friend and colleague of her father. Life in Rochester was good. After Jean graduated from Sarah Lawrence College in New York, she met and married a young lawyer named Frank Michaels, and they returned to Rochester in 1953, to work and raise their family.

Jean loved teaching at Aldrich Memorial Nursery School, and Frank built a law practice in a local Rochester firm. Both were active in community affairs–Frank on the Rochester Public School Board of Education, and Jean on a host of local advisory boards and task forces. Years later, County Administrator Richard Devlin remembers Jean as a champion for the health and welfare of children as well as an exceptional advocate for early prevention and intervention programs. Jean supported programs addressing child abuse and maltreatment because in her mind, it was the right thing to do, but also because of the savings to taxpayers down the road in public health, social services, and corrections. She liked to quote a familiar parable, written by Ronald Rolheiser and found in *A Spirituality of Justice and Peacemak-*

ing, that illustrated the tendency of society to deal with symptoms of a problem rather than the root cause:

> *Once upon a time there was a town that was built just beyond the bend of a large river. One day some of the children from the town were playing beside the river when they noticed three bodies floating in the water. They ran for help and the townsfolk quickly pulled the bodies out of the river. One body was dead so they buried it. One was alive, but quite ill, so they put that person into the hospital. The third turned out to be a healthy child, who they placed with a family who cared for it and who took it to school. From that day on, every day a number of bodies came floating down the river and, every day, the good people of the town would pull them out and tend to them—taking the sick to hospitals, placing the children with families, and burying those who were dead. This went on for years; each day brought its quota of bodies, and the townsfolk not only came to expect a number of bodies each day but also worked at developing more elaborate systems for picking them out of the river and tending to them . . . However, during all these years and despite all that generosity and effort, nobody thought to go up the river . . . and find out why, daily, those bodies came floating down the river.*

Jean scorned short-term fixes on complex social issues and in a casual conversation with a small group of friends that included Olmsted County Commissioner Rosemary Ahmann, declared, "We aren't doing a good job preventing child abuse in this community!" Rosemary's response was to ask Jean if she would chair a Task Force on Family Violence that the County Board planned to establish in response to a community survey identifying family violence and child abuse as top priorities.

The Task Force, staffed by Sheila Kiscaden, began its work in 1979, and fifteen months later shared its findings with the county board and larger community. Jean had a knack for bringing out the best in people, and she clearly understood the close connection between a healthy community and the region's economic success. In Jean's presentation of task force findings and recommendations to the county board, she stressed the need to "break the circle" of violence so that generational abuse and neglect could be stopped. Unlike many studies that end up collecting dust on a shelf, all of the recommendations made by the Task Force were implemented in one form or another.

Charting a new course

Now, here she was five years later in 1985, sitting at the Women's Resource Center weighing her options for what was next. Jean had been a busy mother of four, a dedicated early childhood education teacher, and an active community volunteer. She had developed close friendships with individuals associated with Olmsted County, especially Sheila Kiscaden, who had been encouraging Jean to run for the county board of commissioners. To Jean's surprise, as she and her counselor at the Y began honing in on her interests and all that she had learned as a mother, teacher, and community volunteer, the prospect of running for a spot on the county board seemed a logical next stop on Jean's life journey. In January 1986, Jean and her cavalry of friends, colleagues, and supporters, nicknamed "Jean's Machine" by her opponent, began organizing what was ultimately a victorious campaign to unseat an incumbent on the Olmsted County Board of Commissioners. Asked what it was about the incumbent that made Jean decide to run, she simply says, "He was a very nice man, but too busy with a career and small children. It seemed to me that he didn't really have the time to devote to public service, and I did!"

Jean had served as a volunteer on more than thirteen boards and commissions when she was sworn in at the first county board meeting in January of 1987. Now, she and her husband Frank had become a first in the community. For the first time in the history of the community, a husband and wife were serving as elected officials on two important governmental bodies at the same time. Frank made a decision to retire from the school board in 1988, after twenty-five years of service, declaring that "one Michaels at a time in local government was plenty!" That may have been the end of Frank's career

The January 1987 swearing in ceremony following an election of officers and board members of Olm-sted County. Women pictured (left to right) are Commissioners Carol Kamper and Jean Michaels, County Recorder Lois Finstuen, and Auditor Hazel Pearson. (Courtesy Post-Bulletin Co.)

in elected office, but for many years he served as Legal Counsel to Rochester Township. While the Michaels didn't often disagree as a school board-county board couple, township and county issues were another story. Townships and counties have historically had their differences, and Jean recalls with a smile some interesting pillow talk when the county and Rochester Township were at odds over an issue. Married more than sixty years, Jean and Frank weathered the storms and gracefully balanced parenthood, careers, and elected office with wisdom and humor.

Jean never forgot the priorities she learned as a teacher and maintained a steadfast support of children and families throughout her tenure on the County Board. One of only two female commissioners out of seven, Jean was faced with yearly budget decisions that often seemed in conflict with the high expectations taxpayers had for services and programs. A quick study on complex topics, Jean enjoyed the challenges that came with each new project and did her homework. It was clear to staff members that she came prepared for each meeting having actually read the background material they provided. Jean routinely had questions to ask and referred back to specific pages and lines in documents when she needed clarification on a topic. Like all good leaders, Jean recognized that no matter how knowledgeable she may have been on an issue, she always had something to learn.

Bob Bendzick, the Olmsted County Finance Director, describes Jean as "moving important things forward with civility, and (she) proves that warm, caring people can improve our government. We'd all be better off if we wore little wristbands that asked, 'How would Jean do this?'" As an elected official, Jean was often confronted with difficult choices, but her decisions were a careful blend of fiscal responsibility with, in her words, "the compassion and respect we expect in a civilized society."

Jean's first term as Chairperson of the Olmsted County Board in 1989 was also a first for women in local leadership positions. That year, the Rochester City Council, the Rochester Public Schools Board of Education, and the Olmsted County Board of Commissioners were all being chaired by women. Jean recalls a reception that was held to welcome First Lady Barbara Bush to Rochester, to which Jean and her counterparts on the City Council (Nancy Selby) and School Board (Pam Smoldt) were invited. After they were introduced, Nancy Selby asked Mrs. Bush what she thought of a community where the highest locally elected offices were all being held by women. The First Lady, famous for her beautiful white hair and signature pearls, turned to look directly at Jean, whose white hair was equally as stunning, saying grandly, "You've certainly got the hair for it." Everyone laughed and agreed that Jean had it all–except perhaps the choker of pearls!

In 1998, a community-based long-range planning effort known as 21st Century Partnership identified seven key issues (diversity, rural and small city vitality, education and workforce readiness, children, families and the elderly, crime, and neighborhoods) that the community must address in order to remain economically and socially successful in the twenty-first century. The Rochester Human Rights Commission came under scrutiny on the task force studying diversity because of the city's refusal to include sexual orientation on the list of protected classes. City Council President John Hunziker served on the 21st Century Partnership Steering Committee and strongly supported the inclusion of sexual orientation as a protected class in the city. He was quoted as saying that the lack of support from members of the city council on that issue was one of the "biggest disappointments" of his tenure as a councilman.

No one says that the wheels of change turn quickly, especially in government, but after much public and private discussion, and a great deal of support from Jean, County Commissioner Jeff Thompson, and County Administrator Richard Devlin, a solution was negotiated. In January 2000, the Human Rights Commission leadership was transferred to Olmsted County and sexual orientation was included as a protected class.

County Commissioners not welcome!

Perhaps the best illustration of Jean's willingness to tackle controversial issues affecting the health and well-being of residents and visitors to Olmsted County was her unflinching support of a ban on restaurant smoking in 1996. Olmsted County Administrator Richard Devlin recalls the controversy surrounding the Restaurant Smoking Ordinance and the vehement opposition from a prominent local restaurateur. Richard and Jean optimistically thought that it would be helpful if they could meet with the restaurant owner to discuss the ordinance. The meeting was held at the restaurant, but when it was clear that Jean was firmly in support of the ordinance, she and Richard were unceremoniously escorted out of the building and told that county commissioners were no longer welcome in his establishment. Later the restaurateur called Richard to apologize for his behavior, assuring him that indeed county commissioners were welcome at the restaurant. The Olmsted County Restaurant Smoking Ordinance was the first of its kind in a Minnesota county and a model throughout the state when it was adopted.

Colleagues who worked closely with Jean throughout her seventeen years as an Olmsted County commissioner are unanimous in their praise for Jean's grace under fire and for her natural ability to make friends and find common ground. For many years Jean represented the county on National Association of Counties (NACO) committees that focused on environmental issues. She rose to leadership positions on several of those groups due in no small part to her welcoming demeanor, her genuine interest in others, and her exceptional grasp of the issues. Watching her work a room before meetings with handshakes and hugs was a lesson for staff members in how to set the tone for important relationships, for they will pay dividends when the time comes to bridge political and geographic differences. As a result, Olmsted County was well positioned on the national level to take advantage of important funding opportunities in the areas of water quality and land sustainability.

Jean's career as an elected official ended in 2003, but she remained committed to community service as a volunteer on the Dodge Fillmore Olmsted Community Corrections Advisory Council and with prisoners in the Olmsted County Jail for many years after leaving the county board. Jean's sense of fun, curiosity, eagerness to learn, and obvious interest in others have endeared her to people of all ages, abilities, and cultural backgrounds. Her selfless dedication to the people of her community illustrates her belief that we all share in taking responsibility for one another and especially for the most vulnerable among us—our children. Jean's contagious enthusiasm for life and her active support of the value women bring to the public arena will continue to be an inspiration to girls and women of all ages. Jean Michaels will be remembered as a shining example of the extraordinary contributions women have made in this community. Her final words of the State of the County Address January 1, 2000, epitomize the values she learned early in life—"It is my wish for this new millennium . . . that we treat others as we wish to be treated . . . We can do no better."

Jean and her husband Frank have embarked on a new adventure. They have moved to Duluth to be near their daughter Annie and her family. The Michaels have other retired friends in the Duluth area, and unlike many older adults who do not relish the thought of change, Jean and Frank are looking forward to this new chapter with happy anticipation. They will miss their Rochester friends, but are hoping that the attraction of the North Shore of Lake Superior will be added incentive for lots of visitors. Frank even jokes "it will seem odd to finally, after all these years, be in the company of Democrats!"

In 1987 Jean and Frank Michaels were the first wife/husband duo in local elected office—she on the Olmsted County Board and he on the Rochester School Board. Frank retired from the school board in 1988 declaring that "one Michaels at a time in local government was plenty!" (Courtesy Post-Bulletin Co.)

A Safe Place for Women

Judy Miller, advocate for battered women, became the first Executive Director of the Rochester Women's Shelter in 1981

During the late 1970s, Judy Miller tried for several years to safely and legally get herself and her children away from her violent husband. After the family moved to the isolated area of Zimmerman, in central Minnesota, he had become increasingly violent toward Judy and her oldest daughter. His violent behavior even caused Judy's daughter to run away, but after she returned, the Sherburne County authorities ordered the family into a counseling program designed to teach them how to operate as a positive unit. It was a family violence pilot program and, typical of such programs at the time, the likelihood of a lethal attack by the husband was not taken into consideration. The prevailing belief was that the assault victim was somehow partly, if not solely, to blame for being assaulted. The focus of the counseling sessions was thus aimed at ways to change the victims' behavior rather than that of the batterer.

A few months into the counseling, after Judy had left for work one day, her husband exploded in a rage and tried to strangle their oldest daughter. Her son intervened and the daughter escaped. The youngest daughter hid in a closet while Judy's husband spent the rest of the morning trying to engage their son in fistfights. Late that afternoon, after Judy arrived home, her husband threatened the lives of Judy and her eldest daughter before leaving for his nighttime job.

That night, Judy and the children noticed that he had uncharacteristically left a spare set of car keys on the counter. Some inner strength took over in Judy after she made a phone call to her sister in Rochester. The little group stuffed clothing into garbage sacks, put the cat and the TV on the laps of those in the backseat, and left for

Rochester, fleeing on one of the coldest nights on record in January, 1979. She took a chance that the court would be sympathetic to her action in spite of a Minnesota law making it illegal to move a child more than 100 miles away from an objecting parent.

It was just 8:00 a.m. the next morning when the counselors from the Sherburne County program phoned her sister's home, trying to locate them. Even after explaining what had precipitated their leaving, Judy was gently reminded of the counseling obligations and the 100-mile limit imposed by the court. She offered to bring the children to the St. Cloud offices to meet with the counselors, hoping that if they became convinced it was in the best interest of the children, the counselors would agree to lift the order. For safety, because they had to drive by Zimmerman on the way to St. Cloud, Judy had the counselors promise to keep this meeting a secret until they were all safely back in Rochester.

Her plan worked. Within days, what had been an overwhelming journey into the unknown became a solvable puzzle as Judy and the children began putting their lives back together. Sherburne County counselors closed the case. Her oldest daughter and son got after-school jobs. Judy's family sent her money. She filed for divorce, petitioned the court for a protective order, and signed up for every possible government program in hopes that she and her children would quickly become self sufficient.

The day she applied for Aid to Families with Dependent Children, a welfare program, she was sent to Mayo Clinic Outpatient Services for a medical exam. Her hopes were crushed when the doctor confronted her, asking "What have you done?" He told her she had made the worst mistake of her life and asked her questions about the future that she couldn't answer. Then he told her that she needed the help of someone with more experience in emotional problems and made an immediate appointment for her. Judy got in her car, followed the directions given, and walked into the admittance area of the Rochester State Hospital, not realizing it was a psychiatric hospital.

To this day, Judy remembers the feeling of rising panic as she noticed the two armed guards and the woman at the desk behind glass. The people in the waiting area had vacant looks, and employees spoke to her as if she were fragile. When she attempted to leave, she was told to wait for the doctor so her case could be properly closed. After a long, three-hour wait, a woman named Doctor Uno, who was leaving for the day, noticed Judy and asked if she could help. Taking her into her office, Dr. Uno interviewed her, finally assessing that Judy didn't need the help of the state hospital. Most likely, Judy could be of help to others someday because of her experiences, the doctor said. She gave Judy some referral names and phone numbers.

The way we were

When Judy reached Rochester in 1979, Olmsted County offered counseling services to women like Judy, but no real safety. There was an organization of private homes open for sheltering battered women, but not that would take Judy's son because he was older than thirteen. There was a battered women's shelter in the Twin Cities, but it had a waiting list. The shelter in St. Cloud was too close to the town of Zimmerman. Domestic abuse legislation at the Minnesota Capitol was only a few months into creation. Police enforcement of an order for protection was unreliable.

Yet this was a vast improvement over what had been. As Judy soon learned, in 1976, Nancy Powell, Sheryl Lesch, and Esther Holly from the Minnesota Division of Vocational Rehabilitation had attended the first National Conference on Battered Women in Milwaukee, Wisconsin. These three then met with Marilyn Brodie, Susan Piggott, Kathie Zawistowski, and Carol Ball from Rochester's Chapter of NOW (National Organization for Women) to begin the process of educating the general public about battered women. Very little was known about the battered woman's psyche. In general, it was believed that the mindset and emotional state of a battered woman led her to stay in an abusive relationship out of "learned helplessness," a theory later debunked by Lenore Walker, who had actually authored the theory. Publications of the 1970s attempted to explain the battering of women with existing psychosocial theories that emphasized the faults and weaknesses in a woman's character. Consequently, women's stories of beatings, torture, and life threats were often dismissed as over-reactions or irrational fears.

By January 1977, there was a network of volunteers in the Olmsted County region who aided women and their families when they fled battering. These volunteers also met to discuss various theories of battering. Many believed only the victim knew what she had truly experienced. Others disagreed. But after serious discussion, these volunteers decided to adopt a policy that whenever called upon to address a battering situation, at least three would volunteer to relate to the woman. Olmsted County developed a Family Violence Task Force chaired by Jean Michaels, a future county commissioner. The task force was composed of representatives from the Olmsted County Health Department, the Social Services Department, the Rochester Chapter of NOW, the YWCA's Women's Resource Center, Mayo Clinic's Domestic Relations Task Force, Sunrise Services, the Volunteer Connection, and two representatives from the community at large. They came together regularly for meetings. Rapeline, directed by Carol Huyck, had an office and phone in the county building; the staff agreed to let their phone number be the emergency contact number and refer all pertinent calls to a Women's Shelter group volunteer. Nancy Vollertsen and Mary Alice Richardson, local lawyers, volunteered their services to develop articles of incorporation for a woman's shelter organization. When the Olmsted County Family Violence Task Force issued its final report, it cited the Rochester Women's Shelter as the major service provider addressing family violence in the community, with financial support from community agencies and individuals.

During its 1977 session, the Minnesota Legislature had passed Chapter 428 (SF124), which established pilot programs for emergency shelter, support services for battered women, and funds for community education, data collection, and counseling and training services for displaced homemakers. This bill, authored by Representative Phyllis Kahn and Senator Bob Lewis, provided for four pilot projects in the state: two in the Twin Cities, one in a rural area, which became the Brainerd project, and one other "outstate," which funded Rochester. Thus in 1978, the Rochester's Women's Shelter volunteer group was awarded $50,000 by a unanimous vote of the Minnesota Department of Corrections' Battered Women's Taskforce. Later, the group received an unsolicited $3,000 from the State with a mandate to develop services in Southeastern Minnesota–once known as Region 10 (In 1970, Minnesota Governor Harold LeVander had signed a bill that divided the state into eleven regions. Olmsted County, its ten other surrounding counties, and the fifty-four school districts they contained were part of Region 10).

Called to lead

Soon after arriving in Rochester in 1979, Judy began attending the Rochester Women's Shelter support group. She became a full-time student at Winona State University, but also soon was an active speaker, telling her story to county officials, state representatives, foundations, and service groups. She learned of the Minnesota Coalition for Battered Women, which sponsored her testimony before the Minnesota Legislature, trying to sensitize them to the needs of battered women and their children. Each time she spoke, she met women who either told or knew similar stories, and she became increasingly aware of the many women and children needing safety. There were so few resources for them.

Judy took stock of her skills and realized she had many experiences she could mine for helping others. Her background had included management of a hotel in Denver, fundraising for national non-profits in both Nevada and Minnesota, and political action in Las Vegas and Reno, Nevada. She decided to change her college major from art to business management.

In 1980, for the first time, the Woman's Shelter Board sought and received funding from the United Way of Olmsted County. The Minnesota Department of Corrections designated Rochester's Women's Shelter program as the official Battered Women's program serving eleven counties in Southeastern Minnesota. This designation came with a small bi-annual block grant for administration and non-security costs. Also in 1980, the Minnesota Legislature authorized per diem payments through the Department of Human Services to those who were sheltered throughout the state. With additional funds from the City of Rochester, as well as the Bush, McKnight, and Rochester Area Foundations, the Women's Shelter Board was able to purchase a seven-bedroom house and renovate it as the women's shelter. Several women's advocates were hired, as well as a children's advocate, a secretary, and a bookkeeper.

As with any new organization, internal struggles develop on a board, and the Women's Shelter Board was no exception. Some members wanted greater government funding and more community involvement. Others worried about government interference in the personal lives of women and were concerned about maintaining their privacy. Some on the Board believed the organization should be managed as a collective, while others believed in strict adherence to the corporate code. The divisions continued to deepen. Eventually the priorities and philosophy of the organization were so affected that a consultant from the Twin Cities was hired. Suddenly much of the administrative staff left and the board members had to volunteer to take over the house duties temporarily.

Judy remembers it as a challenging time. The most intimidating task was meeting with the Minnesota Department of Corrections' Battered Women's Advisory Council. "It was like being called to the head of the class for a dressing-down by your classmates. But we were convincing and remained in good standing." All this caused Judy to take a long deep breath and ask herself what kind of commitment was she ready to give. Should she apply for an administrative position? What would be best for the organization? Most importantly, what would be best for that ever-growing crowd of women and children who needed safety? She searched her motives, trying to be honest with herself. "Nothing is completely altruistic," she says. "But I loved the work and the challenge. Others could be hired to do the tasks as well as me, but as far as I knew, no one had the motivation or the 'second chance' experiences that I had been given." She adds, "You have to live through it to know it."

Judy Miller, became the first Executive Director of the Rochester Women's Shelter in 1981. She believes her greatest achievements center around the networking that helped create a pathway for battered women, opening doors for them and giving confidence to their voices.

Like the other board members, Judy volunteered her time at the shelter for six months while the Board's hiring committee searched for an executive director. She continued to drive to Winona for college courses three times per week. Late night hours, weekend study groups, and flashcards on her dashboard got her through those six months with good grades. After the widely advertised six-month search, the shelter's hiring committee decided that the best applicant was their own board member, Judy Miller.

Expanding the focus

Judy was offered the job just in time for the first public march against domestic violence on a dark, rainy, windy Saturday night in Rochester. This event was among many nationwide vigils on October 19, 1981. Women, men, and children showed up in sweaters and raincoats to bravely march from Mayo Clinic to Rochester's Central Park. Sue Bateman, YWCA Director, and Mary Goette, Rochester Community College professor, both members of the League of Women Voters, were the featured speakers. The League was studying battering as part of a women's rights study. The battering of women was now a public issue, exposed as "unacceptable."

It soon became clear to Judy that she would be endlessly swimming against the tide unless she had some paid help. In the

1980s, the state was bursting with women's rights programs that were receiving start-up funds. The Women's Shelter was eager to develop sensitive anti-battering programs throughout Southeastern Minnesota. From the beginning, there had been long-term planning conversations on the shelter board, and anti-battering program growth had been identified as a goal. She believed in advocate personnel who had experienced battering because "they don't let a victim kid themselves for long." She also looked for a creative and articulate person, capable of new ventures–such as Donna Dunn, whom she asked to staff a new position, Community Education Coordinator. Judy worked with the Olmsted County Board, the state legislature, and inter-agency relations with other programs around the state. Judy and Donna, who later directed Olmsted County's Victim Services, shared a compatible philosophy: "No one deserves to be beaten."

In 1982, The Rochester Women's Shelter began a two-year project, funded by the McKnight Foundation, to study Olmsted County's response to domestic assaults. Under the direction of Nancy Kolaas, surveys and personal interviews of criminal justice professionals and domestic assault victims identified ways to improve the system's response to domestic abuse calls. At the beginning of the project, neither the Olmsted County Sheriff's Department nor the Rochester Police separated domestic assaults from the category of neighborhood disturbance. Yet it was known through national statistics that more police were killed while involved with these calls than with most other response incidents. Representatives from law enforcement, the courts, and the Women's Shelter announced the Intervention Project for Domestic Assault (IPDA).

IPDA focused on immediate contact with the victim, coordination with both the prosecution as well as the perpetrator, and networking of the agencies responsible for enforcing domestic assault laws. Quarterly meetings of IPDA agencies were hosted by the Women's Shelter staff, which facilitated the sharing of information. This provided for a review of the handling of a case as well as review of policies and data in cases, which, for example, might lead to changes in training of various personnel. Domestic assault calls to the Rochester Police and Olmsted County Sheriff were finally separated from the neighborhood disturbance category of reporting and given their own classification. Police Chief Patrick Farrell agreed to serve on the Women's Shelter Board of Directors. He further mandated periodic training of all police officers in their response to domestic assault calls. While IPDA was patterned after a Duluth, MN, project, Olmsted County's IPDA was the first criminal justice program to be successfully integrated with a battered women's shelter program. IPDA was one of three Rochester programs presented to an All American City competition held in Houston in 1988. Rochester in fact won the designation of "All American City" by including this project.

The mid- and late 1980s were banner years for the women's shelter programs, and the most memorable in Judy's thirty years of leading the organization. She became a part of an alliance with a Rochester Republican State Representative, Dave Bishop, and Sue Rockne, a renowned woman's rights advocate, shelter board member, and Democrat from Goodhue County. Judy and Sue persuaded Dave that shelters in the state were overcrowded because as the woman resident was ready to strike out on her own and leave the shelter, the only financially feasible place for her to go was back home. In reality, no matter how supportive one's family and friends, with few exceptions, it was difficult for women to put together enough money to pay required deposits plus advanced rents while starting a new job, providing for her children, and striving for independence. As the shelters became overcrowded, there were few options but to return to the batterer.

Dave Bishop authored a bill in the legislature to establish a program to provide transitional housing to women and children of family abuse as they left a shelter program. It was a competitive grant process. Rochester's Women's Shelter was granted a twenty-year, no-pay-back loan through the Minnesota Housing Finance Agency with ongoing funding from the Minnesota Office of Economic Opportunity. These contracts and grants allowed for the purchase of the Transition House, an eleven-bedroom, five-bath house close to downtown Rochester. Women and their children can live here up to two years on a subsidized rent while they go to work or school and plan for their future. Community and church groups redecorate rooms for new residents.

During November 1986, the shelter board and staff learned that a recent former shelter resident, JoAnn Hennum, had been arrested for killing her abusive husband. Judy's first action was to work with JoAnn's attorney to get her released on bail and into Judy's custody at the Women's Shelter. She comments, "It's every shelter advocate's worst nightmare to read: 'woman killed by,' but now we were reading the reverse." Judy and the staff believed that JoAnn had acted in self-defense. Late on Christmas Eve, Judy and Donna Dunn got word that the judge had approved JoAnn's bail and was allowing her to leave jail in Judy's custody. They rushed to check her out and get her to the shelter in time for Christmas Eve dinner. Afterward, Judy and Donna realized they had been so embroiled in helping JoAnn they had forgotten about preparations for their own families' Christmas. Not easily overwhelmed, Judy and Donna contributed

The signing of the Transition House—the first home in Minnesota for families leaving abuse shelters. Left to right: Judy Miller, Representative Dave Bishop, Donna Dunn, Governor Rudy Perpich, Sue Rockne, and an unidentified person.

what they each had in their larders and the two families shared a Christmas meal.

JoAnn Hennum spent three years of an eight-and-a-half-year sentence in the Women's Correctional Facility at Shakopee, MN, after her conviction of second-degree murder in Wabasha County, MN. The Minnesota Court of Appeals, on September 1, 1988, reversed the decision and remanded for a new trial. On further appeal, the Minnesota Supreme Court on June 16, 1989, stated "We affirm the conviction; reverse the court of appeals' order for a new trial; and modify the sentence (to fifty-four months)." Much of the public interest in the case had revolved around the discussion of battered women's syndrome. That did not impact the outcome of either of the appeals, although it was discussed in the decisions as admissible but limited to the general description of the syndrome during expert testimony.

During the trial, Judy and the Shelter staff reviewed the many house rules and expectations along with JoAnn's files from her earlier stay at the Shelter. This was a time of deep soul searching: could they have contributed to JoAnn's being in this position? Judy came to believe that Women's Shelter policies plus behaviors of the criminal justice system and law enforcement contributed to JoAnn being in this position. This review exposed many obstacles faced by JoAnn, including some Shelter policies that had seemed so benign at the time . . . policies that had existed primarily for Shelter convenience. This process opened minds and created a platform for regular reviews of how the Women's Shelter could be welcoming to women of all lifestyles, cultures, abilities and backgrounds, as long as the two elements of non-violence and non-discrimination were present.

In February 1987, Sue Rockne arranged a lunch with Judy and Orville Pung, Commissioner of Minnesota's Department of Corrections. A few weeks earlier, Judy had telephoned the Commissioner with an idea that the Women's Shelter might partner with the Women's Correctional Facility at Shakopee. Recognizing that some women who became incarcerated were there because they were forced or manipulated into crimes by the person battering them, Judy proposed that these women be allowed to serve their last months at the

Rochester Women's Shelter, where they would be carefully monitored. They would seek meaningful employment, attend shelter group sessions, submit to drug tests, and refrain from aggressive behavior. This would prepare them for release and a future. The commissioner decided to try the idea. Judy had to be deputized, and the shelter staff was trained in short-term custody. By July, all criteria had been met and the program–the first of its kind in Minnesota–was fully funded and operational.

As the demographics of women's ages, personal status, and cultures changed over the years, the Rochester Women's Shelter broadened its focus. New immigrant populations appeared, requiring a different response from the Women's Shelter as well as Olmsted County. An International Shelter House was created that allows each culture to have its own room and kitchen in which to make the foods they are used to preparing. Until it is reported by children or hospital personnel, battering of women is the norm in many cultures. The Women's Shelter employs advocates to speak their languages, representing their battering story in court and explaining that these injuries are not tolerated in our country. Judy has used her artistic training as well as her sensitivity to the people of many cultures to decorate this house.

More legislative change needed

One day as Judy sat at the shelter, someone left a package labeled "For Judy" on the front porch–a rare occurrence. Inside a paper bag was a book with carefully underlined passages and some of Judy's clothing. That was the first of many intrusions into her personal life. Someone began stalking her by entering her home not only when she was away, but also when she was sleeping. She refused to let this control her life. Judy worked with a private investigator, and again Representative Dave Bishop became involved as he drafted anti-stalking legislation. Judy and Sue Rockne met with legislators, testified before committees, and networked with other stalking victims to get the best legislation possible. Once the legislation passed and was published with penalties listed, intrusions into her home and life ceased.

Judy Miller has now retired. The programs she initiated or influenced are still operating. Judy believes her greatest achievements center around the networking that helped create a pathway for battered women, opening doors for them. It has given confidence to their voices. She hastens to add, "I have been very fortunate. My three children are all educated and productive adults. I have had the support of a community that was not afraid to embrace self-examination. I have had good mentors and have learned from the best of leaders." In creating a safe place for women–those at the mercy of battering spouses and partners–Judy Miller has created a safer community for all by relentlessly working to change what we are willing to consider "acceptable" family behavior.

"...and a Woman Shall Lead Them."

In 1983 Ancy Tone Morse became the first woman judge in rural Minnesota

As a child, I knew I wanted to be a lawyer," says Ancy Tone Morse, when asked about her trailblazing role as the first female judge in Olmsted County. She had been raised with support and encouragement for her chosen profession. Her father's dad, a graduate of the University of Minnesota law school in 1901, was a pioneer lawyer around Bemidji and International Falls. When roads were non-existent or impassable, sometimes he was required to walk many miles for a court appearance. Her mother, Esther Olson Tone, born in 1908, had also wanted to be a lawyer. But Esther's Scandinavian immigrant parents had their money stolen by a banker. Her mother became a teacher and taught school for over thirty years.

Ancy's father, Aad Tone, Jr., was unable to afford college during the Depression and became a businessman. Both parents saw all three of their daughters graduate from college.

Ancy's grandfather, Aad Tone, Sr., a backwoods lawyer and father of six sons, doted on his first granddaughter. Ancy remembers going with him to the courthouse in International Falls where Grandpa talked about helping people through his legal practice. "He impressed on me what a privilege it was to be a citizen," she recalls.

International Falls might seem like an unusual place for a young girl to develop the determination to enter a predominantly male field in the 1930s and 1940s. But for Ancy, the "Icebox of the Nation" provided some unique opportunities. This Rainy Lake area on the Minnesota/Canadian border was a large outdoor playground where her father taught her to fish and hunt. (As a teenager, Ancy used money earned babysitting to purchase a rifle!) The small-town school experience allowed Ancy to participate in a wide variety of activities and pursuits. When Ancy graduated from International Falls High School, the prescient year book staff wrote next to her name " . . . and a woman shall lead them."

A life member of the Girl Scouts, Ancy was a third grader when she joined her first troop, and she still remembers how wonderful the leaders were. Seven of the girls continued in scouting through high school. It was Ancy, from International Falls, Minnesota, who was chosen as one of the four national delegates to attend the international meeting of the Girl Scouts/Girl Guides at "Our Chalet" in Switzerland.

Ancy remembers feeling "special and empowered" by this experience. After her high school graduation in 1953, the four U.S. girls and their adult leader set sail aboard the S.S. United States to attend the conference–the "Juliette Low Session." In England they had tea with one of Girls Scouts' guiding lights, Lady Baden-Powell, widow of Lord Baden-Powell, the founder of Boy Scouting. They shared the awe and excitement of the British as they celebrated the recent coronation of their new, young queen, Elizabeth II.

Throughout England and France, Ancy became very much aware of the scars of WW II destruction, which had ended only eight years before. Nineteen girls from all over the world gathered in Switzerland for this meeting, representing countries from Sri Lanka to Switzerland. This select group has kept in touch since 1953 via an annual newsletter, having occasional reunions over the years at various locations throughout the world–husbands and families welcome. They have written a book titled *Our Story* about their lives, many of them having become trailblazers like Ancy. As Ancy says, an experience like this "instills great confidence." She would need this confidence as she continued her education that fall at the University of Minnesota.

The trials of an early woman lawyer

In 1953, Ancy entered a six-year college program designed for two years of liberal arts courses and four years of law school. There were very few women enrolled in the law school; she recalls that for the first year, the few female students shared the dean's secretary's lavatory because there were no other facilities for females in the school. Ancy joined a study group and graduated in June 1959, as the only female graduate in that June class. Family members came for the occasion, including her grandfather, the pioneer lawyer—by then confined to a wheelchair—and her in-laws. In 1958, she had married Robert Morse, also from International Falls and a medical student at the University of Minnesota.

After passing the bar exam she was "sworn into the practice of law" before the Minnesota Supreme Court on October 27, 1959– Ancy and 166 men. Applying for jobs in the Twin Cities area, she was often asked during these interviews, "Can you type?" She attained a job with the Hennepin County Legal Aid Association, a valuable learning experience for a young lawyer. One day she was interviewing a client who seemed quite distressed. She asked what was troubling him; he replied that he had hoped to meet with a lawyer. Ancy told him she was indeed an attorney. He gasped, "My God, now I've seen everything!" She also recalls having trouble trying to serve legal papers on a party in the jail. The guards suspected she was a girlfriend of one of the inmates and called her office to check.

By 1963, Bob had completed medical school and was starting a psychiatric residency at Mayo Clinic. (He would later join the Mayo Clinic Psychiatry staff for a thirty-one-year career). When they arrived in Rochester, there were no practicing female attorneys in Olmsted County. She wanted to be home with her two children—two more would arrive in the next few years—and so she started a legal practice from home. Many clients came from her neighborhood, so like her grandfather, she walked to many of her legal appointments. She practiced family law—mostly adoptions and divorces (now dissolutions), along with probate and real estate.

She remembers one early appearance in a Rochester courtroom when she was appearing on behalf of a female client seeking a divorce. The judge was confused and assumed Ancy was the woman wanting the divorce, not the lawyer presenting the case. Finally, he called her up to the bench for a talk. Looking at her over his glasses, he asked, "Have you been to a local bar meeting yet?" he asked. She said "No." He responded, "Well, you'd better come; that'll shake up the boys a bit."

The members of the Olmsted County Bar Association were hospitable and welcoming to this female now in their midst. The wives of the lawyers had created their own organization called the "Barrettes." Once they knew Ancy, they teased Bob that he could join their group any time–they claimed they could really use a psychiatrist. The big social event for the Bar was the Sweetheart Dance in February. Ancy was not affiliated with a firm and thus had no natural group with which to be seated, so Ancy and Bob were placed at a table with other visiting attorneys. That evening, Bob and Ancy Morse met Warren Burger, Harry Blackmun, and their wives. In the following years, Burger would become Chief Justice of the United States Supreme Court, Blackmun a sitting justice of that same high court, and Ancy the first female judge in rural Minnesota. She remembers being "so impressed" with these men, who were so respectful of her as a new attorney and her husband as a medical resident. She savors the evening of conversation over a quiet dinner in Rochester.

Ancy's children grew and so did her legal practice, so she decided in the 1970s to affiliate with the firm Swan, Pougiales, and Gullickson. Ancy modestly attributes her success in family law to the times. Women wanted to have a woman represent them, especially for divorce. When there was a woman attorney available, many clients sought her out. Even men getting a divorce sometimes wanted a woman's perspective and chose her as their attorney.

During the late 1960s and 1970s, the law schools began graduating more women and a few more began coming to Rochester. Three or four would gather for lunch once a month, dubbing themselves WARPS–Women Attorneys of Rochester, Pine Island, and Stewartville. This group grew, and at the present time the monthly Wednesday lunch gathering of women attorneys fills a long table.

Watched from the bench by Judge Daniel Foley, Minnesota Supreme Court Associate Justice Rosalie Wahl swears in Ancy Morse as the first woman judge of Olmsted District Court in the 3rd Judicial District. Ron Seeger of Rochester, president of the Minnesota Bar Association, is at Ancy's right. (Courtesy Post-Bulletin Co.)

Ancy's historic appointment to the bench

In the early 1980s, Minnesota's legal caseload had grown large enough to require a Court of Appeals between the trial courts and the Supreme Court. One of the local judges was appointed to that court, creating a vacancy. Ancy had often handled divorces against a well-known local attorney, Sandy Keith. To Ancy's great surprise, he encouraged her to apply for the open position as Judge of District Court.

Sandy Keith had been active in politics and served in the Minnesota Legislature and later as Lieutenant Governor. He would become a Justice on the Minnesota Supreme Court in 1989 and Chief Justice the following year, serving until 1998. He remembers that Ancy was the first female lawyer ever to call him about a case back in 1968. "I was shocked!" he says. But within a few years they often worked together. "She was an excellent lawyer," he recalls. He encouraged her to apply because many more women were entering the field of law and family law was increasing in the work of the court. "In 1960, only five percent of the court's docket was concerned with family law matters. Today it is forty-five percent," Keith says. Ancy's expertise in the area was valuable.

Keith assisted Governor Rudy Perpich in many of the appointments he made to the bench, including the ground-breaking appointment of Rosalie Wahl as the first female Supreme Court Justice in Minnesota. With Keith's encouragement, Ancy decided to apply. She realized it was an historic act for a woman to apply for a judgeship and it would advance women within the profession, but she did not expect to be selected. When it happened, she was "delighted and amazed" and thus became the first woman appointed to the bench in all of rural Minnesota. Noteworthy support came from endorsement of Ancy by 100 percent of the female members of the Minnesota Legislature through the work of Keith and Senator Nancy Brataas.

About Morse's years on the bench as District Court Judge, Justice Keith says, "She was marvelous. This is the key job; ninety percent of law happens here. She was very good at it." Judicial ethics and behavior became an interest of hers, and she served for many years as a Judge-representative on the Minnesota Board on Judicial Standards, including a period as Chairman. In the criminal law area, she believed in seeking alternatives to jail and prison for appropriate offenders and supported Community Corrections concepts. As the trial courts became more congested and legal expenses soared, she became a strong advocate for settling cases before the trial stage and supported efforts toward mediation and arbitration. She believes the adversary system does not always lend itself to resolution of disputes, especially in the area of family law.

Judicial selection also was a special interest of hers. As an attorney representative she served on selection panels for some judicial appointments. She believes in judicial merit selection and is not in favor of election of judges by support of political party designation.

Reflecting back, Ancy says, "Being a judge can be very lonely. There are very few people with whom you can discuss a decision or a legal issue." She resigned from her memberships and board positions in many organizations. She needed to be "very vanilla" and to avoid any appearance of impropriety or impartiality. And, of course, there was the issue of stress.

Family life and children's activities were very important and naturally served as an outlet or relief from the work of the courts. "When I was stressed I liked to cook, and I still do," says Ancy. Cooking Italian, German, and of course Scandinavian food could become relaxing during a particularly demanding trial. She credits her family–husband Bob and children Kathryn, Karen, Mark, and Kelly–with being an important source of support. Maintaining a sense of humor was also necessary.

"I loved my job, and I loved the District Court," Ancy is quick to say. She truly felt she was there to help people. She stresses that the court environment is foreign to the majority of those who appear there. It is easy for people to be truly frightened; lawyers and judges who are there every day can easily forget that. She concentrated on being "very courteous" to those who were appearing in her court.

Toward the end of her sixteen years on the bench, Ancy had a rare opportunity. In Minnesota, district court judges can substitute in another county's court for short periods. The judge in International Falls wanted to spend a week in the Twin Cities and needed a sub. So Ancy had the opportunity to travel back to her hometown to preside over the Koochiching County Court. The caseload volume was far less, and naturally differed somewhat from Olmsted County. (She remembers meeting "CC," the Courthouse Cat who slept on the windowsills and had the run of the courthouse.) It was an amazing and poignant experience to sit on the bench in the very same courthouse where her grandfather had instructed his young granddaughter about the experience of practicing law so many years before.

Since retiring in 1999, she remains active in the community. Ancy and Bob enjoy their nine grandchildren and pursue a variety of interests. They travel frequently and return to the Rainy Lake playground for several weeks each summer at their island cabin.

"'No' Doesn't Work for Me"

Julie Nigon used creative funding to help refugees assimilate into the Rochester area

In 1980, minorities made up about two percent of Rochester's population; by 2010, that number had increased to twenty percent. A contributing factor was that as the Vietnam War was winding down in the 1970s, Rochester received its first wave of Vietnamese refugees, many of whom were well educated and quickly adapted to the culture. Several years later, Cambodian and Hmong refugees began to arrive, with local churches and social services helping people settle in by connecting them to housing and government assistance. Children in these refugee families entered public schools and learned English, but their parents and other relatives, many from villages with little schooling, had no opportunity to learn the new language.

The Rochester International Association, which traditionally helped foreign visitors and employees of Mayo Clinic or IBM, was intended for people who were extremely well educated, employed, and already spoke English. In 1984, the International Mutual Assistance Association (IMAA) began to help newcomers find housing, jobs, and health care; assist with immigration issues and citizenship classes; and help immigrants understand and cope with American technology, laws, and culture. But during the 1970s, once families were safely housed and their children in school, many adults in refugee families needed a place to learn English.

In l979, Rochester received the first federal funds for teaching English to Vietnamese and Cambodian refugees. The federal government had distributed the new arrivals throughout the country, providing funding for three years to support their assimilation into local communities. Julie Nigon, who was teaching adult literacy at

Rochester School District's Community Education program, organized about fifty volunteers to help the students in an English program for refugees. Sessions were held in a church basement, or volunteers went to the homes of mothers who couldn't leave their young children. Soon the Rochester Refugee English as a Second Language Program and its staff moved into the Northrop Community Education building to join the General Education Development (GED) program and the adult literacy program.

Julie Nigon's approach to teaching acknowleges that facts, formulas, grammar, and information must be in the context of people's lives and what they already know. .

Now under the Northrop Community Education umbrella, the program served nearly fifty adults with low literacy, forty foreign-born new arrivals, and about sixty GED students. Julie taught and managed the program. Today, Julie continues to direct the program, now located at Hawthorne School, which reaches three thousand students a year. Offerings include English classes from pre-literacy to college preparatory, a Hand in Hand preschool program that teaches kids and enables mothers to attend classes, a medical clinic for students and their families, citizenship classes, GED programs for all students, joint classes with Rochester Community and Technical College in specific fields like nursing assistants and welding, and a Career Pathways program that prepares people for job hunting and employment.

New and creative approaches

As Julie's responsibilities grew, she realized that in order to meet the growing demand she would have to rely on more than government funding. She attended a Southeastern Minnesota Initiative Asset Based Community Development class that changed her view on how to write grants. As the instructors of the class emphasized the value brought by the students to the community, Julie began to understand that her job was to help others see those assets and how they could help. As time went on, she learned not to be daunted by closed doors. "'No' doesn't work for me," she says. "I just find a different way to look at it. People want to do the right thing; you just have to present your idea in a way that fits their mission and corporate structure." Because of her creativity in finding funding sources, many of the programs at Hawthorne are supported by grants written by Julie.

Julie and her staff also realized early on that they needed new approaches to teaching. She was inspired by John McKnight, of Northwestern University in Chicago, who told the story of a village that needed a new bridge. When the village elders sought advice from a wise woman, she said, "You know the answer," and left. They returned to her, still puzzled, and she repeated her cryptic advice. Finally the elders sat down and figured out what they needed. In other words, facts, formulas, grammar, and information must be in the context of people's lives and what they already know. They need to see how it fits and how it connects in their lives. That is how Julie and her staff approach teaching.

"Even help and good advice will fail if you don't know what someone is already thinking," Julie explains. For example, the Hawthorne staff had noticed a rather persistent problem with tuberculosis (TB) in some local populations despite free testing and treatment. According to information from the local health department, Rochester's TB rates were approaching those of the Twin Cities. In cooperation with Mayo Clinic, Julie and her staff applied for a National Institutes of Health research grant to conduct community-based participatory research which funded twelve to fourteen focus groups for the purpose of finding out what the community knew about the transmission and treatment of TB. Based on the information, the Clinic and community would develop an action plan. "What they discovered was that people believed you died from TB and that when you got it, you would be socially isolated and no one would feed you," says Julie. "They were afraid to get tested." The school and the Clinic created a video to explain to people that in the U.S., TB was not terminal. Teachers took Mantoux tests for tuberculosis in front of their students before each year's TB campaigns. There has been no active TB since.

Formative years, some thrillingly insane

Julie was born and raised Catholic in La Crosse, Wisconsin. Her mother stayed home with six kids while her father worked as an insurance agent. Both parents were active in politics, and it was common to have visitors in the house discussing civil rights. One night, Julie's father called to say, "Don't go to bed, I am bringing company home." However, her mother went to bed, sleeping through a visit from Robert Kennedy, who talked with the children and even tucked them in bed. Another time, the family invited in a young boy who needed a haircut and a bath. Their caring ways also extended to a rescued possum that promptly had babies and clawed her way out of the family car.

When Julie was eleven, her father died. Her mother went back to school to earn a master's degree and then worked at UW–La Crosse as an English instructor. She expected her children to speak properly and achieve academically, and she edited everything Julie wrote. The children took on the housework, with Julie in charge of the cooking. Her mother's one rule for all six children: Do not embarrass me.

Julie went to St. Catherine's University at age seventeen, graduating in three-and-a-half years with a major in elementary fine arts education. She was hired immediately to teach kindergarten on Saint Paul's west side. Though she could speak French, nearly all of her students spoke Spanish. She had two sections of students and realized that she was in over her head; she refers to the four years there as "formative." During a teaching unit on the Twin Cities, Julie realized that most of her students had never traveled out of their neighborhood, so she wrote and received a grant to take them up in an airplane for a panoramic view of their city. She remembers the field trip as "thrilling and insane." During the holidays, she took fifty-five kids on an escalator up to the eighth floor of Dayton's department store to see the Christmas displays.

Taking on new responsibilities

She married Rochester native Bernie Nigon in Saint Paul and moved to Rochester to teach first grade in Byron for four years. In 1979, after she and her husband adopted the first of their three children, she secured a job in the Rochester Community College's Education Department. She ran the volunteer program for teaching adult literacy. In 1980, she began running the refugee literacy program. In the mid-1980s, with the help of IBM, Community Education experimented with redesigning the teaching software for American English speakers to better serve foreign-born new arrivals and refugees. The first comprehensive computer instruction program was called Success Maker. Later, higher level reading, math, and spelling with assessments were added. GED for all students also came under Julie's direction.

Over the years, Julie's responsibilities expanded to include the Hand in Hand family literacy program, citizenship classes, the on-site clinic, job readiness and job training, English instruction from pre-literate to Level Seven writing, reading and grammar classes, and pronunciation classes. Students have included local residents, foreign visitors, and employees of IBM and Mayo Clinic. Funding for services continues to come from the local business communities, government, and grants.

As she contemplates her achievements, Julie says that it is important to build true partnerships with the community, to teach people in the context of what they know, and to know your place. The students are important, not the teacher. She says, "I loved teaching. I loved new programs and computers. I wanted to teach half-time, but I couldn't do both, so I managed full time." When asked how she manages all the different programs and continually finds funding for them, she replies, "As the school has grown, I have had wonderful help from my staff who have assumed added responsibility for different parts of the program. This shared responsibility makes Hawthorne work."

Just Like One of the Guys

In 1973, Karen Ricklefs became the first woman president of the Rochester School Board since 1923

Newly-elected Rochester school board member Karen Ricklefs was eager to attend her first board meeting. I probably won't say much, she thought. I'll just plan to listen quietly and learn at the first few meetings. Not far into the evening that plan changed. The topic of busing arose and there began a discussion on whether the district should pay for it. The year was 1970, and Rochester didn't provide student busing in the city. Students were able to walk to their neighborhood schools. But with the addition of rural school children now coming into the city to attend "the town" schools, busing had become an important topic.

During the discussion one board member commented, "People who live right across the street from Bamber Valley School get free busing today." Karen and her husband Merlin (whom she calls Rick) lived about a mile from the school–at that time outside the city limits. They paid for busing, so she knew he was wrong and that she had to speak up.

"There's no way that I would let my children walk to school from where we live, because they would be on busy roads that don't have sidewalks. Rick and I pay for our children to be bused to school because walking would be unsafe for them." Her input and comments changed the course of the discussion.

After the meeting, two board members took Karen aside and said, "We have occasionally had a woman on the school board, but we've always considered her the 'decorative' member. We're not used to them saying much."

Karen was quick to reply, "You know, I don't think a single person who voted for me wanted me to be the 'decorative' member."

Six months later, those same two individuals took Karen aside and said, "Karen, you ask the best questions. We've learned so much since you've been on the board." After a pause they added, "You're just like one of the guys."

Karen was used to being one of the guys. One of her favorite stories related to this took place in 1957, when she transferred at the start of her junior year to Iowa State University in Ames, Iowa, from St. Olaf College in Northfield, Minnesota. She was a math major, and before she could continue in that field at ISU she was required to "pass" an interview with Dr. Hinrickson, the head of the math department. Hinrickson was a tall ("really tall" as Karen recalls) man who wore his glasses at the end of his long, hooked nose. This combination of height and the position of his glasses had him looking down at nearly everyone he encountered. As he looked down at Karen he said, "What makes you think you're smart enough to be a math major here?"

The only words of reply that came to Karen were, "Well, I am!" Dr. Hinrickson let her in, and fate would have it that he was her professor for her first math course, Differential Equations. There were forty-two men and one woman, Karen, in the class. Karen recalls that about a month into the quarter, after Hinrickson had picked on her constantly, he assigned two problems to the class. She worked on them all weekend, and it took her both sides of seven pages to write her solution. In class on Monday, Dr. Hinrickson asked, "Did anyone get those problems done?" Karen was the only one who raised a hand. Hinrickson said, "Oh, no. You didn't."

Karen replied, "Oh, I did and I believe they're right."

"Well, put them on the board." There were blackboards on all four walls of the classroom. Karen began writing her solution on one board and commenced to "write her way all around the room." As she began to erase the first board so she could make her second loop, Hinrickson grew impatient. "What's your answer?" Karen told him. She was right. Soon after, Hinrickson hired her to work for him in the math office. At ISU in 1957, Karen, too, had become "one of the guys."

ISU student Merlin Ricklefs was not just one of the guys, but rather a special guy. Karen had intended to return to St. Olaf, but meeting Merlin changed her plans. They fell in love, became engaged, and married September 1958, during their senior year. Following graduation in 1960, they moved to Yorktown Heights, New York, where Merlin began his career with IBM's Advanced Systems Development Division.

In 1961, they moved to Rochester, Minnesota, with the opening of the IBM Rochester Development Laboratory. Karen started substitute teaching in Rochester and then took teaching positions in math at Kasson-Mantorville and Plainview.

Never a question about education

Education was always important to both Karen and Merlin. She credits her parents for instilling this passion within her. Her father, Ole A. Anderson, was the oldest boy in a family of nine. When Ole was a sophomore in high school, his father died and his mother was left with trying to run the farm near Elmore, Minnesota, and support her large family. Even though he didn't want to quit school, Ole knew that if he didn't devote his full attention to farming, his family might lose the farm. When Ole's younger twin brothers became sophomores the next year, they said, "We don't need a high school education. We're going to quit and work on the farm." Ole said, "If you're going to quit, then I'm going back to school." So back to school he went where he attended class, even played–and lettered–on the football team, and received his high school diploma at age twenty. Karen says, "That took a lot of nerve for my father to do that. I'm sure that being older than his classmates was awkward, but education was very important to him."

Ole and his wife, Florence, would have five children. Karen recalls, "There was never a question whether my siblings and I would go to college. It was just assumed, and we never thought otherwise. My parents began taking me to St. Olaf College's Christmas concert from the time I was eight years old. I think they did that to indoctrinate me there. Of course, that was the only school where I applied."

Karen's brother majored in civil engineering at Cal Poly and later became a building contractor. Karen's sister obtained her bachelor's degree in interpersonal communications, her master's degree in organizational behavior, and Ph.D. degree in intercultural communications at the University of Minnesota in five years. Karen says, "My sister was not going to be one of those Ph.D. candidates who never gets around to writing her thesis, so she wrote a chapter every week. I attended her thesis defense. It was a fascinating experience. She has taught and consulted around the world." Karen graduated from Iowa State University with a major in mathematics. Sadly, two of her younger siblings died at early ages (three and thirteen).

By 1970, Merlin and Karen were proud parents of two children and busy with work and community activities. A third child, Kris, was on the way. In 1969, the state of Minnesota had required that all schools be part of a kindergarten through twelfth grade (K-12) district. At that time, the Rochester School District included only the City of Rochester. A number of the elementary school districts around Rochester were only K-6 or K-8, so each had to decide whether to become a K-12 district on its own or join another community with a K-12 program.

The Rochester School Board had six seats, each representing a specific geographic area of the city, but the board was adding a seventh seat that would represent all of the areas outside Rochester's city limits. The Bamber Valley area, where Karen and Merlin lived, voted to become part of the Rochester School District. Karen says, "Education was extremely important to us in the Bamber Valley District. We had chosen to live there because of the excellent elementary school. They paid well and consequently attracted very good teachers." Karen had been active in volunteering at the school, so she decided that she would run for the new open seat.

Karen's baby was two weeks late. At her doctor's appointment, Karen's obstetrician advised that the baby be induced. He said, "Please meet me at the hospital at five o'clock this afternoon, and this evening we'll begin inducement."

When she left her appointment, Karen had a list of things she wanted to do before checking in to the hospital, and one of the items was applying for the school board position. Karen recalls, "I was feeling fine, and I wasn't in labor. So applying was just another item on my list of things to get done before our baby arrived. So I stopped and applied." The next morning after her baby girl (Kris) was born, a *Post-Bulletin* reporter called and said, "Karen, did you really file for the school board position on your way to the hospital?"

Karen said that was true. She recalls, "He acted like he had the scoop of a lifetime. The story ended up having a five-column headline in the Rochester paper, which was probably the best free advertising I could have had in running for office."

Three other men were vying for the seventh seat. Karen received support from several of the other elementary school districts because she had worked with them on a number of community projects. Karen's campaign team put together coffees so that people could meet her. One of the supporters of Karen's opponents said, "She (Karen) has three children; she should stay home and take care of them."

One of Karen's supporters replied, "Well, he has six children, you'd think he should stay home and spend more time with them."

Along similar lines, another of Karen's strong supporters said that someone approached him to say, "Why would Karen's husband let her run for school board?" When she heard this, Karen said, "There's no 'let' in my relationship with Rick. I don't 'let' him do things; he doesn't 'let' me do things. If either of us decides to do something, we support one another."

Karen's campaign emphasized her experience as a math teacher and her involvement in the Bamber Valley Home School Club, YWCA, Girl Scouts, and the American Association of University Women. One of her campaign pledges was "the best quality education available for each tax dollar." She was quoted as saying: "Since I will have children in school for the next eighteen years, I am very much interested in the future of education."

Karen won the election over her three male opponents; she would serve as a member of the school board for the next six-and-a-half years. She recalls attending her first Minnesota State School Board (MSBA) meeting, a two- or three-day event, and standing in

This photograph, captioned "Ricklefs will have children in school for 18 years" appeared in the *Post-Bulletin* shortly after Karen was elected to the Rochester School Board. (Courtesy Post-Bulletin Co.)

the long registration line. When she reached the head of the line, the person doing the registration looked up at her and said, "And whose wife are you?" In the early 1970s, it was assumed–because it was true– that most school board members were men.

Taking stands

Karen has never been afraid of taking a stand. About a year after she was elected to the Rochester School Board, she would voice her concern and lobby at the state capitol against Governor Wendell Anderson's plan called the Minnesota Miracle. The concept behind the plan was that equal spending per student throughout the state would lead to equal educational opportunity. Karen was all for equality, but she felt the plan would not work. She says, "The legislators were so naïve. Rochester was capable of attracting many teachers that had master's degrees, educational specialist degrees, or Ph.D.s. The school system took advantage of these higher level skills by having an eleven-month contract [as opposed to a nine-month contract] available to nearly one-third of the teachers. With the extra two months they could write curriculums (which benefited Rochester students and could be sold to assist and benefit other districts around the country), study for their advanced degrees, teach summer school, or engage in educational travel. This plan cost the district much more than other districts that hired new teachers for only a nine-month schedule every year. The idea that it cost the same to put teachers in any districts' classrooms was just not true. Rochester also had a number of special education programs that attracted special needs students from other area schools. The teacher-student ratio was much lower for these students than in the regular classroom. In addition, at that time we had the Rochester State Hospital. The Rochester School System provided certified teachers to work with the patients there who were under twenty-one. I wasn't certain that certified teachers were necessary in all instances; teachers' aides might have served those needs as well." The bill passed, and Karen spent the next five years lobbying for exceptions.

In July 1973, after three years as a board member, Karen was elected chairman (the term used in the Rochester *Post-Bulletin*) of the Rochester School Board. She would be the first woman president of the Rochester School Board since Amelia Witherstine served in that capacity from 1914 to 1923. Karen recalls, "After I was elected president, the board members were concerned. They said, 'We've never served on a board with a woman president, what are we supposed to call you? Should we call you Madam President? Mrs. Chairman?' I really didn't care what they called me; that was so unimportant to me. I just wanted the meeting to begin. I believe they settled on calling me Madam Chairman."

School Board (and other) articles about Karen in the Rochester *Post-Bulletin* continually referred to her as Mrs. Merlin Ricklefs, in accordance with the newspaper's policy. Karen contacted the paper to ask that they use a woman's first name rather than her husband's. The newspaper declined changing its policy, but it agreed to grant an exception for Karen and a handful of other female community leaders in Rochester.

Karen Ricklefs served on the Rochester School Board from 1970-1976 and became its first woman chair in 1973. (PB)

More leadership roles

In October 1973, Karen was selected to be one of two representatives on the Region 10 Development Commission. Karen was elected to represent the large school districts in the region, a man from Sargeant was elected to represent the small school districts, and there were other representatives from the townships, counties, and cities. Karen attended the first organizational meeting in which offices and officers would be established. As was often the case, she was the only woman in the group. As they began to discuss the positions and who would fill each, one of the men looked around the room and said, "Oh, we have a woman, so at least we can have a secretary." Karen declined that opportunity and was elected vice president. To this day she has a policy that she won't serve as secretary on any group where she is the only woman. "I give men credit for being able to take notes and write well," she says.

In 1975, during Karen's fifth year on the board, her fellow board members nominated her for the Minnesota Outstanding State

School Board Member. She had been the board's treasurer, chairman, and clerk, as well as a member of the Minnesota School Board Association (MSBA) Delegate Assembly for four years. She had been appointed by Governor Wendell Anderson to the Minnesota Environmental Education Commission (MEEC). She was also vice chairman of a state mathematics assessment committee, active in the Minnesota Educational Computer Consortium (MECC) for state school districts, and involved in local teacher and administrative negotiations. Though she didn't win the award, she was honored to be nominated. In 1976, Merlin was transferred from IBM Rochester to IBM Headquarters in Armonk, and the Ricklefs family moved to New York. They returned to Rochester two years later.

During Karen's presidency, she teamed with Dr. Jack Kinder (Rochester Superintendent) and Dr. James Sheehan (Assistant Superintendent for Administrative Services) to propose a Rochester inter-governmental council. Karen recalls how this came about: "There's always a money problem any time you work in government. Dr. Sheehan, Dr. Kinder, and I realized that the city, the county, and the school district serve many of the same people. We thought there must be ways we could cooperate to save money for all of us. We came up with the idea of establishing an inter-governmental council with representatives such as Mayor Alex Smekta, the city council president, county board chairman, county administrator, superintendent, and school board president. We created the council and soon found all kinds of ways to save. For example, we would buy paper supplies in bulk, and we found that we could save quite a bit of money by cooperating."

Karen led the group so effectively that Mayor Smekta proposed that she become the group's permanent chair, a position she held until her move to New York. All were pleased with the cooperation among the various government bodies because there had been a bit of conflict and frustration. Karen said, "We found that when people sit down together, they can find common ground and work effectively. I think when people meet face-to-face it's much harder to take pot shots. People tend to be more positive than negative."

Karen's people skills were developed at an early age. Her parents owned their own businesses in Elmore–first a trucking company and then The Hilltop, which consisted of a car dealership, garage, gas station, restaurant, and motel. Starting at age twelve, Karen waitressed in the restaurant. She learned that as the owner's daughter she was expected to work twice as hard as the other employees. She also learned much about working with the public, because people from all walks of life, with different occupations and education levels and backgrounds, were her parents' customers.

Listen actively; ask insightful questions

Karen's leadership style consists of listening actively and asking good questions. She says, "I like to have all the facts possible before making a decision. If someone were to try to determine my political leanings by looking at the books on my bookshelves, they would have difficulty doing so because I read all the extremes and as well all the middle. I try to have an open mind."

She considers her school board years to be "a great experience, but, of course, frustrating at times." To those who reminded her that serving on the school board was a thankless job, she would counter by saying that she received much positive feedback. Also, she often heard from people who disagreed with her. They would call to say, "I didn't agree with what you decided to do but I respect the reasons why you decided to vote the way you did." She appreciated those comments.

Today, nearly four decades after serving on the school board, there are still reminders of issues discussed and decisions made. For example, Karen recalls a proposal that was made to cut down the hill at Golden Hill Elementary School and develop the land as a flat lot. The citizens in that area were quite upset that they would lose the "Hill at Golden Hill." Karen brought the issue and the citizens' concerns to the board, and the proposal was voted down. She says, "I still think of this when I drive by that neighborhood and see the lovely trees and hill. 'Golden Flats' would not have suited the school."

Karen displays a plaque in her home called Opportunity. Its text, based on the John 9:5 Bible verse, reads:

I shall pass through this world but once. Any good therefore that I can do or any kindness that I can show to any human being, let me do it now. Let me not defer or neglect it, for I shall not pass this way again.

The plaque is especially meaningful to Karen because it was displayed in her parents' home, too. In 1967, they and Karen's thirteen-year-old brother were tragically and instantly killed in a head-on car crash.

Karen reflects, "My school board experience taught me much. For example, I learned how a multi-million dollar enterprise is run. I also learned the difference between being on a board, where policy is set, and serving in administration, where the work is done. I learned, too, that one shouldn't cross that line." Regarding the difficulties of serving and leading in a male-dominated environment, she says, "I never took anything personally. There were things that needed to be done, I thought I could do them, and with very few exceptions, I was accepted. In most of what I've accomplished in my life, it's been done with a male majority. I'm comfortable with it." Karen advises today's women, "If you believe in something, be as well prepared as you can to make a difference. Depending on your interests and your passions, don't stop doing something you believe in just because somebody tells you that you can't–because of gender or any other reason."

Karen continues to passionately support and improve K-12 education across the state. She actively works with legislators and the Minnesota Quality Council to create and promote Minnesota state legislation. She is also co-chair of the Rotary District 5960 Literacy and Education Committee, which has sixty-nine clubs in Minnesota and Wisconsin.

There Must be a Mom I Can Talk To

Joyce Schut turned family struggle into the Rochester Area Alliance for the Mentally Ill

Joyce Schut and her husband, Wayne, raised their three small children in Cuttingsville, Vermont, where without realizing it, she was preparing for future adventures and an unknown horizon in Minnesota. Their house in Vermont was part of Spring Lake Ranch, a therapeutic community founded in 1932 for adults with mental illnesses. For ten years, Joyce and Wayne lived, worked, and played with the residents in a variety of activities and capacities. They made maple syrup, hand cut cords of wood, gardened, cooked, washed dishes, cut ice, played volleyball, swam in the lake, skied, and celebrated holidays.

In 1974, a board of directors from a new, non-profit organization hired the Schuts to begin a similar community in Dodge County, Minnesota. The Schut family moved to Rochester. However, hostile local community reaction prevented the development of the project. It never materialized.

The professional becomes personal

Over time, Joyce and Wayne developed other employment. The children went to Rochester schools and became involved in church, school, and community activities. Their next journey into the world of mental illness came suddenly in July 1985, when their youngest child was sixteen. She drove their car to a church youth gathering. No one has ever managed to put together a clear picture of what happened that night, but something was triggered in her brain. She wandered away from the group and a few hours later was being examined in the Saint Marys Hospital Emergency Room. After much waiting, questioning, and testing it was suggested to Joyce and Wayne that their daughter spend the night in the adult psychiatric unit because there was no space in the adolescent unit. To this day, Joyce asks, "Who would leave an undiagnosed sixteen-year-old in an adult psychiatric unit over a weekend?" Joyce and Wayne took her home and managed to care for their very ill teen. She and they were frightened and uncertain about what was going on in her mind and body. On Monday, Joyce began making phone calls for medical appointments and a possible diagnosis.

It soon became obvious to Joyce and Wayne that the prevailing professional assumptions were that hospitalization was necessary for their daughter and that Joyce was a contributing cause of her daughter's problems. Thus began the long journey into the ever-changing mental health system with its ups and downs, ins and outs, and a frequent lack of compassion or understanding for the young patient or the parents.

After two weeks when they were allowed no contact with their daughter, Joyce and Wayne were permitted weekly visits, but only if they first attended a support group meeting. By this time, the diagnosis of schizophrenia had been made. None of the other youth in the adolescent ward had that diagnosis, so the required support group meetings were not relevant to the Schuts' needs and proved only frustrating. Much later they learned that very few teens are diagnosed with schizophrenia and that services are basically non-existent. Their daughter remained in the hospital for an extremely traumatic eight weeks.

Finding others "in the same boat"

Joyce persistently asked social workers and nurses, "Is there a mom with whom I can talk whose child has similar problems?" She had grown weary of medical jargon, lack of services, and social workers saying, "Try this, try that." She wondered what other parents had done in similar circumstances. But no one could give her names.

In 1986, Wayne was working for Ability Building Center, a non-profit organization in Rochester that provides rehabilitation and

Joyce and Wayne Schut (right) with their daughter. Joyce says of the work involved to form The Rochester Area Alliance for the Mentally Ill (RAAMI): "It was a labor of love. The joys of helping families find each other and providing some hope and direction were great."

employment services for people with disabilities and other special needs. While manning a booth at Rochester Community College, he met Ruth Mueller and Pat Solomonson from the Minnesota Mental Health Advocacy Coalition in Minneapolis/Saint Paul. They were stationed at an adjacent booth. Each was a mother of an adult child who was constantly in and out of psychiatric hospitals. They were hoping to start a Rochester branch of the coalition to provide support, education, and advocacy. "I went to meet them that very evening," says Joyce. A few weeks later they advised Joyce as to the wording for articles of incorporation. Meanwhile, the Schuts had found a few other interested people in Rochester. They spent forty dollars to file for the incorporation and were soon accepted as a Minnesota 501(c)(3) organization. The Rochester Area Alliance for the Mentally Ill (RAAMI) was born in August 1986.

"Starting a new group with only a few people and very limited funds was an enormous challenge," Joyce recalls. "I was fortunate not really to know what we were getting into when we began. We just went along in a one-step-at-a-time fashion. A motto we soon adopted was *"If you don't ask, you know the answer is 'No.'"* The work was all-consuming, with more always to be done than could be done. But, as Joyce says, "It was a labor of love. The joys of helping families find each other and providing some hope and direction were great." Offering encouragement and reminders never to give up were rewarding. "In many ways and at many times we were swimming against the current, which can be exhausting, but always there were others to swim alongside and those who began to understand and offer help and support. Having families get to know each other and become friends contributed greatly to healing and well being."

Wayne became RAAMI's first president. He, Joyce, and Tom and Pam Johnson, who had two teenagers with mental illnesses, held the first RAAMI Board of Directors meeting around the kitchen table at the Schut's home. As secretary, Joyce kept very detailed, hand-written minutes. "We were not alone," comments Joyce. "We immediately became a chapter of the Minnesota Mental Health Advocacy Coalition, which soon changed its name to the Alliance for the Mentally Ill of Minnesota. Also, we joined the National Alliance for the Mentally Ill (NAMI), which had been started in Chicago in 1979 by a group of parents. This made us part of a large network at both the state and national levels. The local work, however, was our responsibility."

The Minnesota organization gave Rochester's new group $200. With the funding, Joyce made and posted fliers and brochures around the city to increase public awareness of RAAMI and mental illnesses. The first official RAAMI meeting was at Rochester Methodist Hospital in September 1986. Ten people attended.

Joyce says, "Our member base included men and women, all of us volunteers, and all with a vision and commitment to make things happen." The RAAMI goals were to educate the community about mental illness, to advocate for change in public policy and legislation to improve the lives of people with mental illness, to provide support and resources to people with a mental illness and their families, and to promote and support research about mental illness.

Spread the word

Joyce organized community education classes, making certain there was a knowledgeable professional or experienced parent, plus a person with a mental illness, in each educational presentation. These classes were available to school teachers and their classrooms (especially health and social studies classes), community groups such as Kiwanis, Rotary, the Jaycees, the League of Women Voters, and church groups—all presented not only to educate, but also to explore how to erase the stigma of mental illness. Help was solicited from supportive mental health workers in Olmsted County, the Zumbro Valley Mental Health Center, practicing psychiatrists, and other interested professionals. Book reports were written for newspaper columns, and avid RAAMI newspaper watchers responded to erroneous media statements about mental illness. A traveling puppet show was developed for elementary students, which was eventually adopted in other states.

Monthly meetings were arranged to educate all who attended RAAMI meetings about the goals. Refreshments were served so people could linger and talk about their possible future involvement or ask questions. In later years, Joyce arranged for expert speakers in various areas who came to Rochester from across the country.

In November 1986, Joyce and Wayne met with Gil Brown, Executive Director of the United Way, to inquire about how to receive United Way funding. Gil answered, "Keep good records of everything you do." Joyce continued to do so and later related them to the stated goals. In 1989, the RAAMI Board submitted its first funding request to the United Way and was granted $12,000. "We were rich!" exclaims Joyce. With that funding, the group acquired its first office, a room rented for fifty dollars per month at Ability Building Center. Also, after years of volunteering for this cause, Joyce received her first compensation as the part-time RAAMI Executive Director.

Mid-1987 brought the passage of Minnesota's sweeping mental health legislative reforms and mandated the creation of each county's mental health services system by 1990. During early RAAMI meetings, members wrote letters to legislators about various mental illness needs, lack of services, lack of insurance coverage , and other needed legislation. Sample letters were devised to encourage others to write, and more than 700 letters were mailed from Rochester to help pass this important legislation.

Because hospitalization often leaves a person with a mental illness feeling very alone, the need for friendship is an important part of a person's recovery. Joyce, with support from other RAAMI members, started a Circle of Friends program after writing and winning a Robert Wood Johnson Foundation grant. The Circle of Friends plan was to find volunteers to become friends to people with mental illnesses and provide enrichment through friendship and meaningful activities. Some of these friendships remain, though the need for additional volunteer friends is acute.

Also initiated at the national level was a local educational program called Journey of Hope, which later became Family to Family. It is a twelve-week course about mental illness written by a family member to educate other family members. Joyce and Wayne took the course, as did other RAAMI members, and then underwent training in order to become teachers. A requirement was that those who taught had to themselves be family members of a person with a mental illness and were required to attend a rigorous training session. RAAMI initially sent two people to be trained. Others went in later years. The training session became one of the very best of what RAAMI had to offer in the Rochester community. Attendees consistently said it was the most helpful thing in their journey towards recovery, acceptance, and wellness. The program continues.

A support group component was later added to the Family to Family program. It was developed by a family member who was also a professional psychologist. Joyce, Wayne, and others took the necessary training and brought the support group component to Rochester. This, too, continues to be offered, and has proved very helpful in problem solving and emotional help for families traveling the journey of life that has been interrupted by a mental illness.

Other RAAMI funding ideas included the Cajun Dinner, featuring local entertainers and cooks; the Flowering of Hope Art Show, demonstrating creative abilities of local people with a mental illness; and the annual Walk for Research around Silver Lake. Joyce says of the latter, "Friendly rivalries came into being, and it became one of our most enjoyable activities over the years, raising thousands of dollars for research."

Joyce says, "Since most RAAMI members were all in somewhat the same boat, we became good friends. The meetings provided times for people to reconnect with each other, make plans for the future, offer support, and provide laughter. There were Christmas parties at members' homes. We traveled together to state or national conventions. RAAMI became part of the fabric of our lives."

Joyce would be the first to say that no one person can do anything without the support of many others and their efforts. The Board of Directors and RAAMI's many active, involved members are the heart of the organization, now called NAMI Southeast Minnesota. However, Joyce's creativity and enthusiasm must be credited for shepherding a parade of professional speakers into the Rochester community to deal with the vast spectrum of mental illness concerns. She brought in three schizophrenia experts: Ron Norris, from Delaware, to speak on children and adolescent issues; Dr. Nancy Andreasen, a well-known researcher from the University of Iowa; and Dr. Fred Frese, a psychiatrist with schizophrenia. There were experts on suicide, obsessive compulsive disorder, and transgenic pharmacology. Also, an individual with schizophrenia shared his recovery experience. A National Depression Screening Day and a fall Candlelight Vigil became part of each year's Mental Illness Awareness Week's offerings.

The National Alliance for the Mentally Ill, the Alliance for the Mentally Ill of Minnesota, and the Rochester League of Women Voters have given awards and recognition to Joyce's leadership in bringing a better quality of life to those affected by mental illness. The League recognized her for "choosing change" and honored "a woman who made a difference" in the Rochester Community.

In a tribute to a ten-year RAAMI Board Member, Joyce expressed a key truth about RAAMI. "For many, joining RAAMI and working for system changes and a more accepting public attitude was a positive way to deal with the pain caused by the intrusion of mental illness into one's family."

Joyce and Wayne's daughter is now forty-three. Medically stable, she has not been hospitalized since 1990. She lives alone in an apartment, owns, maintains, and drives a car, and works at two part-time jobs. She sometimes travels alone by air to visit family members in other states. She has an excellent psychiatrist who is unusually skilled in devising creative medication combinations. That's the upside. The downside is this: she has very few friends and is often lonely. Side effects of the medications cause weight gain and a high risk of diabetes. So, the need for education and advocacy continues, as does the challenge to all of us to be more aware, accepting, and sensitive towards those among us who live with the ongoing challenge of a mental illness.

Changing the Way the World Looks
At Child Care

Tutti Sherlock led the Olmsted County Council for Coordinated Child Care (4Cs), one of the first organizations of its kind in the nation

*This chapter, included with Child Care Resource and Referral's (CCRR) permission, is an expanded version of an article written by writer Penny Marshall from an interview with Tutti Sherlock, Earlene Wickre, and Randy Bachman on September 13, 2008.

In 1972, working in a shoe box-sized office with a minimal budget and one assistant, Tutti Sherlock would begin to change the way the world looked at child care. Through her determined leadership, she– a working mom herself–ensured information was available for parents looking for child care. Her efforts also assisted providers, giving them guidance on everything from making the day care safer to serving nutritious meals.

Born Naomi Bach in Montana to Danish immigrants and raised with strong family traditions, Tutti graduated from the University of Montana–Missoula with a degree in social welfare. She married Thomas Sherlock and moved to Minnesota in 1952. Tutti applied the household skills she learned from her mother to earn the title of Mrs. Minnesota in 1959, a competition which at that time focused mainly on the Domestic Arts. After she, her husband, and their three small daughters moved to Rochester in 1964, Tutti would be given and would capitalize upon opportunities to advocate for the young. She said, "I was motivated by challenges, and I did not like to lose. I thank God for letting me be at the right place at the right time."

Tutti served as a member of a United Way long-range planning committee that authorized a study in 1969 called "Who Cares for the Children: A Study of Child Care in Olmsted County." The results of

Tutti Sherlock (standing) and Earlene Wickre, who began with 4Cs as a secretary in 1974. Earlene recalls, "Tutti was always approachable. We could go to her with anything."

the study showed significant deficiencies in the early childhood care system and child care availability at a time when the number of mothers entering the work force was rapidly increasing. Following that study, Tutti served as representative to a statewide committee that was writing a rule for a new allocation of state money made available to improve child care facilities. "I did that on my own–paid my own way to the meetings and learned a great deal from the Greater Minneapolis Day Care Association, Saint Paul's Resources for Child Caring, and the State Health Department" said Tutti. This, combined with mentoring from Helen Remley of Aldrich Nursery School, prepared Tutti, in 1972, to qualify for application as the first Executive Director of the Olmsted County Council for Coordinated Child Care (4Cs), one of the first organizations of its kind in the nation.

Humble beginnings

The foundation of 4Cs then, and going forward, was to follow the recommendations made by the study, listen to the concerns and issues within the child care profession, and involve leaders from all sectors of the community. "That model of cross-county community representation was used whenever we did planning. Whether it was PAIIR

214

(Parents Are Important in Rochester), use of the sliding fee child care funds, Head Start, or whatever–we made sure we had representation of anyone the program might impact," said Tutti.

Tutti was selected as the agency's director and its first home was a makeshift, part-time office in a small portion of the Zumbro Lutheran Church choir room. From humble beginnings grow great things. Furniture was acquired from the downtown Dayton's store that was relocating to Apache Mall. "A little paint and reupholstering and you'd never have known that the two reception chairs had once been white wrought iron, pink plastic-covered furniture originating from a shoe department," recalled Tutti with a laugh.

Looking back on the first couple of days when 4Cs first opened, Tutti discovered that a major function of this new agency was helping families find and choose quality child care in a very deliberate way–i.e., child care referral. "As a brand new agency, there were no established rules and procedures. But we listened to the parents calling us every day. We listened to family child care providers. We listened to teachers at nursery schools and child care centers and during the next few years, we began new programs and new projects in order to respond to the community concerns and fill in the gaps."

Tutti recalled the reaction to 4Cs within the child care and preschool community. "They were very cautious and not sure if they liked us or not. We were getting community money, and family child care providers thought we were favoring day care centers over their facilities. And maybe we were, to start with. The providers watched how we operated over the next twenty-five years to make sure they were treated fairly–which actually resulted in our improvement. The family child care providers took me to major task because Aldrich, Civic League, and Bethany Nursery School were the only facilities eligible for funding. I went to Olmsted County Social Services and told them they had to open up support for family child care as well. Family child care providers wanted to get their share of our attention, money, and impact. It was a positive effort."

Within a year, Tutti convinced the United Way Board that a child development specialist was critical to 4Cs' mission. They supported the funding of that position, paving the way for Cindy Kroll to be hired as the first Child Development Program Coordinator. "We added a child care development specialist because the quality of child care in the community was a key component in the recommendations from the original study," said Tutti. "And because quality child care was a key component in my thinking and we had a responsibility for the quality of care to the community," she added.

4Cs grew and was able to expand a bit as it left the church choir room and relocated to a Sunday school room. Earlene Wickre began her career with 4Cs as a secretary in 1974. She recalled, "On Fridays we'd have to stack the chairs on the desks, push all the furniture to the other side of a sliding door, and put it all back together on Monday." Earlene had worked at a CPA firm doing tax returns and audits and had college experience in accounting. "The agency had a bookkeeper at the time I was hired," said Earlene. "After a few months of employment, I decided to be bold and went to Tutti suggesting I do the books and she add the ten dollars per hour she was paying a bookkeeper to my salary." Tutti agreed and Earlene was happy to be earning more than $500 per month. "Tutti was always approachable," said Earlene. "We could go to her with anything."

Just out of the military and wanting to return to the Midwest, Randy Bachman found his way to 4Cs in 1975. He and his wife, Klare, were on their way from Missouri to Inver Grove Heights, where he had a job interview, when their car broke down near the Minnesota/Iowa border. "Rochester and Mayo Clinic are close by," said Klare. "Let's go there." Camping at the area KOA campground, Randy donned his suit and arrived at the Rochester unemployment office, where he was referred to 4Cs. After circling Zumbro Lutheran Church several times because there was no sign indicating 4Cs as an occupant, Randy made his way inside, found the office, and told Earlene that he was camping at the KOA and that he should be hired. He eventually was hired, creating yet another turning point for the organization. Tutti found temporary and unique low-cost housing for Randy at the home of her widowed neighbor Francis Gooding, also known as the "Grand Dame" of Rochester.

"The environment was rich for what we were doing," recalls Tutti. "Historically, child care and children in general were the least important issue for any other organization–public or private. No one in the community paid much attention if new child care initiatives were being funded at the state or federal level. The Rochester School Board and staff of the Olmsted County government were often very supportive of our initiatives as long as we were responsible for them, brought money into the community, and 4Cs would be in charge." She pulled them all together

"We may have been the first organization in the nation to pull so many early childhood/child care entities together under one organization," said Tutti. "One of the first projects we brought to the community was a parent education program in 1974–Parents Are Important in Rochester (PAIIR). The state allocated a small amount of money to initiate a model for a parent education program. The state issued six grants–two to the metropolitan area, two to suburban, and two to rural communities. We wrote the grant for PAIIR via the school district and were one of the first six programs to start in the State of Minnesota. We managed PAIIR for the next eleven years."

After the launch of the PAIIR program in 1978, the county asked 4Cs to manage the federal, state, and county dollars designated to help low income families pay for child care. "We were the only county in the state managing the money in this way," said Tutti.

One of the things that excited Tutti was a challenge, such as the sliding fee scale. Tutti felt it was an injustice that a mother would lose eligibility for the program if she got a pay raise and, as a result, would have to endure the entire cost of the child care. Tutti pursued a state grant so that the fees could slide and the mother would only pay more for child care as her earnings grew. "We were a pilot program for the first use of Minnesota state money for a sliding fee scale program, which became the beginning of Minnesota's child care program for the cost of child care for low income families," said Tutti.

Early in his career at 4Cs, Randy approached Tutti with a dilemma for which there seemed to be no easy solution. Tutti responded, "Whenever you're faced with a dilemma like this, step back and ask yourself, 'What's in the best interest of the child?' It might not be very good for others, like parents, teachers, or government, but it must be the right thing for children."

"That has always stuck with me," said Randy. In a short time, Randy's job description grew. "It was exciting," he said. "Tutti gave permission for us to grow and stretch. I went from someone who was focused on individual kids and families to focusing on what could be done to build community support."

"Randy was innovative and I would say–go for it," said Tutti.

Further innovation

Earlene remembered the establishment of a library, thanks to a small amount of grant money. "The library was a strategy to get child care providers to come into the office so they could feel like we were a team, based on quality," she said. The toy library followed, allowing providers to check out toys, just like books–things they would have liked to have but couldn't afford. It was a way to provide variety and quality equipment in a cost effective way.

Acquiring a nutritionist through a Comprehensive Employment and Training Act (CETA) grant in 1978 resulted in 4Cs becoming the first agency in the State of Minnesota to implement the federal child care food program (CCFP, now know as Child and Adult Care Food Program). "It took a lot of innovation to develop the program but having a funded staff person developed it quickly and well," said Tutti. "The implementation of the Food Program was to become one of the most effective methods that we had to improve the quality and the value of licensed family child care."

It wasn't long before Tutti acknowledged the question, "What do families do when their children are sick and they still need to go to work?" She worked to inspire Olmsted Community Hospital to do a pilot program. A facility called "Under the Weather" was designed to provide care to sick children and is the influence for the sick child care programs that exist today. Once again, Tutti went back to the core principal of listening to parents and responding with a solution. Even though much time has passed, people still express thanks and acknowledgement for their efforts. "We did our jobs passionately," said Earlene. "I met a woman recently who said, "You may not remember me, but you saved my life.""

A paramount concern of Tutti and her staff was to assure that anyone, regardless of who they were, who walked into the 4Cs office felt good about their experience. "It made no difference if it was a single mom on welfare or the president of Norwest Bank," said Tutti. "People were respected and valued regardless of who they were and, because of this, they trusted us," said Earlene. "And we never ignored the children. In fact we went out of our way to make sure they didn't feel excluded in the process of helping the parent."

As the agency grew, it changed its name and collected a host of addresses. Since it began, the agency has been in two locations in Zumbro Lutheran Church, the United Way building at Northgate Plaza, the United Way Building on West Center Street, and the Olmsted County State Hospital facility. Today the agency enjoys its own building. In 1980, the Olmsted County Council of Coordinated Child Care became Child Care Resource and Referral, Inc.–frequently called CCRR or sometimes C2R2.

Tutti was diligent about learning and staying on top of what was going on, locally and nationally. "But she always made sure the rest of us kept up too," said Earlene. "Because she insisted on staff development, I went to places like New Orleans, Boston, and San Francisco for conferences and co-chaired a regional conference held here in Rochester with Tutti. This was amazing for a small nonprofit organization, but it paid big benefits."

4Cs made its mark with the media as well. Earlene remembers taking calls from publications like *Working Woman* magazine in reference to the agency's work. A member of the community was even flown to New York City to appear on the *Early Morning* show to talk about Rochester's unique and comprehensive child care system.

Find the gaps, fill them in

Why has this been such a successful organization? Clearly the leadership of Tutti Sherlock made a huge impact. "I always looked for people who had passion and were willing to take risks," said Tutti. "You had to look at the gaps and then fill them in. The reason we were able to put all these things together was because we were an early entrée and no one else was ever interested."

"Tutti took risks," said Randy. "And we were a small enough organization starting out that we could take advantage of not having to go through a string of committees."

Employers became aware and accepting of companies taking responsibility for hiring working mothers. "They began providing services to employees who had young children and paying us to provide those services–such as IBM," said Tutti. "That pushed us into thinking about how we were doing things. Our first computer was a gift from IBM in 1984, and making that transition in the operation of our office was a significant step. The President of our Board of Directors at that time was an assertive manager from IBM. He basically ordered me to throw away our paper records and rely only on the computer! We obeyed and it pushed us into a whole new realm of productivity and ready to work with other employers such as Mayo Clinic." Initially, the entire child care referral program was converted from a small two-drawer file cabinet and numerous files of parent information forms to two large, floppy diskettes–one for the program and one for the data.

Again, Tutti went back to listening to the people and looking at the gaps. This time it was the need for school-aged child care. Although local principals didn't think care for school-aged children was needed, a survey showed that kids were going home to empty houses. Tutti pursued a national grant from the Ford Foundation designating funding for one elementary school to start a school-aged child care program. "We didn't need to run the programs, but the schools needed to have them," said Tutti. "Today, they're in nearly every school."

Head Start was another program initiated by 4Cs. Tutti persevered with a state representative to Congress to find out why Head Start didn't exist in Olmsted County. The program became eligible in 1984 for communities where it had never been, and 4Cs developed the program there just like they had PAIIR, the Child Care Food Program, and many others.

The legacy of Olmsted County Council for Coordinated Child Care is rich, extensive, and unique. Tutti was an instigator and proficient at recognizing needs and getting the right people to the table to implement efforts. She paid a lot of attention to who served on the board–always looking for the right balance of parents, providers, and members of the community. She provided the right combination of leadership and environment to mobilize the community at that time. For Tutti, a large part was passion–passion in the people she recruited and passion for the cause.

The Rochester Child Care Resource and Referral agency would grow to a staff of more than 150 and a budget of thirteen million dollars. Following her leadership at the county level, Tutti spent several years encouraging the rest of Minnesota and the entire United States to adopt the concept of child care resource and referral (CCRR), as the system needed to improve dramatically the early childhood/child care system. She pursued a grant from the State of Minnesota to begin developing CCRR across Minnesota. In coordination with the Minneapolis and Saint Paul organizations, this was successful, and it continues to play an important leadership role in the Minnesota child care system.

In 1986, Tutti took the model of Rochester Child Care Resource and Referral to the national stage. She became the first president of NACCRRA (National Association of Child Care Resource & Referral Agencies) and in a volunteer position began organizing, designing, and developing this national organization. Today there are CCRR organizations in every state and a very successful national CCRR agency located in Washington, D.C.

Tutti retired from CCRR in 1999 after serving as executive director for twenty-seven years. She remained an advocate for children her entire life. When Tutti died in December 2009, Rochester *Post-Bulletin* columnist Jill Burcum eulogized her with these words: "The word visionary is often overused, but Tutti Sherlock was one. She began her work in an era where it wasn't common to have both parents work outside the home. But she saw the changes ahead and [took] commonsense steps to help families continue to thrive. I'm one of the many moms grateful for her work and to have known her."

The Community Partner and Advocate

Marilyn Stewart, first female chair of the Rochester Area Chamber of Commerce, was a tireless advocate for higher education and other quality-of-life improvements in her community

The year was 1989. A hush fell over the 100 women gathered at the Twin Cities Chapter of the Women's Council of Realtors luncheon as the first female president of the Minnesota Association of Realtors stepped forward to speak. The women had every reason to expect that she would congratulate them on their organization, the size signifying the power of women in the profession. After all, the speaker had gained valuable leadership and organizational knowledge herself while participating in a host of all-female organizations: Girl Scouts, Job's Daughters, her college sorority; and, since moving to Rochester, AAUW, Zumbro Valley Dental Auxiliary, PEO Chapter, St. Luke's Church Women, and the Civic League Day Nursery Board.

But Marilyn Stewart had a surprise for this audience. After relating recent activities of the Minnesota Association of Realtors, she calmly advised them to get out and join their Chambers of Commerce, their local economic development boards, and their Rotary Clubs. They would accomplish much more as women in business than they would within this all-female organization, she argued. Business women needed to create partnerships with men and with all the diverse players within their communities. She pointed to her own recent experience of joining the Rotary Club of Rochester as part of the first group of women admitted to that previously male-only bastion. (She would later become its first female president.) She told them about her appointment to the Rochester Area Chamber of Commerce Board of Directors.

"It was not what they wanted to hear," says Marilyn, looking back. "But I was right: the Women's Council of Realtors has faded away, and not because there are fewer women in the profession!"

223

Early partnerships and the community of Rochester

Marilyn Stewart has always been about "partnerships," as she terms the multiple allies she has cultivated over the years while leading many community projects. In a June 2010, Rochester Chamber of Commerce publication, *Advantage*, Marilyn is quoted as saying, "Partnerships can make anything possible. I get involved because I care about the community and want to make it better. In today's world, partners have to work together to get us where we want to go. That's what makes Rochester a very special place."

According to Marilyn, her most important and longest partnership is with her husband, Jack. She dismisses those who ask how they met with, "It's a long story," but goes on to relate it anyway. They met on a bus while she was on her way back to the University of Minnesota from Thanksgiving break with her parents in Mankato. There were only two vacant seats. "Naturally I took the seat next to the handsome young man in the blue shirt," she says. Jack, a recent graduate of the University of North Dakota, had boarded the bus in New Ulm, his home town, and was headed to Minneapolis to apply for Naval Officer Training. While they really enjoyed talking with each other, it wasn't love at first sight. However, the next year they were an item, just as Jack received word that he was to be sent to Korea.

Jack was overseas, but his fiancée was being introduced to Rochester as a newly-graduated first grade teacher. The Rochester position was a plum job: a top school district in the state, a brand new elementary school (Washington), and an eleven-month contract. But this was to be a short stay, an "appetizer" for later, when she and Jack moved back to Rochester after several years of his naval intelligence work at the Pentagon. During that time Marilyn taught in Maryland and Virginia, followed by four years staying home with babies in Minneapolis while Jack completed U of M Dental School.

Eventually, back to Rochester they did come. "I really wanted to put down roots," Marilyn states, "unlike my own childhood of frequent moves. And I was starved for involvement because I never felt that I fit into the neighborhood we lived in while Jack was in dental school." They did some research and narrowed the choices to Boulder, Colorado; Appleton, Wisconsin; or Rochester.

She will never forget the Rochester First National Bank's approval of loans for Jack's dental practice and a house with a fireplace, screened porch, and a tree taller than she was. But the particulars of the house mattered far less than the friendliness of the neighbors. Years later, as a realtor she would say, "Buy the neighbors, not the house." How true in their case, as their neighbors–the Laedtkes, Kempers, Kyles, and later the Baileys–all became lifelong family friends.

Even though she had small children, Marilyn plunged into service organizations. "I wanted to get involved in making my community better," she says. She joined AAUW in 1961, and became chair of the House Tour, the Fashion Show, and new member recruitment before becoming president in 1964. She credits mentors like Eleanor Stroebel, Inez Schafer, and Betty Christian with showing her how to lead an organization, recruit, assign, and stay organized. She and Jack also met the Gibiliscos the first Sunday they attended the Episcopal Church. Dr. Gibilisco was a Mayo dental surgeon and would become one of the important "partners" to work on a University of Minnesota Branch in Rochester. Since Jack and Marilyn were not affiliated with either Mayo or IBM, the community's two major employers, they lacked the contacts enjoyed by other Rochesterites. Neighborhood and community activities were thus even more important for them.

Equal pay for equal work

As to why she got involved in so many community organizations, Marilyn just says, "One thing leads to another. I have been active since I was a teenager." Her daughter, Nancy, once asked, "Mom, do you always have to be president? Can't you just bring cookies and sit in the back row?" "Of course I did that too," laughs Marilyn. But once her children were all in school she began to think she'd like to focus again on a career. As a former teacher, she received a letter from the Rochester School District, inviting her to a recruitment event on teaching learning-disabled children. She had a disturbing conversation with another invitee who said, "Your husband is a dentist. Why would you take a job away from another?" Marilyn points to this as a galvanizing moment. She wanted a job on her own and didn't want to worry about reflecting on her husband, or he on her. "I was liberated before it was the rage," she says. "It worked for me because Jack is my great support system." At a Boy Scout event somewhat later, another father said to Jack, "You are going to have to rein in your wife." Jack recalls that he didn't respond, knowing the man was "dead wrong."

Marilyn chose real estate for her next career because it seemed to be the one professional business opportunity in which women would be paid the same as men for the same work. And what an excellent fit for a person who loves architecture, her community, and wants to "share and sell it" to newcomers!

"It was not as though there were so very many choices for women then," Marilyn reflects. Today, with her skills and interests she might have chosen antiques, architecture, or even law. But at the time she saw the usual "women's careers" as teaching, nursing, and secretarial work. She relates the story of a neighbor, Ann Goldston, a pediatrician who had to practice in Austin, Minnesota, since her husband was already on the Mayo Clinic staff. There were many barriers for women pursuing what were not traditionally female careers.

Marilyn took classes quietly at the University of Minnesota Extension Division at the Friedell Building in Rochester and passed her exams in the Twin Cities. "I live in a city of highly educated people. Education at all levels has always been important to me," she explains. Marilyn's commitment to professional education was her route to leadership in realtor organizations at both the state and national levels. Her position as "Education Chair" brought her to the attention of the president of the state realtors' organization. At a Legislative Day at the Capitol, Jim Stanton asked her to run for President of the Minnesota Association of Realtors (MNAR). "I'm not ready," she recalls telling him, although she had been on the Board of Directors for three years. She had also been named "Realtor of the Year" in 1988 and "Rochester Realtor of the Year" in 1985 by the

Rochester Area Association of Realtors for whom she had already been president. But she did consent and became the first female president of MNAR in 1989.

Marilyn was a top agent for K and K Realty throughout the 1970s and 1980s, becoming the principal broker/owner from 1982 to 1993. She was also an exceptional realtor for hundreds of families relocating to or within Rochester. Marilyn understood that realtors work with the most important investment for most families–their home. In keeping with her philosophy that making a home is as much about the neighbors and the community as it is about the trees and square footage, she asked sellers to write short paragraphs about their neighborhoods, including phone numbers of neighbors willing to be contacted. She gave that information to potential buyers so they could check out the neighborhood, urging them to drive through the neighborhood at different times of the day to get a feel for the place.

Because she was so well known in the community, she was frequently called upon to give what she calls "my twenty-five dollar tour of Rochester" to spouses of candidates being interviewed for executive level positions. While one member of the couple was being interviewed, Marilyn did her best to "pitch Rochester" to the spouse. Recently she provided this service for Joan Munoz, wife of Rochester's new school superintendent. After her afternoon tour, Marilyn was so impressed with Joan that she emailed a School Board member she knew and said, "If the candidate is anything like his wife, grab him. They will be great ambassadors for the school district!"

Eleanor Kirklin, one of the two original (1949) owners of K and K Realty, "was a walking history of Rochester," says Marilyn. "She called houses by the owners' names." Eleanor was the kind of mentor that Marilyn tried to emulate for her own agents. When Edina Realty approached Marilyn in 1993 to buy the business, Marilyn turned to Eleanor for advice. "Maybe this is the next step in growth," Eleanor suggested. K and K Realty had four agents when Marilyn joined in 1972; now, in 1993, there were seventeen–all women and all holding real estate professional certification. "I would applaud your decision should you make it," Eleanor said. Marilyn sold to Edina Realty, continued "to run the show," built a great new office building, and grew Edina Realty Rochester to an even more profitable firm with 100 agents and staff until her recent retirement. In 1986, she received the first-ever Athena Award, in recognition of an outstanding female boss, mentoring female employees, to be offered by the Rochester Area Chamber of Commerce. Marilyn had indeed passed on the great mentorship she had received.

Strategic planning for the community: Don't forget higher ed!

In 1985, Marilyn was asked to join the Rochester Area Chamber of Commerce Board of Directors, "probably because K and K Realty had been named 'Business of the year,'" recalls Marilyn. Anyone knowing her past would bet on her becoming president, or in this case chair, of the organization within a short period of time. But that didn't happen until 1990, when she was asked and responded, "Yes, and I do know how," instead of "I'm not ready," as she had once told Jim Stanton.

Before her chairmanship, but while an active member of the Chamber Board of Directors, she was involved in perhaps the largest community-wide strategic planning that Rochester had ever undertaken. Since the failure of urban renewal in the late 1960s, there had been no comprehensive plan for downtown development, economic growth, or community problem solving. During the mid-1980s, the two major employers were not growing very rapidly, and local governments and developers were approaching development in a piecemeal fashion. In late 1985, the Rochester Chamber of Commerce, partnering with the city, the county, the school district, major employers, and the *Post-Bulletin*, contracted with Arthur Andersen to guide them in an intensive long-range planning effort to be known as FutureScan 2000. The federal funding for the huge local flood control had just been achieved, so downtown development could move ahead with some certainty, if only the community could reach consensus on what was needed. The plan was to have a wide scope: "To insure the future vigor of the area's economy and quality of life."

The project's steering committee of forty led by Chair Al Tuntland, a local businessman, included Marilyn Stewart. Chamber Executive Mark Ricker and Diane Langton staffed the effort, eventually including more than 150 local people on the task forces. The community was polled to help identify the four or five most crucial issues to be addressed. Marilyn recalls being surprised how many business people did not think higher education, specifically a U of M branch for Rochester, was an important topic. Her hard work lobbying the Chamber members on behalf of this issue paid off. The five topics eventually selected for study and recommendations were: economic diversification, downtown redevelopment, higher education, housing affordability, and local government structure/cooperation.

This is one strategic plan that did not gather dust on the shelf. Many of the recommendations were acted upon in one way or another, several during Marilyn's Chairmanship at the Chamber of Commerce from September 1990 to September 1991. Marilyn remembers the inception of the idea of a joint city-county government center in a rundown area just across the river from the downtown. The Downtown Redevelopment Task Force had recommended: "Plan for a local combined government services campus in downtown Rochester." At the time, Olmsted County needed to expand its jail, and Mayo Clinic wanted to expand its campus to the current courthouse property. The county board had to decide: should the courthouse be moved and the land sold to Mayo Clinic, or should just a new jail be built at a remote location, or should all county services be moved out to the county-owned portion of the old state hospital on the east edge of Rochester?

At a Chamber of Commerce meeting when Marilyn was chair, the idea was hatched to locate the county courthouse, jail, and offices with room to expand for a City Hall in the rundown area that was now buildable, thanks to the 1986 passage of the long sought federal funding for the flood control project, protecting much of downtown Rochester. She gives credit to Dan Berndt, a board member and prominent local attorney. Of course the idea required a lot of lobbying of city council and county board members, but most were much at-tuned to the need for downtown redevelopment thanks to involve-ment in the FutureScan 2000 project. The Olmsted County Board voted 4-3 to proceed with the development of the downtown site, rather than the old state hospital campus. In 1993, the doors opened on the county side of a new government center (the city added its of-fices a few years later) connected to the downtown over the river by skyway, another idea championed by Marilyn. She particularly wanted to see a skyway to the Civic Center after attending a conven-tion in Duluth, which already had skyway connections.

The most important outcome to this story came from the rec-ommendations from the Higher Education Task Force, led by Larry Osterwise, the IBM Rochester General Manager. "We recommend (the number one recommendation of this task force) that FutureScan 2000 Implementation Action Committee create a local organizational structure called 'Greater Rochester Area University Center' so that the Rochester Community has a single focus to represent it on all higher education matters." Thus GRAUC was born, became the cat-alyst for effective community education and advocacy for higher ed-ucation in Rochester, and provided the next and most memorable outlet for effective community action by Marilyn Stewart.

"I hope we live long enough to see a U of M Rochester Branch!"

Why did Rochester need GRAUC? Why did Marilyn's children refer to her endless meetings in the Twin Cities, around the region, and in Rochester on behalf of higher education as "GRAUCing"? Because, for historical, political, institutional, and of course financial reasons, there had been no four-year college or university situated in Rochester. Until GRAUC, there had been no unified advocacy for the higher education needs of the community. Senator Brataas and her successor Senator Kiscaden, along with Representative Bishop, had been lonely, although always vocal, voices at the legislature on this issue. But institutional and political forces for "no change"–for no full University for Rochester–were incredibly strong. In their book *The*

University of Minnesota 1945-2000, authors Stanford Lehmberg and Ann Pflaum credited, in addition to the local legislators, "such community volunteers in Rochester as realtor Marilyn Stewart, retired IBM manager Don Sudor, and former Mayo faculty member Joseph Gibilisco with further long term efforts to enhance higher education in Rochester." But Marilyn's vision–and that of other members of the community–for higher education was not being achieved in a very timely manner, despite GRAUC's efforts.

In Minnesota there are numerous state universities and full scale branches of the University of Minnesota, but Rochester, the state's third largest city with the state's largest private employer, had a two-year community college and a vocational-technical training institution. Rochester also boasted the largest training program (Mayo Clinic) for specialty medicine in the nation under an agreement with the University of Minnesota (U of M), and beginning in 1972, Mayo Medical School. Because there was obviously a "market" for higher education in this growing community, Winona State University (WSU) began offering upper-division and graduate courses in Rochester in the early 1980s. In 1984, WSU formalized with Rochester Community College (RCC) a "two plus two program" for four-year degrees. The sale by Olmsted County of the former State Hospital in 1985 provided the opportunity, through legislative work by Representative Bishop and Senator Brataas, which allowed the use of $5.8 million from that sale to pay for a new building adjoining RCC to house WSU classes.

In 1966, the U of M Regents had established a Continuing Education and Extension program in Rochester that offered limited courses. In a May 9, 1986, *Post-Bulletin* story, Regent Dave Roe, retired President of the Minnesota AFL-CIO was quoted as saying, "My wish is that back in 1966 when there was a move for an actual university campus here, they should have provided that." In the same story, President Keller noted that the University should expand programs in Rochester, but they would need more money. A real U of M branch in Rochester was Marilyn's wish as well, and she promoted her view in GRAUC. "I wanted the 'answer' to be a real branch of the

University of Minnesota (not just more incremental collaboration between MNSCU institutions such as WSU and RCC in Rochester). But it had to come from the members of GRAUC, not me. The day it finally happened at a strategic planning workshop, I called my three-Advil Day."

There had been studies and studies and studies. As far back as 1972, the Minnesota Higher Education Coordinating Commission used a panel of higher education consultants throughout the nation who, according to a July 28, 1972, *Post-Bulletin* article, "prefaced its recommendations by urging the state to 'take a deep breath and imaginatively re-group and re-focus its educational resources in southern Minnesota.'" The report further noted that cooperatives are hard to govern and that university branches in other states are not strong and are slow to react to community needs. Then they dropped the bombshell that probably poisoned relationships between Rochester and Winona for a generation: move the four-year state institution from Winona to Rochester and move the two-year community college from Rochester to Winona! Needless to say, the idea was not executed.

GRAUC kept the issue of higher education for Rochester front and center in the community and at the legislature through the 1980s, 1990s, and into the new century. When Rochester sales tax extensions were granted by the legislature, they always included locally generated tax money for local higher educational purposes, which was highly unusual for state institutions. In the 1999 session, the legislature finally passed (although it didn't fund) enabling legislation to create a Rochester Branch campus of the U of M. Then the political winds began to change. Governor Pawlenty, a Republican who wished to champion Rochester, was elected in 2002, and promoted, in 2003, the Minnesota Partnership for Bio-technology and Medical Genomics, a state-funded research collaboration with Mayo Clinic and the University of Minnesota. In 2004, for the first time in memory, two of the four state representatives and one of the two state senators representing the Rochester area were elected on the DFL (Democratic) or Independence ticket. Now both parties saw an electoral opportunity in Rochester and were interested in responding to this long-held desire of the community. In 2005, during his State of the State Address in Rochester, Governor Pawlenty stated his priority: a four-year university in Rochester. The Governor appointed an eleven-member Rochester Higher Education Development Committee (RHEDC), in response to the legislative appropriation of $3.2 million for this purpose. RHEDC was charged with bringing a blueprint to the legislature in 2006 to meet the growing need for baccalaureate and graduate programs in biosciences, business, and technology.

Who should be on the RHEDC? The wrong individuals could torpedo the outcome. At the last minute, Marilyn submitted her application by e-mail at the urging of her husband. "I don't need another job," she said thinking of her twenty-four/seven real estate business. "You have the history and a responsibility," Jack told her. She had a pleasant interview that ended with what she thought was "a royal kiss-off." "I was told there were so many good people applying, that they did not know how they would be able to choose." So she quickly told the interviewer some people that the governor should really consider, including Wendy Shannon and Drew Flaada, active and informed community leaders. She was surprised to receive a call asking if she were still interested in serving, and if so, would she be the chair and come to the Rochester airport at seven o'clock the next morning for a press conference with Governor Pawlenty and Susan Heegaard, Director of the Minnesota Office of Higher Education. "Of course I said 'yes' and began preparing some remarks. Jack had to drive me because my legs were still bandaged from vein surgery earlier that week."

"All of the activities I had performed in my community led to that 2005-2007 chairmanship," she said. "This was my greatest achievement." According to Marilyn, each RHEDC member was a leader, but they all became partners on the team. This dynamic had much to do with Marilyn's leadership style and efforts. They had to build the case. It certainly was not enough that Rochester wanted a full university branch, no matter how needed. The case had to be made that U of M Rochester would benefit the entire state. She had to calm the dissenters, some of whom were represented on the committee. The State, represented by Jayne Rankin from the Department

Of her many accomplishments, Marilyn is most pleased with her leadership of the eleven-member Rochester Higher Education Development Committee (RHEDC). She says, "All of the activities I had performed in my community led to that 2005-2007 chairmanship. This was my greatest achievement."

of Finance, was not interested in massive outlays of money in these tight budget years. The U of M, represented by past Regent Chair Dr. David Metzen, was concerned about weakening its core institution with an expensive new branch. The State University System (MNSCU), represented by Dr. Robert Hoffman, past Chair of MNSCU Trustees, did not want to see its institutions in Winona or Mankato or the Rochester Community College weakened by competition. She had to guide this group, with open meetings no less, toward a vision of the kind of four-year university that could be built in Rochester, fit within these parameters, and bring economic development to the state. Supportive Dr. Robert Bruininks, President of the University, whom she always introduced as our "best friend from up north," had told her, "It won't be easy."

Marilyn called upon her training, organizational skills, multitude of friends in the right places, and ability to win over people with one-on-one communications—either with her or with the right "partner" chosen by Marilyn. The committee met weekly at 7:00 a.m. at the Edina Realty offices "because it was free," laughs Marilyn. Local committee members Dr. Claire Bender (Mayo Clinic), Al Berning (Pemstar entrepreneur), Al DeBoer (attorney), Drew Flaada (IBM), Dwight Gourneau (retired IBM and National Science Foundation), and Dr. Wendy Shannon (Superintendent, Byron Public Schools) carried a heavy load. They were aided by the many people, like Kathy Meyerle, Jim Clausen, and former Senator Nancy Brataas, that Marilyn appointed to subcommittees on program, facilities, finance and governance. Frequently Marilyn called upon her friend, Dr. Patty Simmons, U of M Regent from Rochester, when she needed someone to consult regarding protocol and procedure with Regents or U of M officials.

Because she gathered the right people together, there were "aha" moments that brought the vision closer to reality. Marilyn recalls one such meeting with Walt Ling, IBM State Executive; Dr. Hugh Smith, Mayo Clinic CEO; and Dr. Zigang Dong, Executive Director, Hormel Institute, Austin, MN. They became excited discussing all the research collaboration between their three institutions and suddenly realized how their research would be enhanced with a U of M Branch downtown, where institutional partners would be just a few steps away by skyway! If current research at these three institutions could be leveraged at the new U of M Branch, far less infrastructure would be needed, there could be financial savings, and a strong partnership could be created. Not only would this save the new university branch money; it would also make it unique in the state, the nation, and perhaps in the world. There would be no question of competition with other MNSCU or U of M campuses, which had their own, different missions. This new school would focus on the health sciences, research, genomics, biomedical informatics, technology, and entrepreneurship. It would be new, unique, focused, leveraged on community partnerships, and jump-started with eleven million dollars from the City of Rochester's sales tax. The Rochester Higher Education Committee had built the case, had calmed the dissenters, and proceeded to sell the vision to the community, the U of

M Board of Regents, and the Minnesota Legislature . . . one Power-Point presentation after another.

Wendy Shannon, recently reflecting about her role on the committee said, "In my life to date I have never had such a synergistic experience. I credit much of the result of our work to one phenomenal leader, Marilyn Stewart. What was so unique about this experience? I believe it was because of Marilyn's belief in excellence. An anonymous quote says, 'Excellence is caring more than others think is wise, risking more than others think is safe, dreaming more than others think is practical, and expecting more than others think is possible.'"

"As we write the history of UMR, Marilyn will be recognized as a founder of the institution," says UMR Chancellor Stephen Lehmkuhle as quoted in the Rochester Chamber of Commerce *Advantage* newsletter, June 2010. "It was her passion, commitment, and tenacity that created a new institution, but she also infused these same attributes into the DNA of this embryonic university. As we now write our future, I predict that it will also be our passion, commitment, and tenacity to student learning and building our community that will make us a great university–and one that lives Marilyn's legacy each and every day."

"Never doubt that a small group of thoughtful, committed citizens can change the world. Indeed, it is the only thing that ever has," said Margaret Mead. Thanks to Marilyn Stewart's leadership, the small group mushroomed into a crowd of community advocates and partners, making Rochester the great community it has become in which to live, work, *and* go to college!

The Melanin Lady

Jackie Trotter raised Rochester's diversity consciousness

J ackie Trotter and her husband, Virge, were newlyweds when they moved to Rochester in 1965, after he was offered an engineering job at IBM. The south side of Chicago, where they had been born and raised, was home to many African-American families, whereas Rochester had but a dozen. After the Trotters settled in Rochester to raise their sons Skip, Chris, Jack, and Gene, Jackie began to teach children about black people and black culture. She explained the role melanin played in making humans different colors; it was because of this that the children nicknamed her "The Melanin Lady." Over time, she talked to children in all of the public schools in Rochester.

In the spring of 1965, Jackie became a founding member of the local chapter of NAACP. After attaining her social work license, she became the Rochester Public School's first African-American social worker. In the early 1990s, she helped develop the Diversity Council's Prejudice Reduction workshop curriculum, which is still being used in area schools, and she chaired the committee that did the first survey of inclusivity in the Rochester Public School curriculum.

Raised to do good

Jackie credits the examples set by her parents for her belief in the power of education. Her parents had graduated from high school and her dad had gone to college for two years. Her father became a mailman, her mother a clerk for the Internal Revenue Service. Jackie lived with her parents and three younger brothers in an almost completely

237

black neighborhood which included many extended family members living nearby. One uncle owned a dry cleaner and another was vice president of an African-American insurance company. Because of the segregated nature of Chicago, a wide range of professions was represented in her neighborhood, with doctors living on the same street as stockyard workers.

Even before she really knew what college was, Jackie always knew she would go to college because her parents told her so. An uncle sold her parents an insurance policy that would mature when she was old enough for college. Though at times it was difficult to scrape together the eighteen dollars and seventy cents per regular payment, her parents did so; consequently, the insurance policy made it possible for Jackie to go to the University of Illinois.

As important to her family as education was religion. Growing up Catholic, Jackie grew to believe that people were put on this earth for a reason. Her mother was a kind and generous person who did not tolerate meanness and who believed that "we were supposed to try and do good." If Jackie happened to be on the phone with a girlfriend and made an unkind remark about someone, her mother made her hang up. Her father was a member of a social club with other high school classmates that met for over fifty years, raising money for student scholarships.

Places were limited where black families could live and send their children to school. Jackie attended a parochial elementary school where most of the students were black. The nuns, all white, were very strict and the classes were large. Jackie liked to talk and the nuns scolded her, but when she and her brothers complained, her parents insisted that they needed a good education and they were there to learn what the nuns had to teach them.

Jackie's parents talked very little about race. She knew white people were different, but she rarely saw them in her neighborhood. One time when she was nine, she and her parents were in a downtown Chicago department store elevator. All the other people, who were white, glared at Jackie's father, who looked white, and her mother, who looked black. It was scary to suddenly realize that the white people were angry because they thought her parents were a mixed-race couple. She still remembers those glares.

When Jackie was about to enter her freshman year of high school in the mid-1950s, the family moved to a different section of Chicago. The new neighborhood was shifting from white to black, thanks to Eisenhower's new highway system, which meant that housing areas for whites were opening up in the new, segregated suburbs outside of Chicago. White real estate agents warned white homeowners that black families were moving in and that they should sell fast, often for less money than the property was worth. Then the agents raised the prices and sold to black families.

When Jackie began attending the local high school, the student body was about twenty percent black. The white students and teachers made it clear they did not want black students by not speaking to them and treating them with distain. There was only one black employee in the school. There had once been many after-school activities when the school was all white; now there were only football games and one prom. One day, as Jackie helped her teacher carry books back to the classroom, he threw one of the books against the wall, frustrated that the district would send only used books from the white schools. If black students wanted to stay after for practice or work in the library, they had to walk home and risk being accosted by gangs of white boys. Jackie remembers pushing aside the attitudes of her classmates and just concentrating on doing what she needed to do. By her junior year, there were enough black students walking together to protect themselves from being attacked. Upon her graduation from high school, the school was eighty percent black.

Virge went to the same high school in the class ahead of Jackie. He played on the football team and she was in the band. They both attended the University of Illinois in Chicago and then, after the death of her mother when Jackie was eighteen, transferred to the main campus at Champaign-Urbana.

In college, she discovered that Abraham Lincoln, the Great Emancipator, had not freed all of the slaves. She also noticed that her textbooks did not have pictures of people like her unless they were slaves. As a young teen, she loved to read, checking out "loads of books" at the Chicago public library. One day she took the wrong "El" train and looked up to see a car full of white people. This was in 1955, during the time of Emmet Till's killing. (Till was an African American boy who was murdered in Mississippi at age fourteen after reportedly flirting with a white woman.) Frightened, she left the train at the next stop and found her way to the right train back to her neighborhood, possibly unnoticed because of her light skin.

When Jackie and Virge were dating, they went to a local public beach in Chicago called Rainbow Beach, historically frequented exclusively by whites. They believed they had a right to be there since their parents paid taxes along with everyone else. Still, people walked by, giving them dirty looks. One man swore at them. Later, when it came time to search for a job, she read the ads in the Chicago Sun-Times and the Chicago Tribune. Many of the want ads had "White only" so she knew that she could not apply.

Work together to get things done

Virge graduated from college as an aeronautical engineer. Though he received many job interviews, the jobs had always been "recently filled." Finally, he went to a minority hiring fair, was selected for an interview at IBM-Rochester, and then was chosen for the job. Virge retired after a successful thirty-year career at IBM.

Jackie had always loved to read, but now books became her education. With her mother no longer living, she learned to cook and take care of babies by reading books. She remembers being up all night crying the night her first son was born because she knew that some people would hate this baby. She knew she would have to do something because she believed that if people only knew more, they would not be prejudiced.

Jackie and Virge eventually had four boys. There were only two other African-American children at Holmes School when her first son went there, but in the late '60s and early '70s, IBM made a commitment to hire more minorities. About 120 black families moved to

Rochester over a period of ten years. However, only nine of these families remain. Some left to be near family; most left because they felt their careers would not flourish in Rochester. Most who left went on to successful careers in other places.

In 1965, Mr. Howard Naves, who ran one of two boarding houses where black patients could stay, asked Jackie and others to help start the local chapter of the NAACP. Jackie agreed to help, as it was a way to get out into the community and do some good as her parents had done. Then, shortly after the assassination of Dr. Martin Luther King in 1968, some community women were concerned about the presentation of women, Native Americans, Jewish Americans, and African Americans in textbooks and teacher's guides. Phyllis Layton, Elaine White, Sue Bateman, Ann Sheehan, Judy Zachary, Nancy Hart, and Jackie sat around each other's kitchen tables and surveyed educational materials. Though a top administrator had assured them there was no problem, the women noticed that in history texts, blacks were only mentioned as slaves; one book even used the adjective "happy" in reference to the slaves. Jackie wrote the committee's final report, which insisted that children needed to see positive images of themselves in the curriculum in all their classes. Ann Sheehan, Judy Zackary, and Jackie were then asked to write curriculum on diversity. They split their payment of $200; Jackie bought a bike with her share. She has never forgotten how well that group of women worked together for change and how she learned from each one of them. She believes that is what women do: work together to get things done.

Public schools, the foundation of democracy

In the early 1970s, Sue Bateman, the Rochester YWCA Director, asked Jackie to teach pre-school classes at the Y. It was at the Y that Jackie developed lesson plans on melanin. Several years later, her first-grade son, Jack, came home upset that classmates kept feeling his hair. He said he was going to beat them up if they touched him again. Jackie realized she needed to do something. She visited Mrs. Luneman, her son's teacher, asking if she could come in and talk to her son's classmates. After that, she talked to the personnel director about visiting other classes. He agreed, but "only if the teacher wants you there." Eventually, all the public schools in Rochester invited Jackie to speak to their children. She did so for more than twenty years. During this time the students nicknamed her "the Melanin Lady."

In 1989, students were fighting in a local middle school. The superintendent pulled together a steering committee with representatives from the Intercultural Mutual Assistance Association (IMAA), the county, the police, the NAACP, the schools, and other community organizations to determine what could be done. The steering committee evolved into the Diversity Council. Jackie and Elaine White attended training in Allentown, Pennsylvania; upon their return to Rochester, they began leading the Prejudice Reduction Workshops. As participants shared with teachers, their audience was transfixed by stories of how people had been made to feel "less than." Jackie and Elaine went on to present to groups for Olmsted County, Mayo Clinic, and local churches. In 1991-1992 they rewrote the curriculum, recruited more people to teach, and began presenting to classes at the two high schools and then the middle schools. The Prejudice Reduction Workshops continue today in area schools.

Believing that African American students needed to see someone who looked like them working in the schools and knowing she needed the proper credentials, Jackie returned to school for a school social worker's license. She became the Rochester District's first African American social worker. The first year, she worked half-time with her position split among three schools. The next year, she became full-time at two schools; the third year, she worked full-time at Gage, where she stayed until she retired in 2007.

Jackie believes that a public school is one of the few places where we can truly learn about each other and learn to live together. "Good, well-funded public schools are the foundation of a democracy," she says. "They are particularly critical for poor children and children of color as a place to learn the skills for being contributing members of society. It is also critical for all children to see people of color and other cultures in teaching and counseling positions."

Jackie profoundly respects how hard public school teachers work. Many of these teachers welcomed the chance to expand their horizons and consider new ways to be more effective with their increasingly diverse group of students. She also felt she had the support of her administrators. She continues to tutor as a volunteer and welcomes each occasion when a child's face lights up at seeing someone who looks like him or her. She believes that the price of freedom is eternal vigilance and that we must always be looking for ways to support and improve public education.

1984 photo of Jackie, Virge (right) and their children: Gene, Chris, Skip, and Jack. Jackie talked to children in all of the Rochester public schools about black people and black culture and was nicknamed the "melanin lady."

She Put the "Community" in Community Corrections

Barby Withers helped inmates gain a voice

In the early 1960s, the Minnesota Department of Corrections established the Youth Vocational Center (YVC) on an early warning radar base that had been abandoned by the federal government near Rochester in Viola Township. The YVC was a vocational training school for adjudicated delinquent teenage boys from across the state. Ken Schoen, the director who would become a pioneer in alternative corrections, had the idea to hold dances for the boys in the center, to help them develop social skills. Needing a person to help run the center, he called someone known for getting things done, whose family had a history of service, and whose daughter was the right age for recruiting girls to the dances. He called Barby Withers.

Barby remembers that early dance as being "so successful" that she was subsequently asked to do many other things for the YVC. In 1969, Schoen returned to Rochester to run a program known as PORT (Probationed Offenders Rehabilitation and Training). Unlike YVC, PORT was a program located in the community, serving the community, and operated by the community. The program took an innovative approach to sentencing people convicted of nonviolent crime. The Rochester *Post-Bulletin* explained the program in an article dated May 14, 1973: "What it means is that a person could be sentenced for a lesser crime to a PORT program, but could keep his job. He would maintain family ties but would be kept at night in a minimum security institution, subject to intensive group therapy and counseling. Proponents contend that community systems have two major advantages–they are cheaper and 'graduates' are less likely to repeat as criminals."

Again, Barby became involved, and PORT became her main volunteer activity. The program operated in the Rochester area with much volunteer help from Barby and others for more than twenty years. As she says, "I'll try anything once, and if it works I'll do it again."

"Out of fear and misunderstanding, few people will venture from their comfortable surroundings to work with individuals who have been 'in trouble' with the law," Schoen recently observed. "But those who do will make a difference." Mr. Schoen became the "architect" of the Community Corrections Act (CCA) of 1973, for which PORT was the blueprint. Soon after, he served as Commissioner of Corrections for the state of Minnesota. He once described the CCA as providing a "comprehensive strategy" for "existing fragmented policies." Barby too would graduate–to working with youth, women, and inmates confined to the county jail. She visited with people in jail, where as she points out, "Some people are not guilty, but they have to wait in line."

Those who worked with Barby recognized that she had a special ability to gain the confidence of the inmates. Dorothy Callahan, another longtime volunteer in the jail, recalls, "If there was tension between staff and an inmate, Barby could get to the heart of it and close the gap. She is a very direct woman."

Eventually, Barby began taking some youth into her home, her goal to give them six weeks in a supportive environment. She feels young people can learn from being in someone else's home. The youth she housed didn't get into trouble while they were with her. As Barby says, everyone needs someone to turn to when they are in trouble. "Young people need someone to connect them to reality."

Isabel Huizenga became the first female chair of the Community Corrections Advisory Board in 1976. Isabel was a natural for the leadership position because she had a master's degree in social work and had worked in the field in Chicago. The Advisory Board represented Dodge, Fillmore, and Olmsted Counties. Isabel remembers a sheriff from another county saying he would never allow citizens to visit inmates in his jail. The staff in Olmsted County, on the other hand, was ready to support direct citizen involvement because people like Barby had already been participating in direct contact since the 1960s.

Do something nice for somebody every day

Barby was born in Rochester and graduated from Rochester High school in 1945. She inherited her desire to help others from her parents. Her father, Dr. John Mayo Berkman, was an internal medicine doctor at Mayo Clinic, a nephew of the famous Mayo brothers. He started to treat young women with an unusual wasting problem, a condition that would eventually be called "anorexia nervosa." Barby

Barby was born in Rochester and graduated from Rochester High School. She inherited her desire to help others from her parents.

remembers coming home to dinner and finding a young female patient at the table. Her father often brought home patients who even stayed a few days. The family recognized that surrounding them with domesticity was helpful to these people. Barby would offer the same "medicine" to young people in the jail decades later.

Barby's mother, Margaret Sherman, was very active in the Universalist Church. "My mother was a saint," says Barby. She remembers her involvement with the Woodworth Club House, a pioneering facility for child care that would become the Civic League Day Nursery. Both Barby's grandmothers, Gertrude Mayo Berkman and Catherine Sherman, were active in the Club House. Barby remembers her mother saying, "Every day, try to plan to do something nice for somebody, and if there's a heaven you'll get there." Barby continues to live by her mother's rule.

Some of the first individuals that Barby helped leave the jail were women about to give birth. She made sure they had an alternative place to bear their children, and the staff was supportive of her efforts. Also while helping in the jail, Barby recognized that the staff was sometimes too busy to sit and talk with inmates informally. Frequently the people confined needed to talk, but the administration did not have the time. Barby proposed a board of citizens to fill that need. One of the big advantages of having citizens listen to inmates and their concerns was that they could offer confidentiality, something the staff could not legally offer. That was how the Citizen's Review Advisory Board came about. The acronym, CRAB, is descriptive of what the board's existence allowed the inmates to do.

Barby thinks the CRAB may be unique. It is unusual for jail staff to trust outsiders to listen to complaints that may be critical of the staff. Early on, Barby had to fight even to name the group. Some people wanted to name it the Citizen's Review Advisory Panel, but that acronym was not advisable, Barby argued. The staff conceded and the CRAB committee was born.

Today the five-person committee is down to one–Barby. Still available to take calls from any inmate who wishes to speak to her, she averages about two per week. She recalls one young man who was highly intoxicated when brought in. He was despondent about the loss of his overcoat. Barby listened to his story and went out to search for the coat. She found it at the bar and returned it to him. This is a typical story for Barby. Her role as ombudsman and liaison is still going strong.

Dave Rooney, the Director of Corrections in Olmsted County for many years, says the work of Barby and the other volunteers was "very useful." "Olmsted County Jail was the first county jail in the state to measure humaneness," he says. Once a quarter, citizens would visit to make observations. "It's because of Barby that the program developed. It was her idea and her leadership that kept it going."

The prisoners' retreat

In the 1990s, after Olmsted County built a new jail, Barby and Dorothy Callahan were able to realize the long-held dream of creating an adequate library for the jail. They both sat on the committee to plan the new space. "We had to fight to get everything we got," recalls Dorothy. Barby remembers finding a large old wooden desk abandoned in the basement; it is still the check-out desk at the jail library. Originally the inmates could visit three times a week, though they have recently been reduced to twice a week. "Many of [the detainees] say it's what keeps them sane," says Dorothy. Adds Barby, "They become different people when they walk through the library door. They can just relax and be friendly."

Barby is proud of the changes that have happened in the Olmsted Jail over the years. She is still part of a group of fourteen female volunteers who help the staff run the library–a place the inmates call a "retreat." Stacy Sinner, who became the first female Captain in the Olmsted County Sheriff's Office in 1999 and now serves as the first female Director of Detention Services, said, "This job would be much more difficult without the dedication of the volunteers who help detainees in so many ways." There are currently eighty-six active volunteers in the jail. Of the library, Stacy says, "The library is the finest jail library in the state–maybe in the nation."

Barby appreciates the way the staff has always welcomed the volunteers, since they are basically unpaid outsiders. Stacy Sinner said this about Barby: "She has been the perfect advocate for detainees. She has the communication skills to create a situation where the staff and the inmate work toward a common goal of not re-offending. She is selfless." Her commitment to community corrections has not gone unnoticed. Among her many awards, she is most proud of being selected one of the "Points of Light" under President George H.W. Bush's program. In 1997, she accomplished the rare feat of being recognized by all three levels of government in the same year. On May 21, at the national conference of the American Jail Association in Salt Lake City, Utah, she received the Volunteer of the Year Award. On June 3, the Olmsted County Sheriff's Office presented her with a commendation for her volunteer work. Finally, on September 18, 1997, she was given the Volunteer of the Year Award by the Minnesota Sheriff's Association.

Barby still receives phone calls from those she has helped over the years. She estimates a month doesn't go by without hearing from someone who wants to say "Hello" and tell her how they are doing now. She continues to treat people from the jail just like everybody else. Her passion to be involved in service is undimmed after all these years. "I have this need to do something for somebody in trouble. I have to help."

Barby, sitting in the jail library, has a need to do something for somebody in trouble. "I have to help."

Women You Know Who Contributed to Public Policy

1970-1990

We may have inadvertently omitted Rochester women you know you made public policy contributions. These blank pages are provided so that you might add your own stories about them.

Appendix: Rochester Women Leaders in the Public Sector, 1970-1990

(Note: This listing is a "best effort" based on the records that have been preserved and discovered by our researchers. We apologize to anyone who served but has not been listed, and to any organizations or boards we have missed. Names are listed chronologically within categories.)

Women elected officials in local government

City of Rochester *(From City Clerk's records.)*
- **Carol Kamper**, first woman Rochester City Council Member; Ward 6, elected 1971-1976
- **Nancy Selby**, first woman Rochester City Council President; At-Large, elected 1988-1994

Olmsted County *(From Olmsted County Board minutes and Rochester Post-Bulletin.)*
- **Rosemary Ahmann**, first woman Olmsted County Commissioner, elected 1972-1980, chair 1976, 1980
- **Carol Kamper**, Olmsted County Commissioner, elected 1976-2002, chair 1979, 1983, 1987, 1994, 2000
- **Lois Finstuen**, first woman Olmsted County Recorder, elected 1978-1992; having been appointed upon the former Recorder's retirement in 1977
- **Joan Sass**, Olmsted County Commissioner, elected 1980-1984, chair 1984
- **Hazel Pearson**, first woman Olmsted County Auditor, appointed 1985 and elected 1986-1990
- **Jean Michaels**, Olmsted County Commissioner, elected 1986-2003, chair 1989, 1996, 2001

Rochester School District 535 *(From Superintendent's Office records and School Board minutes.)*

- **Karen Ricklefs,** first woman Rochester School Board chair 1973-1974, elected 1970-1976
- **Janet Kneale,** elected to Rochester School Board 1973-1982, chair 1978-1979
- **Sally Martin,** elected to Rochester School Board 1974-1980, chair 1977-1978
- **Nedra Wicks,** first appointed to Rochester School Board 1976, continued in elected position through 1982, chair 1979-1980 (Her appointment in 1976 resulted in four of the seven seats held by women for the first time.)
- **Margaret Ellen Frye,** elected to Rochester School Board 1982-1991, chair 1985-1986
- **Susan Rogers,** elected to Rochester School Board 1983-1985
- **Molly Naylor,** elected to Rochester School Board 1984-1987
- **Pam Smoldt,** elected to Rochester School Board 1986-1992, chair 1989-1990, when all three leaders of Rochester local governments were women
- **Kay Batchelder,** elected to Rochester School Board 1987-1993, chair 1990-1991
- **Sherry (Moon) Stevens,** elected to Rochester School Board 1988-1993, chair 1991-1992
- Women elected to the Rochester School Board between 1914 and 1970 included: **Mrs. H. (Amelia) Witherstine** (served as chair 1914-1923), **Mrs. M. Montgomery** (1923-1925), **Helen B. Judd** (1924-1931), **Elizabeth Lowry** (1932-1937), **Mildred Hargraves** (1944-1948), **Phoebe Walters** (1947-1953), and **Elizabeth Drips** (1960-1970)

State of Minnesota
- **Nancy Brataas,** first woman Minnesota State Senator elected in her own right, 1975-1992
- **Ancy Morse,** first woman Judge, appointed and then elected to Minnesota Third Judicial District 1983-1999

Women candidates: first–although unsuccessful–for these offices
(*From Rochester* Post-Bulletin.)

- **Sister Alcantara Schneider**, first woman to run for a State House seat from Rochester, in 1976 on the DFL party ticket, losing to incumbent Dick Kaley. Her obituary states, "I felt called to do it for the sake of women."
- **Jesse Howard**, first woman to run for Mayor of Rochester in 1977, losing by just thirty-one votes to incumbent Alex Smekta
- **Sally Martin** would have been the first woman to run for Minnesota's First Congressional District seat from a major party, had she been endorsed by the DFL in 1978. She lost the endorsement battle.

Women department heads/directors in local government

City of Rochester (*From records supplied by City Clerk and Rochester Librarian.*)
- **Elfreda Reiter,** Rochester City Clerk, 1956-1973
- **Carole Grimm,** Rochester City Clerk, 1973-1994, instrumental in voter registration and education drives with the League of Women Voters, especially after the changes to the state law allowing same-day registration and voting
- **Phillis Goedert Wilson**, Rochester Head Librarian, 1970-1982
- **Judith Keller Taylor**, Rochester Head Librarian, 1982-1998
- Women serving as Rochester Head Librarians prior to 1970 included: **Edna Emerick** (1895-1923), **Grace Steffens** (1930-1943), and **Lucille Gottry** (1943-1968)
- **Elisa Umpiere**, first woman Rochester Police Officer, appointed after time period of 1992, recently promoted

Olmsted County (*From Olmsted County Human Resources and Olmsted County Board minutes.*)
- **Nancy Vollertsen**, first Personnel Director for Olmsted County, 1978-1982
- **Jeanne Haben**, first woman Olmsted County Court Administrator, 1983-1998
- **Patricia Carlson**, first woman Director of Olmsted County Community Services, 1988-2002

- **Mary Callier**, first Olmsted County Associate Administrator, 1989-2011
- **Mina Wilson**, first woman to manage Olmsted County Community Services Income Maintenance Division, 1989-present

Rochester School District 535 *("Directors" and Principals from the Superintendent's Office collection of internal phone books from 1960-1990, located by Wendy Edgar. Many of those listed continued their careers beyond 1990.)*
- **Ruth Hahn**, Elementary Principal at Lincoln School, 1960-1973
- **Nydia Klepper**, Elementary Principal at Gage and Ben Franklin Schools, 1968-1984
- **Ottie Applen**, Director of Student Accounting, 1970-1975
- **Carolyn Richards**, Student Services and Transportation Manager, 1978-1987, Transportation position started in 1984
- **Virginia Dixon**, Special Services (Special Education) Director, 1980-1987
- **Kathryn Schultz**, Elementary Principal at Folwell and Elton Hills Schools, 1984-1990
- **Diane Ilstrup**, Secondary Principal at Kellogg Junior High and John Marshall High School, 1984-1990
- **Vivien Johnson**, Elementary Principal at Pinewood, Golden Hill, and Sunset Terrace Schools, 1986-1990
- **Nancy Kaldor**, Secondary Principal at Mayo High School, 1986-1990
- **Fran Robb**, Elementary Principal at Hawthorne, Folwell and Golden Hill Schools, 1986-1990
- **Earlene Wickre**, Student Services and Transportation Manager, 1987-1990
- **Diane Schwinghammer**, Elementary Principal at Folwell School, 1989-1990
- **Patricia Moen**, Director, Secondary Operations, 1989-1990, instrumental in creating a Diversity Council
- **Marge Kirchhoff**, Interim Regional President of Rochester Technical College, 1990

Some women leaders in area higher education

- **Geraldine Evans**, President of Rochester Community College, 1982-1992, during a period of rapid capital growth and cooperative agreements with Winona State University (WSU)
- **Mary Rieder**, Winona State University (WSU) Professor of Economics, and a developer of an MBA program in Rochester in the early 1980s. She championed closer ties between WSU and Rochester and later in the 1990s, ran twice on the DFL ticket for Congress from the Minnesota First Congressional District.
- **Margaret Thompson**, first Registrar for the newly created Mayo Medical School in the early 1970s. She was instrumental in the lobbying effort (she referred to herself as the token Democrat, not the token woman, in this group) to get state support for a new medical school, and state capitation payments for the students. She was often called "Mrs. DFL" during the same period that Nancy Brataas held a similar unofficial title for the local Republicans.

Women members of selected local government boards
(some of these records are sketchy)

City of Rochester
Rochester Charter Commission (*Incomplete minutes of attendance for this period, discovered in long-term storage from previous City Attorneys' files at the Rochester Airport.*)
- **Margaret Spoo**, 1967 minutes
- **Ms. Sortie**, 1973 minutes
- **Ms. Rudlong**, 1973 minutes
- **Mrs. John (Marjorie) Adams**, 1976, 1977 minutes, chair 1976
- **Mrs. Diane Casper**, 1976-1977, 1981-1982 minutes, secretary
- **Mrs. David (Jane) Toft**, 1976 minutes
- **Sister Ellen Whelan**, 1976, 1977 minutes
- **Mrs. Schwartz**, 1980 minutes
- **Diane Anderson**, 1980-1981 minutes
- **Jo Linnes**, 1980-1982, 1984 minutes, treasurer, 1987 term expired

- **Kay Batchelder**, 1980, 1981 minutes, secretary
- **Ann Cronin**, 1980, 1982 minutes
- **Ann Aaro**, 1981, 1982 minutes
- **Alice M. Olson**, 1981, 1984-1987 minutes, resigned
- **Genevieve Rice**, 1982, 1984-1988 minutes, resigned
- **Nancy Vollertsen**, 1982, 1988-1990 minutes, chair 1984
- **Esther Pfeifer**, 1984-1987 minutes
- **M. Elaine Prom**, 1984, 1988-1990 minutes
- **Marianna Wilson**, 1984-1987 minutes
- **Ann Chafoulias**, 1984-1987 minutes
- **Jane Callahan**, 1988-1990 minutes
- **Amy Caucutt**, 1988-1990 minutes
- **Patricia Gastineau**, 1988-1990 minutes
- **Martha Sessler**, 1988-1990 minutes

Rochester Civic Music Board *(Lists of members in Music Department are not saved with dates of service.)*

Downtown Development District Advisory Board *(Formed in May, 1975. Required by state law to advise on any tax increment finance districts and must have a majority of members who represent downtown businesses with additional members from city, county, school district, HRA and planning departments. Partial records located by Doug Knott, City of Rochester.)*
- **Peggy Miller**, member of original board 1975
- **Mary Lee Healy**, appointed 1975-1983
- **Rosemary Ahmann**, County Commissioner appointed 1975
- **Joan Sass**, appointed from HRA 1976-1980 and as business representative through 1981
- **Marjorie Larison**, appointed 1976
- **Carol Kamper**, County Commissioner appointed 1978-1984, 1988, 1989
- **Carolyn Richards**, HRA appointed 1984-1992
- **Cynthia Daube**, business representative appointed 1990

Rochester Housing and Redevelopment Authority (HRA) *(Information supplied by Olmsted County HRA staff and the minutes of the Rochester HRA from 1972-1990. City HRA merged with Olmsted County HRA following 1994 state enabling legislation. Five member board enlarged/reorganized to seven members in 1974.)*

- **Mrs. Paul Ludowese**, served in 1972, resigned in 1974
- **Katherine Sholtz**, served 1974-1976
- **Jane Belau**, served 1975-1979
- **Carolyn Richards**, served 1976-1990 and perhaps longer
- **Joan Sass**, served 1976-1985
- **Marianne Hockema**, served in 1982
- **Lynn Egan**, served 1982-1988
- **Margaret Thompson**, served 1985-1988

Rochester-Olmsted Council of Governments (ROCOG) *(A metropolitan planning organization was required by all communities with greater than 50,000 residents by the 1963 Federal Highway Bill. In 1970, Rochester's population was 53,766, so the Governor approved such an organization in 1971. ROCOG was formed in 1972 with members from City of Rochester, Olmsted County, area townships, small cities, school boards and citizens. Names of members were found in ROCOG minutes 1972-1990.)*

- **Carol Kamper**, Rochester City Council 1972-1975; Olmsted County Board 1977, 1981, 1984
- **Rosemary Ahmann**, Olmsted County Board 1975-1976
- **Isabel Huizenga**, citizen 1975-1979
- **Sally Martin**, Rochester School Board 1976-1977
- **Geraldine Hennessey**, citizen 1979-1990
- **Joan Sass**, Olmsted County Board 1981-1984, chair 1983
- **Kay Diffley**, Stewartville City Council 1981-1982
- **Gretchen Keefe**, Stewartville School District 1981-1986
- **Jean Michaels**, Olmsted County Board 1987-1989, she served while her husband Frank was the chair
- **Nancy Selby**, Rochester City Council 1989-1990

Rochester Park Board (*Information from Rochester Park & Recreation staff.*)
- **Mary Ayshford,** served 1972
- **Susan Lemke,** served 1973-1999
- **Mary Sue Snyder,** appointed 1990
- A woman who served on the Park Board before 1970 was **Alberta Chance,** 1967-1968

Rochester Planning and Zoning Commission (*From minutes of Planning and Zoning Commission meetings, supplied by staff of Rochester-Olmsted Consolidated Planning Department.*)
- **Marilyn Wick,** served 1972-76
- **Margaret Brimijoin,** served 1975-1978
- **Roberta Herrell,** appointed late 1978; served through 1982
- **Cynthia Daube,** first woman chair 1981-1982, served 1979-1987
- **Amy Caucutt,** served 1983-1989, chair 1985-1986
- **Mrs. Lora Schwartz,** appointed 1988
- Women appointed to the Rochester Planning and Zoning Commission before 1970 included: **Mrs. Russell Ewert** (1960-1965) and **Mrs. Ray B. Wheeler** (1966-1967)

Committee on Urban Design and Environment (CUDE) (*From records supplied by Rochester-Olmsted County Consolidated Planning staff. *CUE disbanded sometime prior to 1981 and was reinstated at that date. Starred names were on the last known CUE membership list; however, records do not indicate appointment date. This group chiefly acted as an advisory committee to the Rochester Planning and Zoning Commission.*)
- **Shirley Baldwin,** appointed 1971
- **Louise Hill,** appointed 1971 and 1985, champion for historic preservation and the River Trail system in Rochester, accompanying flood control project in the 1980s
- **Marilyn Lundquist,** appointed 1971
- ***Mrs. Joe Bendry,** appointed before 1981
- ***Mrs. Chris Chesebro,** appointed before 1981
- ***Rose Sadler,** appointed before 1981

- ***Susan Lemke**, first woman chair, appointed before 1981
- **Marion Keith**, appointed 1981
- **Florence Sandok**, appointed 1981, leader for a host of other environmental issues
- **Mary Jones**, appointed 1981
- **Jan Reid**, appointed 1982
- **Leslie Sonnenklar**, appointed 1982
- **Beverly Nelson**, appointed 1982
- **Suzanne Greenleaf**, appointed 1985
- **Sara Qualey**, appointed 1985
- **Doris Folger**, appointed 1986
- **Jane Kansier**, appointed 1986
- **Lora Schwartz**, appointed 1988
- **Suzanne Ramthun**, appointed 1990

Rochester Police Civil Service Commission *(Information from the staff of the Rochester Police Department.)*
- **Mary Goette**, Political Science and Psychology instructor at RCC, a specialist in Public Personnel Administration, appointed to the three-member Rochester Police Civil Service Commission while the Joy Fogarty legal challenge on sex/age discrimination was still pending in 1979. Served until 1990
- **Mary Ellen Grobe**, appointed 1990

Rochester Public Library Board of Trustees *(Information from the Rochester Public Library staff. The majority of the nine-member board were women from 1979-1985, and also in the mid-1920s.)*
- **Mrs. F.F. Borg**, served 1959-1977
- **Mrs. E.D. Bayrd**, served 1967-1982
- **Audrey Anderholm**, served 1973-1976; 1979-1987
- **Carrie Adamson,** served 1976-1981
- **Jan Larson**, served 1977-1986
- **Margaret Thompson**, served 1979-1985
- **Faith Reilly**, served 1979-1988
- **Mrs. Marion Bagne**, served 1980-1989

- **Maaja Washington**, served 1982-1986
- **Mrs. Bix Stewart**, appointed 1985-1991
- **Jill Beed**, appointed 1988-1991
- **Diane Schwinghammer**, appointed to serve 1989-1992
- Earlier women on the Library Board included: **Mrs. J.R. Eckman** (1958-1966), **Mrs. Edward Degel** (1923-1959), **Mrs. W.F. Braasch** (1911-1933; 1935-1959), **Mrs. Harry Gimbert** (1927-1935; 1938-1959), **Mrs. T.R. Lawler** (1912-1958), **Mrs. S.C. Furlow** (1912-1930 . . . some terms may have been her husband), **Ellen Crabb** (1923-1926), **Mrs. E.F. Cook** (1920-1923), **Louise Thompson** (1913-1920), **Clare Blakely** (1902-1915), **Helen Nowell** (1904-1912), **Mrs. Martin (Margaret) Heffron** (1901-1912), **Mrs. Christopher Graham** (1904-1910), **Mrs. H. C. Butler** (1895-1904), **Mrs. H.W. Garrett** (1895-1904), **Mrs. E.W. Cross** (1895-1904), **Mrs. J. Edgar** (1895; this is when the records begin.)

Rochester Public Utilities Board (*Information from Rochester Public Utilities staff and internet queries. A woman serving on this board prior to 1970 was **Belva Snodgrass**, a former Rochester High School Principal, from 1922-1956, and the founder of the first Rochester Girl Scout Troop in 1927. There were no other women until after 1990 on this board.*)

Olmsted County
Olmsted County Agriculture Extension Committee (*Information collected from minutes of the Olmsted County Board, appointments, and information on a sheet entitled, "1979-1980 appointments to all county boards" found in Planning Advisory Committee records.*)
- **Mrs. Ralph Wiehr,** appointed 1971 and reappointed through 1974; 1975 reappointed to 1977
- **Mrs. Duane Bierbaum,** appointed 1971-1973; reappointed 1974-1976
- **Geraldine Hennessey,** appointed 1976-1979; reappointed 1980-1982
- **Mary Jane Irhke,** appointed 1978-1980; reappointed 1981-1983; continued until retiring in 1985
- **Carol Kamper,** County Commissioner appointed 1978, 1979, 1981, 1982, 1987

- **Rosemary Ahmann**, appointed as County Commissioner 1980
- **Brenda Rossman**, appointed 1983-1985; reappointed through 1987
- **Joan Sass**, County Commissioner appointed 1984
- **June Haine**, appointed 1984-1986; reappointed 1986-1989
- **Nola Salisbury**, appointed 1986-1988; reappointed 1988-1991
- **Virginia Wentzel**, appointed 1987-1990; reappointed 1990-1993
- **Jean Michaels**, County Commissioner appointed 1988, 1989
- **Marguerite Uthke**, appointed 1990-1992

Community Action Program (CAP) Board *(Information from Olmsted County Board minutes. Created as an Olmsted County entity in December 1982, with a three-year term for members. Enabling legislation allowed this CAP to merge with Olmsted County Community Services.)*
- **Joan Sass**, County Commissioner appointed 1983, 1984
- **Esther Covert**, original member appointed 1982
- **Rose Ronnenberg**, appointed 1984
- **Sister Alcantara Schneider**, appointed 1984
- **Jane Campion**, representative from Community Social Services Advisory Board (CSSAB) appointed 1986-1987
- **Lois Bruce**, appointed 1986-1988; reappointed 1988-1991
- **Mary Kramer**, appointed 1986-1988; reappointed 1988-1991
- **Rose Sadler**, representative from CSSAB appointed 1988 to unexpired term ending 1989

Dodge-Fillmore-Olmsted Community Corrections Advisory Board *(from DFO Community Corrections Advisory Board minutes and letterhead supplied by Olmsted County Corrections staff. This was the first local community corrections board organized in Minnesota after 1973 enabling legislation. Board includes judges, prosecutors, defense attorneys, probation officers, victim services, law enforcement and citizens to develop and support local programming for prevention and offenders.)*
- **Isabel Huizenga**, first woman chair 1978, appointed to first Community Corrections Advisory Board for Olmsted County in 1974, served 1974-1979
- **Jane Duncan**, served 1974

- **Anna McGee,** served 1974-1979
- **Rosemary Ahmann,** County Commissioner 1974, 1979-1980
- **Donalee Butler,** served 1976-1978
- **Jean Olson,** served 1976-1980
- **Mary Ann Ward,** served 1976-1979
- **Carol Kamper,** County Commissioner 1978, 1990
- **Bev O'Malley,** served 1978-1979
- **Dorothy Callahan,** served 1980-1989, chair 1983, 1990
- **Olive Soli,** served 1980-1982
- **Beulah Eisenman,** served 1982-1983
- **Joan Sass,** County Commissioner, served 1983-1984
- **Carol Gunderson,** served 1983-1986
- **Leona Kleine,** served 1984-1986
- **Dr. Joyce Penniston,** served 1985-1989
- **Pauline Huse,** served 1985-1986
- **Linda Erstad,** served 1987-1989
- **Lori Batts,** served 1987-1989, chair 1989
- **Bonnie Heidtke,** served 1987-1990
- **Rozella Maust,** served 1987-1990, chair; late 1989
- **Ancy Morse,** Judge 1987-1990
- **Sara Chase,** served 1989-1990
- **Mary Goette,** served 1989-1990
- **Judy Hanson,** served 1989-1990
- **Dr. Janice Andrews,** served 1990
- **Susan Lange,** served 1990

Olmsted Community Hospital Board *(Information from minutes of Olmsted County Board. The hospital was owned and operated by Olmsted County during this period; the board had nine members, including two Olmsted County Commissioners.)*
- **Frances Harley,** appointed 1976, resigned 1977
- **Donna Kennedy,** appointed through 1979 to fill Frances Harley's seat
- **Joan Sass,** County Commissioner appointed 1981
- **Carol Kamper,** County Commissioner appointed 1982, 1986, 1988, 1989

- **Karen Ricklefs,** appointed 1982-1985
- **Carrie Fritz**, appointed 1987; reappointed 1997-1990
- **Janice Kaplan**, appointed 1987 to unexpired term through 1988; reappointed 1988-1991
- **Jean Michaels**, County Commissioner 1987, 1988, 1990
- **Jane Belau**, appointed 1987-1990

Olmsted County Community Social Services Advisory Board (CSSAB) *(Information from Olmsted County Board minutes. CSSAB of seven members was created July 1979, with first members appointed December 1979, for three-year terms, except County Commissioners who served one-year appointments. Expanded by two members April 1982; expanded to total of twelve members February 1990.)*
- **Carol Kamper**, County Commissioner appointed 1979, 1981
- **Jean Michaels**, appointed 1979; reappointed 1982-1984 and 1985-1987
- **Rose Ronnenberg**, appointed 1979; reappointed 1983-1985
- **Elizabeth Schmuck**, appointed 1979; reappointed 1982-1984
- **Joan Sass**, County Commissioner appointed 1981, 1982, 1983, 1984
- **Jane Campion**, appointed 1982-1984; reappointed 1985-1987
- **Maggie Brimijoin**, appointed 1982 to unexpired term; reappointed 1983-1985 and 1986-1988
- **Jean Meyer**, appointed 1985 to unexpired term; reappointed 1986-1989
- **Doris Oehlke**, appointed 1986-1988
- **Rose Mary Sadler**, appointed 1986 to unexpired term; reappointed 1988-1991
- **Kristine Lenz Litzow**, appointed 1987 to unexpired term; reappointed 1987 through 1990
- **Lynda Hyberger**, appointed 1987-1990; reappointed 1990-1993
- **Jane Macy-Lewis**, appointed 1989 to unexpired term; reappointed 1990-1993
- **Camtu Nguyen**, appointed 1990-1992
- **Nedra Wicks**, appointed 1990-1992
- **Diane Carlson**, appointed 1990 to unexpired term

Olmsted County Board of Health (*Information collected by staff at Olmsted County Public Health Services Department.*)
- **Mrs. Russell Billings**, served 1970-1974
- **Rosemary Ahmann**, County Commissioner 1973-1974
- **Carol Kamper**, County Commissioner 1975-1976
- **Doris Oehlke**, served 1975-1981
- **Sheila Fort**, served 1975-1977
- **Sister Alcantara Schneider**, served 1978–1984. She was Executive Secretary of the congregation of the Sisters of St. Francis and 1976 candidate for Minnesota State Legislature.
- **Glynis Sturm**, served 1982-1987
- **Janet Johnson**, served 1984-1988
- **Jeannette Krom, M.D.**, served 1988-1989
- **Lynn Frederick**, served 1989-1992

Advisory Committee to Board of Health, changed to Community Health Services Advisory Board in February 1983 (*Information from minutes of Olmsted County Board, appointments; two-year terms divided between six providers and six consumers.*)
- **Helen Ratchford**, appointed 1977 to unexpired term; reappointed 1978-1980
- **Mrs. Rosalie Sziarto**, appointed February 1977 to unexpired term through December 1977
- **Ms. Sheila Anderson**, appointed 1977-1978
- **Mrs. K.T. Mewhorter**, appointed 1977-1978
- **Mrs. Barb Mix**, appointed 1977 to unexpired term through 1978
- **Sharon Ormsby**, appointed to unexpired term 1977; reappointed 1978-1977
- **Ellen Evans**, appointed 1979-1980; reappointed 1981-1983
- **Sister Jean Keniry**, appointed 1979-1980; reappointed 1981-1982; 1983-1984
- **Barbara Moulton**, appointed 1980-1982
- **Dr. Julie Abbot**, appointed 1982-1983; reappointed 1984-1985; 1986-1987
- **Carolyn Richards**, appointed 1982-1983; reappointed 1984-1985; 1986-1987

- **Barbara Birkeland**, appointed 1983-1984
- **Lois Rink**, appointed 1984-1985; reappointed 1986-1987
- **Sharon Tennis**, appointed 1984-1985; reappointed 1986-1987
- **Myra Ahearn**, appointed 1984 to unexpired term; reappointed 1985-1986; 1988
- **Judith Thistle**, appointed 1984-1985; reappointed 1986-1987
- **Margie Loprinzi**, appointed 1987-1988
- **Janet Jones**, appointed 1987-1989

Legal Assistance of Olmsted County (*Information collected from minutes of the Olmsted County Board, appointments.*)
- **Sue Scribner**, appointed 1976-1977; reappointed 1978, resigned 1979
- **Joy Fogarty**, appointed 1979 to unexpired term; served through 1981
- **Ann Kelly**, appointed 1976 to unexpired term through 1977; reappointed through 1979
- **Jane Donadio**, appointed 1981-1984
- **Kathy Renaux**, appointed 1982-1985
- **Linda Lancaster**, appointed 1984-1987
- **Adelaide Reese**, appointed 1985-1988; reappointed through 1991

Olmsted County Park (*and Recreation*) Board (*Information collected from minutes of the Olmsted County Board, appointments.*)
- **Georgia Nelson**, appointed 1974-1976; reappointed 1977-1979
- **Diane Fynboh**, appointed 1975-1977; reappointed 1978-1980
- **Rosemary Ahmann**, County Commissioner appointed 1978
- **Kathryn Resner**, appointed 1977-1979; reappointed 1980-1982
- **Kathryn Micka**, appointed 1979 to unexpired term; reappointed 1980-1982 (eligible for another full term)
- **Kathryn Stebbing**, appointed to second full term 1983-1985 (may be same person as Kathryn Micka)
- **Carole Wade**, appointed 1986-1988; appointed to unexpired term 1990-1992
- **Marjorie Jirele**, appointed 1987-1989; reappointed 1990-1992
- **Carol Kamper**, County Commissioner appointed 1988, 1989

- **Charlotte Metzger**, appointed to unexpired term 1988-1989
- **Carol Berseth**, appointed 1988-1991

Olmsted County Planning Advisory Commission (*Information collected from minutes of Olmsted County Board, appointments, and from Rochester-Olmsted Consolidated Planning Department staff. Created May 1963, with five members; raised to seven members in 1967. A county zoning ordinance adopted December 1969. Two-year terms extended to three years in 1977.*)
- **Mrs. Gail Forstie**, appointed 1973 to fill unexpired term of **Caroline Berkman** through 1975
- **Rosemary Ahmann**, County Commissioner 1975
- **Carol Eppen**, appointed 1976-1978
- **Jean Meyer**, appointed 1977-1979
- **Doris Blinks**, appointed 1978-1980; reappointed 1981-1983; served through early 1985; chair 1982-1983 during adoption of Olmsted County's zoning ordinance
- **Mary Sue Snyder**, appointed to unexpired term 1982; reappointed 1983-1985; 1986-1988; chair 1985

Olmsted County Sheriff's Civil Service Commission (*Information collected from minutes of the Olmsted County Board, appointments.*)
- **Rachel Z. Fisher**, appointed 1975-1977; reappointed 1978-1980
- **Sister Ellen Whelen**, appointed 1981-1983; reappointed 1984-1986
- **Judy Olness**, appointed 1986 to unexpired term; reappointed 1987-1989; 1990-1992

Social Services/Mental Health Board (*Information from minutes of Olmsted County Board. These three women, along with three men, were appointed August 1976 until December 1976.*)
- **Elizabeth Schmuck**
- **Jane Belau**
- **Evelyn Hunter**

Solid Waste Advisory Board (*also called Solid Waste Management Board*) (*Information collected from minutes of the Olmsted County Board, appointments.*)

- **Martha Kuehn,** appointed 1986-1988
- **Monica Frytak,** appointed May 1988 to unexpired term through December 1988; reappointed through 1991
- **Jean Slockbower,** appointed May 1988 to unexpired term through December 1988
- **Marcia Brown,** appointed 1988-1990
- **Carolyn Richards,** appointed 1989-1992
- **Joyce Fenske,** appointed 1990-1992

Olmsted County Welfare Board *(Information from minutes of Olmsted County Board. Olmsted County Board assumed the functions of the seven-member Welfare Board, which had consisted of the five County Commissioners and two citizens by resolution in December 1979.)*
- **Rosemary Ahmann,** County Commissioner, served 1973-1979
- **Evelyn Hunter,** served 1972-1976
- **Jane Belau,** served 1973-1979
- **Carol Kamper,** County Commissioner served 1976-1979

Olmsted County Zoning Board of Adjustment *(Information collected from minutes of the Olmsted County Board, appointments.)*
- **Ann den Tex,** appointed 1975-1977; reappointed 1978-1980
- **Doris Blinks,** appointed 1981-1983
- **Mary Sue Snyder,** appointed January 1984 to unexpired term through December 1984; reappointed 1985-1987; 1988-1990

Zumbro Valley Mental Health Board *(Information from Olmsted County Board minutes. Seven members from Olmsted, four members from Goodhue, and three members from Fillmore counties for two-year terms.)*
- **Ann Hambright,** appointed 1974-1976
- **Elizabeth Schmuck,** appointed 1975-1977; reappointed 1978, resigned 1979
- **Carol Kamper,** County Commissioner appointed 1980, 1989
- **Lynette Hjalmervick,** appointed 1980; reappointed 1981
- **Judith Keller Taylor,** appointed 1983-1984; reappointed 1985-1987; reappointed 1988-1990

- **Pat Foster**, appointed 1984 to unexpired term; reappointed 1986-1988
- **Carole Downie**, appointed 1987 to unexpired term; reappointed 1988-1991
- **Mary Keyes**, appointed 1987-1990
- **Joyce Schut**, appointed to unexpired term 1988 through 1990

<u>Olmsted County Task Forces and Commissions</u>
<u>with non-recurring appointments</u>
(In roughly chronological order, from information found in Olmsted County Board minutes, appointments. These bodies were created to investigate a specific problem or develop a specific policy. Also includes some on-going committees that seldom included women appointees.)

<u>Committee on Future of Olmsted County</u> *(Committee of twelve appointed April 1975.)*
- **Carolyn Richards**, appointed as chair
- **Dorothy Callahan**
- **Jo Linnes**
- **Martha Kuehn**

<u>Human Services Advisory Committee</u> *(Committee of fourteen appointed August 1976, to complete its work by December 1976.)*
- **Isabel Huizenga**, appointed as chair
- **Mary Oveton**
- **Eleanor Kirklin**
- **Marilyn Igel**
- **Sheila Anderson**

<u>Needs Assessment Advisory Committee</u> *(Committee of seven community members and a County Commissioner created July 1977, to serve until March 1978, to oversee a large scale local research project on what community needs existed in social services, health and corrections. This was the forerunner of the Family Violence Task Force, another attempt at large scale interagency cooperation.)*

- **Isabel Huizenga**
- **Marilyn Igel**
- **Elizabeth Schmuck**

911 Planning Committee *(Created or first mentioned, January 1978.)*
- **Priscilla White**, appointed as chair 1978
- **Jean Templeton**, appointed 1978

Feedlot Committee *(Appointments on April 1978.)*
- **Doris Blinks**
- **Mary Sue Snyder**

Citizen's Task Force on Recycling *(Twenty appointed March 1980, to create options to landfill.)*
- **Amy Caucutt**
- **Nancy Ann Moltaji**

Family Violence Committee *(Created and fifteen appointments made May 1980, one month after the Family Violence Task Force, whose thirty members led by Jean Michaels had worked for fifteen months, had presented their forty-five recommendations to the County Board. All findings, according to Sheila Kiscaden, Task Force staff, were implemented in some way; chief among them support for a women's shelter. I can find no record of members appointed to original task force in County Board minutes. However, background on purpose, accomplishments, comprehensiveness of membership, and award from the Association of Minnesota Counties in 1979 can be found in the Olmsted County SCAN [internal newsletters] of December 1979 and June 1980. This committee must have been formed for oversight.)*
- **Jean Michaels**
- **Pat Finley**
- **Pat Scott**
- **Joyce Carlson**
- **Marty Roemer**

- **Liz Losenski**
- **Lois Kredemacher**
- **Dorothy Drummond**, appointed 1980
- **Lois McDougall**, appointed 1980
- **Dr. Virginia Dixon**, appointed May 1982 for a two-year term beginning July 1982
- **Ann Haas**, appointed 1982-1984
- **Ruth McCaleb**, appointed 1982-1983

Youth Services Task Force *(Committee of ten, created December 1980.)*
- **Lynn Anderson**
- **Anita Walker**
- **Mary Wellik**
- **Dr. Kim Miller**
- **Gail Jardine**
- **Suzanne Greenleaf**, appointed January 1981
- **Marian Van Dellen**, appointed June 1981

Rochester State Hospital (RST) Task Force *(Committee of twenty-four appointed July 1981.)*
- **Jane Campion**
- **Ann Ferguson**
- **Geraldine Hagedorn**
- **Janet Kneale**
- **Connie Tooley**
- **Nancy Stanley**
- **Nancy Vollertsen**, appointed 1981

Crisis Project Committee *(Created May 1983, with eight members from other county committees; ZVMH, CSSAB, DFO, and two citizens.)*
- **Maggie Brimijoin**, CSSAB
- **Dorothy Callahan**, DFO
- **Pat Keith**, citizen

Fairgrounds Task Force *(Committee of six created May 1983.)*
- **Brenda Rossman**
- **Evelyn Hunter**

County Government Study Commission *(Fifteen citizens were appointed by Judge Ring on June 9, 1983, to study Olmsted County's structure, following a petition, and to make recommendations in accordance with Minnesota Statute 375A. They recommended four possible changes which went to referenda vote in November 1984. One passed, expanding the County Board to seven members.)*
- **Carolyn Richards**, Vice Chair
- **Carol Kamper**, County Commissioner
- **Joan Sass**, County Commissioner
- **Kay Batchelder**
- **Gretchen Keefe**
- **Margaret Brimijoin**
- **Connie Steward**

Campus Advisory Board *(Committee of fourteen created March 1984.)*
- **Jane Campion**, elected co-chair by the group
- **Joan Sass**, County Commissioner appointed

Jail Study Advisory Board *(Created June 1984. Board expanded to include two citizens and charged with development of a plan for a Detention Center in May 1986.)*
- **Joy Fogarty**, appointed November 1985
- **Carol Kamper**, County Commissioner appointed 1986
- **Joyce Penniston**, appointed 1986

Highway Steering Committee *(a.k.a. Steering Committee for Roads, created October 1984.)*
- **Joan Isaakson**, appointed May 1985

Mental Retardation Implementation Task Force *(Created May 1985, with ten members.)*

- **Ann Ferguson**
- **Kay Fockler**
- **Julie Harris**
- **Mina Wilson**
- **Sue Bateman**
- **Carol Carryer**
- **Buff Hennessey**

Mental Health Action Plan Task Force *(Twenty-nine members appointed November 1985. Minutes of May 30, 1989, note that nine new members were appointed as recommended by CSSAB.)*
- **Sharon Danaher**
- **Jo Stevens**
- **Eleanor Martini**
- **Kathy Monet**
- **Lois Linn**
- **Gerry Hagedorn**
- **Cathy Shea**
- **Chris Ness**
- **Julie Harris**
- **Barb Peterson**
- **Brenda Otto**
- **Fran Robb**
- **Maggie Smith**

Water Policy Advisory Committee *(Members appointed by County Board in 1987; plan presented December 1989, as required by new state statute.)*
- **Doris Blinks**, appointed Water Coordinator June 1986; appointed chair of newly formed Water Policy Advisory Committee 1987
- **Jean Michaels**, County Commissioner appointed 1987
- **Mary Sue Snyder**, appointed from County Planning Advisory Commission 1987
- **Amy Caucutt**, appointed from City Planning and Zoning Commission 1987

Task Force to Critique County's Bonded Indebtedness (*Created August 1988.*)
· **Gay Segar**

Hiawatha Valley Resource Conservation and Development Commission
· **Doris Blinks,** appointed to first three-year term 12-31-87; reappointed 12-8-87 through 12-90
· **Priscilla Van Grevenhof,** appointed to unexpired term 1990; reappointed 1990-1993

School District #535
Bond referenda campaign co-chairs (*Not officially affiliated with the school board, nor funded by them. This information found in select School Board minutes.*)
· **Nedra Wicks,** campaign co-chair for successful new junior high election May 1978
· **Kay Batchelder,** campaign co-chair for successful levy override election May 1984
· **Sue Lemke,** campaign co-chair for unsuccessful levy override election December 1986
·**Margaret Frye,** co-liaison from School Board on successful levy override election May 1987
·**Betty Beck,** campaign co-chair for successful levy override election May 1989

Citizen's Advisory Council (community education) (*First appointed on November 1974, and called "Readiness Advisory Board," contained six staff and three ex officio members including Tutti Sherlock, as well as the following women, but no men, citizens. This information found in select School Board minutes.*)
· **Carol Johnson,** chair
· **Gina DuShane**
· **Julie Edstrom**
· **Hattie Kramer**

- **Cathy Frame**
- **Mary Kay Sidell**
- **Donna Brewster**
- **Janet Jones**
- **Sandy Hirsche**
- **Carla Morrey**
- **Mary Ellen McTighe**
- **Shirley Babbit**
- **Denise Greer**
- **Michelle Andrus,** student appointed 1975 for two years
- **Carol Kamper,** ROCOG appointed 1975 for two years
- **M. Elaine Prom,** homemaking teacher appointed 1975 for two years; appointed 1976 for two years; also appointed to third three-year term 1982
- **Sue Bateman,** YWCA appointed 1975 for two years; appointed 1976 for two years
- **Julie Finnie,** student appointed 1975 for two years
- **Pauline Walle,** *Post-Bulletin* appointed 1975 for two years
- **Dee Hettig,** Central PTA appointed 1976 for two years
- **Barb Fedders,** student appointed 1976 for two years
- **Nedra Wicks,** AAUW appointed 1976 for two years
- **Diane McElmury,** law enforcement; JSVP appointed 1976 for two years
- **Jane Leonard,** student appointed 1976 for two years
- **Vicki Brunner,** student appointed 1976 for two years
- **Martha Smith,** student appointed 1976 for two years
- **Judith Voss,** appointed 1982 to three-year term
- **Sharon Barsness,** appointed 1982 to three-year term
- **Sue Lemke,** appointed 1982 to second three-year term
- **Jane Flickinger,** appointed 1982 to second three-year term
- **Mary Alice Pappas,** appointed 1982 to second three-year term
- **Martha Tullius,** appointed 1985-1988
- **Lisa Wagner,** appointed 1986-1989
- **Debbie Anderson,** appointed 1986-1989
- **Shirley Whitney,** appointed 1988-1991

Citizen's School Facilities Task Force *(Ad hoc in 1976 and re-instituted before bond referenda in 1987.* **Nedra Wicks** *was co-chair in 1976 and she and* **Pam Smoldt** *were members of the ten member 1987 group. This information found in select School Board minutes.)*

Financial Advisory Committee *(Became a standing committee December 1976, with eight male members. On October 3, 1978,* **Adelaide Reese** *was appointed to fill a vacancy. This information found in select School Board minutes.)*

Instructional Advisory Committee *(Appointed in 1979 and 1980; predated the Community Curriculum and Instructional Advisory Council (CCIAC) which began in 1998. The following citizens joined ten staff members. This information found in select School Board minutes.)*
- **Mrs. Suzanne Sterioff**, elementary parent appointed 1979
- **Mrs. Phyllis Layton**, junior high parent appointed 1979
- **Mrs. Betty Beck**, senior high parent appointed 1979
- **Mrs. John Callahan**, senior high parent appointed 1979
- **Shirley Lund**, appointed 1979
- **Pat St. Martin**, appointed 1979
- **Jacqueline Underwood**, appointed 1980

Special Education Task Force *(A fifty-member committee appointed September 1979, with eighteen citizen members. This information found in select School Board minutes.)*
- **Ms. Lois Braasch** and **Ms. Dana Ihrke**, Zumbro Valley Association of Children with Learning Disabilities
- **Ms. Ann Ferguson** and **Ms. Carol Carryer**, Olmsted ARC
- **Mrs. Joan Gravett**, Civic League Day Nursery
- **Ms. Sally Laney**, Aldrich Memorial Nursery School
- **Ms. Paula Sullivan**, Olmsted County Public Health
- **Ms. Mina Wilson**, Olmsted Day Activity Center (DAC)
- **Ms. Maureen Hart** and **Ms. Rosemary Wilson**, parents

Rochester Area Council of PTSAs Presidents *(From a plaque in the hall of the School District Administration Building and from select School Board minutes.)*

- **Deedee Odell**, 1987
- **Sharon Tuntland** and **Maggie Gowan**, 1988-1989
- **Sharon Schmoll**, 1989-1990
- **Kathy Maegerlein** and **Wendy Andersen Postier**, 1990-1991

Women members of selected community boards and advocacy groups

(Rochester has long been a community of "organizations", institutional and ongoing, as well as ad hoc and project specific. Women were often among the leaders of these. The following are a sample only, included because many impacted the stories in our chapters and based on our access to information. We know many have been omitted. Please add your own examples, as you may have done with the last chapter of this book, which was left blank for the reader to complete.)

<u>ARC</u> *(formerly Association for Retarded Citizens during this period, but post-1991 became simply Arc . . . not an acronym. The information on influential women leaders in the local ARC comes from Buff Hennessey. I added her name as I know her to have been and continue to be a leader in Arc.)*

- **Diane Sauter**, 1970-1971
- **Sonja Dunn**, 1970-1971
- **Karin Siggelkow**, 1970-1971
- **Mrs. Dave Grimsrud**, 1970-1971
- **Anne Milam**, 1970-1971
- **Helen Towey**, 1970-1972
- **Ann Ferguson**, president 1971-1972
- **Sandy Sutton**, 1971-1972
- **May Ross**, president 1976-1977
- **Mary Sorenson**, president 1979-1980
- **Janet Johnson**, president 1982-1984
- **Kay Fockler**, president 1986-1988
- **Lynette Knapp**, president, 1988-1990
- **Roberta Postier**, 1988-1990

- **Phyllis Larson**, 1988-1990
- **Val Koster**, 1988-1990
- **Ann Larson** (now **Archer**), 1988-1990
- **Kit Strelow** (now **Hawkins**), 1989-1990
- **Mickey Prince**
- **Marilyn Fryer**
- **Carol Carryer**
- **Elisabeth (Buff) Hennessey**

Building Equality Together (BET) (*Formed in 1989, according to an August 29, 1990,* Post-Bulletin *article "in response to racial conflicts in Rochester Schools," and titled "Youth Concerns/Human Rights Inter-agency Committee", the group's name was changed to BET in 1990, and it became the Diversity Council in 1994. The following women were on the first board, according to Kami Jordan of the Diversity Council and additional* Post-Bulletin *article September 4, 1990.*)
- **Patricia Mohn**, chair
- **Elaine White**, secretary
- **Jackie Trotter**
- **Patricia Carlson**
- **Laura Williams**
- **Val Haugen**
- **Rose Davis Harmon**
- **Mary Sorenson**
- **Judy Harris**
- **Dorothy Drummond**
- **Marie Alexander**
- **Susan Hacking**
- **Roberta Stevens**
- **Maggie Gowan**
- **Julie Edstrom**

Channel One Food Shelf (*Formed in 1980 by* **Marge Allen** *and* **Flo Barker** *to reduce food waste and feed the hungry, especially seniors. Originally housed in the YWCA, they fed twenty- seven families in the first month. By 1990, in new facilities, they fed 2,200 families per*

month. Information from October 28, 1989 and November 6, 1990 Post-Bulletin *articles.)*
- **Marge Allen**, founder and first Executive Director 1980-1989
- **Betty Beck**, Executive Director appointed 1990

Dyslexia Institute of Minnesota (the Reading Center) *(Became a nonprofit in 1989, although tutoring began in 1950s, according to an October 6, 2011* Post-Bulletin *article celebrating its sixtieth anniversary.)*
- **Paula Rome**
- **Jean Osman**

Earth Day, April 22, 1970 *(The* Post-Bulletin *reported on several local activities on the first Earth Day. The following women were mentioned.)*
- **Mrs. Robert Bornberg**, with baby in stroller, was identified among a dozen members of the Fellows' Wives group, demonstrating in front of a local grocery store for expanded use of recyclable packaging.
- **Mary Place**, Junior at Mayo High School, was a coordinator for "Earth Week," whose activities included placement of several waste receptacles in youth-frequented areas and leading a petition in opposition to non-returnable/non bio-degradable soft drink containers.

Friends of Oxbow Zoo *(Group created to advocate, fund-raise and recruit volunteers in the 1980s.)*
- **Carmen Nomann**, co-chair for first group

Friends of Quarry Hill *(Group was formed in 1985 to aid Quarry Hill, a joint environmental learning center sponsored since the early 1970s by School District #535 and City of Rochester. These Board Members' names came from Pam Meyer at Quarry Hill.)*
- **Joan Fowler**, 1986
- **Karen Grant**, 1987

FutureScan 2000 Steering Committee and Task Forces, 1985-1987
(From Task Force Reports of FutureScan 2000 at the Rochester Public Li-

brary. FutureScan 2000 was organized jointly by the City, the County, the School District, the Post-Bulletin, and the Chamber of Commerce, along with major employers to do long range planning for the community.)

- **Marge Allen,** diversification/jobs task force member
- **Gail Baker,** housing affordability task force member
- **Betty Beck,** downtown development task force member
- **Lisa Blanchard,** downtown development task force member
- **Maggie Brimijoin,** local government structure task force member
- **Gerri Brown,** higher education task force member
- **Dorothy Callahan,** steering committee and loaned executive on Housing Task Force
- **Jane Campion,** higher education task force member
- **Amy Caucutt,** housing affordability task force member
- **Elizabeth Conklin,** diversification/jobs task force member
- **Cynthia Daube,** steering committee
- **Geraldine Evans,** steering committee and higher education task force member
- **Margaret Ellen Frye,** steering committee and local government structure task force member
- **Marsha Hall,** higher education task force member
- **Susan Hegrenes,** steering committee
- **Julie Hein,** downtown development task force member
- **Susan Hemphill,** local government structures task force member
- **Jane Hendricks,** higher education task force member
- **Bobbie Herrell,** downtown development task force member
- **Shirley Hill,** steering committee
- **Carol Kamper,** chair, local government structure task force
- **Judi Kurth,** steering committee and vice chair downtown development task force
- **Mary Ellen Landwehr,** local government structure task force
- **Diane Langton,** Assistant Project Manager
- **Susan Lemke,** higher education task force member and sub group convener
- **Anna McGee,** steering committee and housing affordability task force member

- **Missy Meredith**, steering committee
- **Paula Meyers**, steering committee
- **Ruth Nevling**, steering committee
- **Carolyn Richards**, steering committee and housing affordability task force member
- **Elizabeth Ritman**, housing affordability task force member
- **Connie Steward**, local government structure task force member
- **Marilyn Stewart**, steering committee
- **June Stoehr**, diversification/jobs task force member
- **Nedra Wicks**, local government task force member
- **Janice Wilson**, diversification/jobs task force member
- **Sarah Yurkovich**, steering committee

Governor's Task Force on the Disposition of the Rochester State Hospital 1982 *(From the original report found on the internet.)*
- **Jane Campion**, chair
- **Sheila Kiscaden**, staff
- **Rosemary Ahmann**, citizen
- **Nancy Brataas**, State Senator
- **Lee Luebbe**, Winona County Commissioner
- **Joan Sass**, Olmsted County Commissioner

Greater Rochester Area University Center (GRAUC) *(Records supplied by GRAUC executive, Jim Claussen, from 1987 original Board of Directors and Board of Providers and other early sources.)*
- **Nancy Brataas**, State Senator 1987-1992
- **Carol Kamper**, Olmsted County Commissioner 1987-1990
- **Geraldine Evans**, Board of Directors and Board of Providers 1987
- **Kristin Ritts**, Board of Directors and Board of Providers 1987
- **Carol Lund**, Board of Providers 1987
- **Jane Toddie**, Board of Providers 1987
- **Nancy Selby**, Rochester City Council President 1989-1990
- **Dr. Mary Rieder**, Winona State Professor 1989-1990
- **Pam Smoldt**, Rochester School Board President 1990
- **Dr Wendy Shannon**, 1990

Intercultural Mutual Assistance Association (IMAA) Board of Directors (*Formed in 1984 with fifty-one percent of the members "non-caucasian," according to information from Bunly Sui and Ponloeu Chim. They noted that first women board members included: **Marie Alexander**, who with Jim Jones was the driving force for refugee resettlement in the community, **Dung Nguyen, Cam Do, Yuwatey Sui**, and **Sheena Loth**. Bunly recalls **Esther Covert** as the first Staff. He referred to **Phyllis Layton** as a long time advocate of enhanced intercultural relations through the Rochester International Association.*)

Olmsted Citizens for a Better Community (*Citizen group formed to oppose the sale of former State Hospital property to the Federal Prisons 1983-1984. The group advocated, ran a plebiscite, and sued. Information from* Post-Bulletin *articles.*)
· **Joyce Martin**, president

Rochester Area Alliance for the Mentally Ill (RAAMI) (*Women on first Board of Directors named in 1986, from information from Joyce Schut. The group became a chapter of The Minnesota Mental Health Advocacy Coalition and the National Alliance for Mentally Ill.*)
· **Pam Johnson**
· **Joyce Schut**

Rochester Area Economic Development Inc (RAEDI) (*Formed as a result of FutureScan 2000 in late 1985. Information supplied by RAEDI staff from their records.*)
· **Jane Belau**, one of the four officers who incorporated RAEDI on November 6, 1985; Board of Directors (fourteen members) until December 31, 1986
· **Judy Kurth**, one of the four officers who incorporated RAEDI on November 6, 1985, Board of Directors (fourteen members) until December 31, 1989, served as vice president in 1987 and president in 1988
· **Carol Kamper**, served on the first Board of Directors, fourteen members, during 1986

Rochester Area Foundation *(Information from records provided by staff member Ann Fahy-Gust.)*
- **Eleanor Kirklin**, 1972-1982
- **Margaret Thompson**, 1975-1980; 1982-1992
- **Barbara Withers**, 1976-1982
- **Isabel Huizenga**, 1976-1980; 1986-1996; and Executive Director for several years
- **Vera Elgin**, 1981-1992
- **Ann Ferguson**, 1982-1992
- **Betty Beck**, 1985-1992
- **Suzanne Norris**, 1985-1992
- **Jean Freeman**, 1985-1992
- **Dorothy Callahan**, 1989-1994
- **Anna McGee**, 1989-1993
- **Marilyn Stewart**, 1989-1996
- **Nedra Wicks**, 1989-1992
- **Jane Campion**, 1990-currently Emeritus

Rochester Better Chance *(Formed in 1973/1974 to help young people with potential by providing room, board, and mentoring for up to nine boys from around the country, who become students at Rochester's John Marshall High School to get "a better chance" at furthering their education. As DeBorah Green wrote in the March 6, 1990, Post-Bulletin, It also "gives the community a chance to put verbal support to multicultural activities into action." According to a March 7, 1975, Post-Bulletin article, the following women were named as the second year's officers and board members.)*
- **Mrs. Craig (Betty) Beck**, president
- **Mrs. Earl (Anna) McGee**, vice president
- **Mrs. Neal (Jackie) Olson**, secretary
- **Mrs. Starr (Lynn) Kirklin**, treasurer
- **Mrs. Donald (Connie) McIlrath**

Rochester Nuclear Freeze Committee 1982 *(There have been many "peace" organizations over the years. This is one example from a Post-Bulletin article naming the co-organizers of a new group.)*
- **Marian Van Dellen**

United Way Olmsted County *(United Way Staff and Rochester* Post-Bulletin.*)*
• **Isabel Huizenga,** first woman president of local United Way in 1973

Women's Shelter (Marilyn Brodie House) Board of Directors
(This information came from Judy Miller and Women's Shelter records. In 1976 an original group formed to generate support in the community: **Nancy Powell, Sheryl Lesch, Ester Holley, Marilyn Brodie, Susan Piggott, Kathie Zawistowski,** *and* **Carol Ball.** *An interim Board included:* **Bonnie Westra, Marilyn Brodie, Jeanne Anderson, Marian VanDellen, Flo Barker, Mary Beeman, Phyllis Acker, Rosemary Ahmann,** *and* **Evon Mitchell.** *The following women served on the Women's Shelter Board from 1978-1990)*
• **Lyla Bendsen,** 1978-1980
• **Mary Ann Frye,** 1978
• **Virginia Grabowski,** 1978
• **Carol Huyck,** 1978-1980
• **Evon Mitchell,** 1978
• **Mary Overton,** 1978-1982
• **Stephanie Podulke,** 1978-1982
• **Liz Schmuck,** 1978-1982
• **Mary Deling,** 1979-1983
• **Jan Link,** 1979-1982
• **Judy Miller,** 1979-1980
• **Charlotte Anderson,** 1980-1982
• **Betty Bach,** 1980-1990
• **Mary Kay Bouise,** 1980-1981
• **Mary Duggan,** 1980-1989
• **Peggy Henry,** 1980
• **Judy Horsman,** 1980-1982
• **Wanda Keefe,** 1980-1981
• **Debra Langer,** 1980-1982
• **Sue Rockne,** 1980-1990
• **Joy Johnson,** 1981-1985
• **Sally Martin,** 1981
• **Dorothy Gores,** 1982-1984

- **Roxanne Mindeman,** 1982-1985
- **Roberta Skow,** 1982-1986
- **Kay Batchelder,** 1983-1985
- **Maureen Plitzuweit,** 1983-1986
- **Margaret Boddy,** 1984-1990
- **Ellen Henderson,** 1984
- **Marlise Riffel-Gregor,** 1984-1990
- **Carol Gross,** 1985-1990

Women leaders in local partisan politics

<u>**Olmsted County Chairs and Associate Chairs for the Major Political**</u>
Parties *(There are many women who managed campaigns or worked behind the scenes, so this is a truncated listing of local women active in leadership roles in the DFL [Democratic Party] and the IR [as the party was known for much of this period in Minnesota]. This information found in Rochester* Post-Bulletin *stories following local conventions.)*
Olmsted County DFL (Democratic Party in Minnesota)
- **Mrs. Richard (Marian) Van Dellen,** chairwoman 1972-1974
- **Marian Van Dellen,** assistant chair 1974-1976
- **Kay Resner,** chair 1976-1980
- **Sister Honore Cashman,** associate chair 1980-1984
- **Mary Berg,** associate chair 1984-1986
- **Sally Blanton,** associate chair 1986-1988
- **Roberta Stevens,** associate chair 1988-1990
- **Janice Reed,** associate chair 1990, elevated to chairwoman when Dr. Bob Baker, chair, took leave of absence

<u>**Olmsted County Republicans, or IR**</u> *(Nancy Brataas was State Chairwoman 1963-1969.)*
Mrs. Charles (Dorothy) Boughton, chairwoman 1971-1975
Mrs. George (Bonnie) Kerr, chairwoman 1975-1977
Lavern Orwoll, chairwoman 1977-1981
Kathy Nass, chairwoman 1981-1983
Jan Gallagher, chairwoman 1983-1985
Darlene Schmidt, co-chair 1985-1987
Gail Baker, co-chair 1987-1989
Dee Hettig, co-chair 1989-

Presidents of three local women's organizations involved in public policy

<u>Presidents of Rochester AAUW</u> *(From Diane Hellie's records of local AAUW history files.)*
· **Mrs. Richard Lundborg**, 1970-1972
· **Mrs. Richard Selby**, 1972-1974
· **Mrs. Merlin Ricklefs**, 1974-1976
· **Mrs. Arnold Hill**, 1976-1978
· **Mrs. Lawrence Barsness**, 1978-1980
· **Mary Sue Snyder**, 1980-1982
· **Mrs. L. Thomas Lemke**, 1982-1984
· **Dr. Mary Burritt**, 1984-1986
· **Dr. Wendy S. Shannon**, 1986-1988
· **Majel Ann Hall**, 1988-1990
· Women who held this post in the 1960s were: **Mrs. W.B. Thurber, Mrs. Charles F. Stroebel, Mrs. J.L. Stewart, Mrs. Ferd Anderholm**, and **Mrs. A. Howard Sather**

<u>Presidents of NOW</u> *(According to Joy Fogarty, the first group of fifteen to twenty women was convened in 1973 by Diane Fass through a newspaper advertisement. Founding members included:* **Mary Kay Bouise, Ginny Grabowski, Peggy Henry, Cindy Hunstiger, Mary Klukow, Marilyn Brodie, Joy Fogarty, Julie Gilkinson,** *and* **Diane Fass.** *Joy remembers being president several times, as was Mary Kay.* **Marilyn Brodie** *chaired the Battered Women's Task Force which resulted in the establishment of the Women's Shelter named in her honor.* **Mary Kay Bouise** *and* **Joy Fogarty** *chaired the Rapeline Task Force which established the first rape call in emergency line run out of NOW members' homes. The first group of advocates working with law enforcement were:* **Connie Fossun, Ilona Westwood, Cindy Hunstiger,** *and* **Joy Fogarty.** **Julie Gilkinson** *organized the first all-women's volleyball tournament in the city with proceeds going to women attending Rochester Community College. In August 1981, AGOG (All the Good Old Girls) was organized by NOW members with* **Romayne Thompson** *as the paid administrator.* **Diane Fass,** *also a past president, recalls* **Donna Mujwid,** *another past president and* **Roberta Skow,** *who was also a key driver for WIBO.)*

Presidents of Rochester League of Women Voters *(From Kathy Maegerlein from Rochester League of Women Voters records.)*

- **Mary (Don) Wick**, 1969-1971
- **Linda (Dick) Woodhouse**, 1971-1973
- **Sue Scribner**, 1973-1977
- **Amy Caucutt**, 1977-1979
- **Maggie Brimijoin**, 1979-1981
- **Jane Toft**, 1981-1984
- **Dorothy Callahan**, 1984-1986
- **Marcia Brown**, 1986-1989
- **Jan (Fandel) Hastings**, 1989-1991
- **Jane Callahan**, 1991-1993
- Women who held this post earlier included: **Mrs. Chas. Mayo** (Olmsted County chair in First District 1919), **Mrs. G.B. New** (1934, the same year that **Mrs. E. Starr Judd** organized first daytime unit), **Miss Lillian Glasser** (in 1936, she organized an evening unit), **Mrs. Otis Hanson** (1937), **Mrs. H.W. Feldman** (1937), **Mrs. Glen (Bessie) Withers** (1940, met at YWCA with eighty-one members and she later went on State Board), **Mrs. K.M. Simonton** (1941, offers nursery and membership of 110), **Mrs. H.E. (Marian) Essex** (1942 morning unit), **Mrs. Malcolm (Mildred) Hargraves** (1942-1948 evening unit president and in 1948, State League president and recipient of Minneapolis *Tribune* Gold Key Leadership Award), **Mrs. E. Cutshall** (1943, League begins monthly UN luncheon and radio program), **Mrs. C.E. Betcher** (1944, League begins one executive Board of both units), **Mrs. Russel Wilder** (1945-1946, League goes to nine units), **Mrs. M.N. Walsh** (1947 and membership at 120), **Mrs. H.K. Grey** (1948), **Mrs. Arnold Dahl** (1949 with membership at 221), **Miss Katherine Kilbourne** (1949), **Mrs. K.M. Simonton** (1950), **Mrs. John Grindlay** (1951), **Mrs. A.G. (Janice) Karlson** (1952), **Mrs. James W. (Mary Margaret) DuShane** (1953-1955), **Mrs. John Silliman** (1955-1957), **Mrs. Robert Faucett** (1959-1961 and state treasurer until 1964), **Mrs. William H. Price, Jr.** (1961), **Mrs. George (Peg) Spoo** (1961-1963), **Mrs. John Adams** (1963-1965), **Mrs. Thomas (Carolyn) Richards**, 1965-1967), **Mrs. David (Rosemary) Ahmann** (1967-1969)

Acknowledgments

Many people made this book possible, beginning with the twenty-five women who graciously allowed us to include their stories. They gave of their time, stories, pictures, and personal papers. None we selected refused to participate!

Others who knew these women and their accomplishments were willing to provide quotes, anecdotes, and leads to information that were helpful rounding out our chapters.

This book was written by volunteer authors, many of whom are members of the Rochester League of Women Voters, and all of whom personally knew the women they interviewed. The authors and their chapters are: Sheryl Barlow (Joy Fogarty), Maggie Brimijoin (Rosemary Ahmann, Cynthia Daube, Julie Nigon, and Jackie Trotter), Marcia Brown (Judy Miller and Joyce Schut), Jane Anderson Callahan (Doris Blinks, Dorothy Callahan, Sue Lemke, Ancy Morse, and Barby Withers), Amy Caucutt (Jane Belau [with Mike Ransom], Nancy Brataas, Jane Campion [with Mary Gorfine], Carol Kamper, Sheila Kiscaden, Sally Martin, Marilyn Stewart, and Appendix), Mary Gorfine (Jean Michaels), Elisabeth (Buff) Hennessey (Ann Ferguson), Mike Ransom (Karen Ricklefs), Jeanne Ronayne (Donna Dunn), Priscilla (Pixy) Russell (Sister Generose Gervais), and Lori Sturdevant (Introduction).

We had wonderful and patient editors: Suzanne Kelsey, Priscilla (Pixy) Russell, Diane Paradise, and Mike Ransom. We thank Sheryl Barlow (Business Development Director) and Sarah Link (Graphic Designer) at CWS, Inc. of Rochester, MN, for their development of cover graphics and branding elements.

Great helpers in so many departments of our three local governments as well as many non-profit organizations in Rochester allowed access to minutes, records, and internal newsletters; located minutes and records; and sometimes actually did the searching for information directly for us.

Rochester Public Library Reference Department staff, and staff from the Minnesota Legislative Reference Library, provided advice on where to look for records pertaining to our subjects in this period. They often unearthed key facts and records that were no longer available from original sources.

Post-Bulletin Co.'s microfilmed back issues of newspapers, found in the Rochester Public Library, were extremely useful because they so thoroughly covered local news of this period. When ours and our subjects' memories were inexact, a check with Post-Bulletin Co. news articles allowed us to be more accurate. The Post-Bulletin Co. also gave us access to some of their internal files and pictures.

And especially thanks to Amy Caucutt, who "gave birth" to the project and worked determinedly on it from start to finish; Mike Ransom, who kept us moving and on track; and to the Rochester League of Women Voters and the Minnesota League of Women Voters Education Fund, who supported the project officially and financially.